2000
PASSING THE MARKER
(Understanding the New Millennium Energy)

**Kryon
Book VIII**

International Kryon Books

See (www.kryon.com) for more info

Spanish
Kryon Books - One, Two, and Three

Coming:
Japanese!

Hebrew
Kryon Books - One, Two, Three and Four

Hebrew
Kryon Books - Five, Six, Seven and The Indigo Children

Italian   **Greek**
Kryon Parables   Kryon Book One   Kryon Book One, & The Indigo Children   **German**

International Kryon Books
See (www.kryon.com) for more info

French
Kryon Books - One, Two, Three and Five

French
Kryon Books - Six, Seven, and The Indigo Children

Danish
Kryon Book One

Hungarian
Kryon Book One, and The Indigo Children

Chinese
Kryon Books - One and Two

Turkish
Kryon Books - One, Two, Three, and Six

millennium (me-lèn´ê-em) noun
plural—*millenniums* or *millennia* (-lèn´ê-e)

(1) A span of one thousand years.
  (2) A hoped-for period of joy, serenity, prosperity,
    and justice.
    (3) A thousandth anniversary.

PASSING THE MARKER

Understanding the New Millennium Energy

Kryon Book VIII

Publisher: **The Kryon Writings, Inc.**

1155 Camino Del Mar - #422
Del Mar, California 92014
[www.kryon.com]

Kryon books and tapes can be purchased in
retail stores, or by phone. Credit cards welcome.
(800) 352-6657 or E-mail kryonbooks@aol.com

Written by Lee Carroll
Editing by Jill Kramer
Copyright © 2000—Lee Carroll
Printed in the United States of America
First Edition—First Printing—August 2000

ISBN# 1-888053-11-9 : $14.00

Table of Contents

continued...

Table of Contents . . .continued

. . . In sincere gratitude to
Luise Hansen

From the Writer
"Passing the Marker"
Kryon Book VIII

Lee Carroll

Preface

Preface
"Passing the Marker"
Kryon Book VIII

From the writer . . .

Welcome to Kryon Book Eight! Like so many other books being released at this time, this work is dedicated to the new millennium. The title, *Passing the Marker,* is Kryon's description of our movement into this new energy of 2000, and has been a subject discussed by Kryon for almost 11 years now. If you pick this book up after the year 2000, you can be sure that it will still be relevant to the events that are ongoing.

From the inception of the writing of Kryon Book One, *The End Times*, in 1989, the subject of Kryon's teaching has all pointed to what is happening right now, and also for the next 12 years (up to the year 2012). Whereas I normally do not release a Kryon book each year, the information coming in is profoundly different, and it almost demands to be published at this time.

There is a lot of joy in this book! If you are new to channelling or Kryon, you might find this information a whole lot less spooky than you thought. Channelling is starting to feel far more *Human*, as we begin to meld into what Kryon calls "our Higher Selves," or "the divinity within." I guess that means that as we draw closer to the God-Self, we start to really *feel* the information from the other side. It becomes closer to us— more familiar, and is much more like a phone call than a supernatural visit from beyond.

The joy, honor, and congratulations you might feel emanating from this book is due to the fact that we have now passed into an energy that was Kryon's main message back in 1989. Eleven years ago, he told us that the doom-and-gloom prophecies did not need to come to pass. He told us that we were sitting on the edge of Human evolution, and that we could potentially see it in everyday life—in the news, in the weather, and in ourselves.

Here is a magazine article I wrote in 1999 called *"Did You Notice?"* It tells a story with an important message.

Did You Notice?

I can remember with great vividness the feeling of beginning my lecture in 1995. Those who had gathered at the United Nations committee room 7 were there to hear a message, but the one I was about to give probably wasn't what they had anticipated. How would they take my message of new hope at this prestigious, but troubled, organization, constantly in turmoil and unresolved conflict? For that matter, what was a California metaphysical channel doing talking to diplomats about the state of the world?

I began my lecture by telling them: "In the Middle East, where the prophecies had told us that the sands would be running red with blood right now, instead there are two former enemies making water rights together!" I continued by telling them that the "doom-and-gloomers" may have the popular airwaves and movies of the week, but the overview of the reality of the state of the world was far more hopeful and moving in a new direction. It is far more dramatic and commercial to frighten than to soothe, and the marketers were giving us just what they knew would frighten us.

Whereas just ten years ago the shouts in the Middle East were "revenge" and "deserved lands," today they are deciding what lands to give away, which areas to retreat from, and are saying, "How can we make this work?" Did you notice?

Whereas just ten years ago we had a Cold War that constantly kept us wondering if our kids would make it at all, today we are sending 1.5 billion tons of wheat to a troubled Russia—the place where the "evil empire," the former enemy, used to be. Did you notice?

Whereas just ten years ago there was a raging 30-year Guatemalan civil war, one that had already claimed the lives of more than 50,000 citizens, family members each one, today there is peace. They called off their war in 1997. Did you notice?

Whereas just ten years ago there was no glimmer of anything but hatred and killing between two Christian religions in Ireland, today both sides are still trying to claim that peace is better than war, and are working to change the paradigm of how to handle their differences. Did you notice?

Ten years ago we had vast armies and even vaster weapons depots. Today we have less then a third of the armies and are wondering how to disassemble a stockpile of weaponry that is rusty and unusable. The subject of funding has changed from "how to afford to build bigger ones," to "how to destroy the old ones." Did you notice?

Whereas just ten years ago we were reeling in the horrible predictions of the upcoming millennium prophecies that were being given by old prophets and new, today we stand with none of them having come to pass in the time frame we were told they would. Did you notice?

Something is happening. The consciousness of humanity is beginning to change—slowly, but certainly. The proof is *in, if you choose to look around. The subject is peace, not "who is right or wrong." Communism has almost disappeared by mutual demand of the people, and now most of the world's turmoil is tribal. Most of the strife is over how to bring many opposing sides back to the peace table. Did you notice?*

By invitation, I have returned two more times to the United Nations, the latest being at the end of 1998. Now they expect to hear the "Good News," and I often have a room filled with smiling faces. They have seen the overview, too. In the building in New York where there never seems to be agreement or resolution, they are seeing a consciousness shift. Humans on Earth are beginning to hate less and love more. There is more patience. There is more hope. There is more compassion. They are changing their desires and passions from "what can we get," to "how can we compromise so that everyone wins."

Oh, sure, the old guard from the past is still trying to get back to the way it was, with car bombings and desperate, terrorist acts, but the chiefs keep coming back to the table to smoke that pipe again. Oh, sure, the marketers are pumping up the doom programs and movies to make us wonder if we are going to make it, but their storylines are now outdated and trite compared to the real miracles at hand.

Former political prisoners are now heads of countries. Long-term despots and tyrants have been overthrown by their own populations. Our current Pope is preaching forgiveness and is suddenly outspoken in areas that were never seen before in the Catholic church. People of high consciousness are working on a Council of Elders, a wisdom council made of indigenous peoples of the world—one that might even counsel the United Nations! Did you notice?

I looked up the word millennium in the dictionary. It had two definitions: (1) A span of one thousand years; (2) a hoped-for period of joy, serenity, prosperity, and justice. Did you know that?

In December 1999, a number of us gathered to watch the world pass into the new millennium. We celebrated the fact that whereas others chose to worry, we chose to be peaceful, trusting in a force far grander than fear. We actively chose to trust in the God within us—that spark of grandness that will always choose love over hate, peace over war, forgiveness over revenge. We trusted in a new kind of Human—one who we are currently seeing all over the world—representing a true evolution of the Human Spirit.

What's in These Pages . . .

Again, most of this book was transcribed from live channellings all over the world. The difference this time is that these channellings are dated for you, and represent a lineage of energy that is sequential. That is, you get to see the channellings as we approach the millennium, pass the marker, and move into the new energy.

Also, as before, I wish to mention Kryon's style. He often offers a loving, congratulatory message in the first ten minutes of every channelling. It's quite powerful. Some of these messages are for new ears each time, but will be redundant if repeated over and over in these pages. As before, I removed some of the similar comments to conserve space. Sometimes spiritual core information is reiterated from city to city. Again, I left in some of that duplication since we need to hear it presented over and over.

Chapter 1 presents an explanation and description of some very confusing and difficult issues, but ones that Kryon deals with throughout this book. The discussion of reality, time, and multidimensional issues are difficult concepts. These concepts are needed, however, before the channellings begin. Don't pass this chapter by. It's a necessary treatise to try and simplify some very basic concepts, but ones that we don't normally get into.

As the new millennium energy works with us, we are going to have to grasp the fact that what we saw as our old and constant reality is now changing to become something else. How does this work? How can time itself be variable? This chapter is my attempt to explain things that are almost inexplicable, but which have attributes we are going to use on a daily basis.

Chapters 2 through 7 present the channellings before the millennium change.

Chapters 8 through 12 present channellings given after the passing of the marker, up through June of 2000.

Chapter 13 contains two Kryon concepts that are expanded on by Jan Tober (co-author of the book *The Indigo Children,* and a partner in the Kryon work). Many have heard of The Death Phantom (Shadow Termination is what Kryon called it), and Jan explains it from firsthand experience. Following that is a great interview by Rick Martin of *The Spectrum,* a Las Vegas newspaper, in which Jan presents additional information about the Indigo Children, one of our most popular subjects.

Chapter 14 features writings from three individuals who are doing a profound follow-up on information that Kryon channelled at the United Nations in 1998: Marc Vallée, and Woody and Catie Vaspra. Kryon spoke about the creation of a Council of Elders on the planet—an indigenous group of tribal leaders who might supply the rest of the world with wisdom about our times—information we need right now.

Sometimes people wonder if good ideas ever get manifested. Well, here you will read about people who are actually putting into motion what Kryon suggested. It's quite startling to think that many of the indigenous chiefs of the world are actually waiting for us to contact them! Why? Because their prophecies said we would!

Chapter 15 is a scientific update on some of the issues that Kryon may have spoken of in previous Kryon books as well as this one. These are usually channelled concepts that have been validated since the last Kryon publication. It also contains a discussion regarding my continuing search for evidence of the magnetic properties of DNA . . . something that is beginning to be a real possibility. It's always fun to watch mainstream science verify some heretofore spooky channelled stuff, and we've got it in this chapter!

Chapter 16 is a compilation of some of the Kryon news, ways to get on-line with us, and a section featuring Kryon products and how to obtain them.

Following that is something I've wanted to give the Kryon readership for some time—a complete *master index* of the entire set of Kryon books! This book is included in it, also. For those who have all the Kryon books, finally you have a master index that bridges the gap between all of them. This will make it much easier to look up subjects spanning the Kryon series, One through Eight.

Finally, I give you the *Index* for this book alone.

As I write this Preface, Jan Tober and I have just returned from a tour of French Canada and Europe (May 2000) with Robert Coxon (Canada's bestselling New Age recording artist); and Gregg Braden (geologist, lecturer, and author). Within a ten-day period, we collectively made presentations in front of more than 5,300 people (in Montréal, Canada; Brussels, Belgium; and Paris, France). The meetings were amazing in their energy, and we were all overwhelmed by the love we received.

For years I have wondered who else might possess the message of Kryon—one that said we had the ability to change our future through Human consciousness and compassion—one that said that the real power of the divine is within us. Now I have received a gift: Gregg Braden's research and profound information shows that the divine message I have been receiving for the past 11 years is also present within ancient lost texts of recently discovered scriptures!

The Isaiah Effect (decoding the lost science of prayer and prophecy), by Gregg Braden, is one of the best spiritual books released in the year 2000. Within these pages there is evidence that information offered by Kryon, which has allowed us to change our reality, was also presented to us long ago in the scriptures of the prophets. Within Gregg's book, you will find compelling proof that the compassion of a Human Being can change the reality of Earth—and that this has been a sacred, lost message!

As Gregg, Jan, and I presented together, we were aware that from completely different perspectives, we were giving the same exact message. Gregg, the geologist and computer systems designer; and Jan and myself, spiritualists and channels, were all offering a profound truth—that *you* are powerful, and that much has been hidden in that respect. We are here to find the love and compassion that resides within the divine spark of humanism—something that has been hidden well as part of our test.

Dear reader, I am filled with joy to be able to again give you what has become my contract on Earth—to try to pass the loving information and compassion from a wonderful angel named Kryon . . . to your eyes and hearts.

—Lee Carroll

"Hard Concepts"

Lee Carroll

Chapter One

"Hard Concepts"
By Lee Carroll

I find that my life as a channel is one that deals mostly with translation. The translation of what Kryon has called "The Third Language" is the translation of the voice of Spirit into a Human language. In my case, it's that of English. I know that some of you are reading this book in one of the 11 other languages that are authorized to publish these writings, so you are reading a translation of the translation!

During these last years, Kryon has continually channelled concepts that are very difficult to comprehend in any language. I wanted to begin this book by giving you my impression and explanation of some of the most difficult concepts Kryon has ever delivered. In doing so, I hope to make some of the channellings that follow more decipherable and easier to understand.

I speak now of several concepts, and also of a metaphor that Kryon has presented over and over. In this discussion, I will deal with the following ideas as channelled by Kryon: (1) "now" time (and variable time); (2) Human reality; (3) dimensionality and the metaphor of the train; and (4) the eternal Human soul—all very lightweight subjects, huh?

Now Time

Okay, time is time. I look at the clock, and it always goes at the same speed. In addition, those scientists who measure time for a living have given us atomic clocks—calibrated to finite physics and accurate to within seconds within thousands of years. So, you might say that time is absolute, and science has shown it, right?

Actually, the reverse is true. Time is variable, and science has proven that, also. Kryon says that we live in 4D. Scientists actually label it as "three-plus-one," but I'm getting ahead of myself since the dimensionality discussion is yet to come. I have to let you know within this discussion that Kryon considers time to be one of the four dimensions that we, as Humans, recognize as our reality. Recently, so have physicists. Kryon also states that each of these four dimensions are variable and conceptual in nature: height, width, depth, and time. These are the four. Also note that none of them identify *things*—they are concepts. But more on that later.

Although our clocks go at a precise speed, seemingly only in one direction (forward), one of our greatest scientists theorized otherwise. In 1917, Albert Einstein gave us the Theory of Relativity, which explained variable time. Now, I'm not going to try to explain $E=MC^2$ in these pages. I'm the channel, not the scientist (aren't you glad?). But I'd like to let you know the core issue that Einstein brought to us.

He said that time was variable (or relative) depending on how fast you're going. He gave us the paradox of the clock. This is a fun fictional example about space travelers leaving Earth and traveling at almost the speed of light to a faraway place, then returning. When they return from their journey, everyone they left behind on Earth has aged greatly! Time seemingly had sped up for those on Earth, or had perhaps moved slower for the traveler. Yet in each case, the clocks they had with them seemed to stay consistent for each group! What happened (according to Einstein) is that the variable of speed made a difference in the fabric of time. Therefore, time was relative to speed. This sounded good to physicists but wasn't able to be proven until small particle acceleration revealed that Einstein was correct. At about the same time, astronomers also showed Einstein's theory about gravity bending light to be true. Therefore, we know from a master scientist that time is indeed variable.

I have another metaphor about this that will relate later during our discussion of the train of reality. Two trains leave the station at the same time. One goes faster than the other and arrives at the destination before the other. The clocks on both trains always read the same, but one train gets there first. You might say, "Of course it did. That only makes sense." However, the reality of our Human train only sees time as "the clock." We don't perceive a dimension that allows for another kind of interdimensional time—the speed of the train we are on.

Why go through this story? So that you will understand more about NOW TIME and REALITY. NOW TIME has been mentioned over and over in the Kryon works. From the beginning, Kryon told us that we were in a false, manufactured time called LINEAR time. The time frame of God is NOW. For us it is linear. It may be "false" according to Kryon, but to me, it's the way things work. To me, all things move along a straight path. As they move along this path, a time line is created representing what I did yesterday (the past), today (now), and what I plan for tomorrow (the future). Can there be anything more common and understood than this? Kryon, however, calls it a manufactured attribute for our 4D lives. In addition, Kryon goes on to discuss (in the science channellings) differing time frames in other parts of the "see-able" universe.

Kryon tells us that the "joke" is that we are already in the NOW, but that our linear perception is something that is "pasted on top of it" to make us comfortable. He asks this: *What do you call the present?* The answer, of course, is that we call it TODAY, or NOW. He goes on to ask, *When you get to tomorrow, what will you call it?* The answer is again, TODAY, or NOW. Then he asks, *And tomorrow (which will become your today), when you look backwards in time, what did you call the past when you were in it?* The answer, again, is TODAY, or NOW. Kryon points to this and says that no matter what Humans consider as being past or future, it is always expressed as TODAY or NOW at the instant of its expression. Therefore, NOW is always your reality and mine, and the past and future are only concepts. So, you are always in the NOW.

I know that this sounds esoteric, but it's kind of funny! It means that the only reality we have is NOW, and that yesterday and tomorrow are only pretend. Kryon says that we should look at that, since it is the basis of spiritual NOW time. This discussion is not scientific, but spiritual, since NOW time is needed for a Human to "sit in the Golden Chair" that Kryon speaks of. It's part of the new millennium energy, and it requires Humans to relate to it. Let me explain what Kryon calls the difference between the reality of NOW time and the illusion of linear time. It's my best shot, but remember that the whole thing is interdimensional in concept; therefore, it is difficult at best for a linear mind to grasp (especially mine).

NOW time is in a circle. Everything that ever was or ever will be is there in some form. We stand in the middle of the time circle. The things that we did are still in the NOW with us. (Do you have any photos of what you did awhile back? Or how about memories?) They are still with you right NOW and make up your reality. The future, although not manifest in your reality, exists as "potentials of manifestation" in your NOW circle. Therefore, they are also with you in the NOW. This entire NOW circle is biased with an energy called OUR

REALITY, which is made up of the present, our past, and the potentials for our future. Kryon goes on to say that as we manifest the potentials (or not), the bias of OUR REALITY box changes.

As you change the potentials of this NOW mixture, you also change actual reality for yourselves. Kryon tells us that the lightworker is a "reality shifter" who is able to change humanity and the planet we live on by changing the NOW. This, of course, has been the theme of Kryon since 1989. When reality shifts for us, attributes of time tend to shift, also, although like the speeding travelers in Einstein's example, we can't see it since everything around us is also coming along for the ride.

LINEAR time is what you are used to. YESTERDAY is what happened and can never be repeated. TODAY is what is happening to you now—your reality—and TOMORROW is unknown and only a concept of hope. But the concepts are all happening in an infinite serialization of moments in the NOW. You just read that, right? Hey . . . that was your "now," and in a moment, you will read the next paragraph, and that will be your "now" as well. So where is the real "now"? It's wherever you are!

In NOW time, your existence is a complete snapshot of the energy of the existing past, the existing present, and the existing potential you have created for the future. Therefore, there is a balanced, complete picture of who you are and who you may become. It is also a picture of self-control, enablement, and wisdom. This NOW existence creates a Human who is able to live with the past through the eyes of one who knows the *why* behind it, and can be peaceful with the present through the eyes of one who knows the *potential* of *why* for the future. This is a Human who realizes that the circle is also small enough to be understood, and that all of it—past, present, and future—is known in an interdimensional way. This Human also understands that his NOW circle belongs to him. This creates wisdom and peace. What you have created, you can control and are responsible for. Reality isn't something that is "doing something to you."

Instead of the linear Human, bemoaning the past and trying to deal with it while balancing the present and fearing the future, the NOW Human is peaceful with the concept that says: "All things I ever was or ever will be are contained in an energy of me, right NOW. Therefore, I have all the tools and equipment to walk into any potential I have generated or will ever generate." The linear future may seem to be unknown in its manifestation, but the energy of it isn't unknown at all. This creates a *"been there, done that"* feeling for the enlightened Human—even if the event coming up doesn't really seem to be "known" yet. Kind of like a movie: You have been told how it ends, but you don't know the details yet.

Did you ever meet a person who felt peaceful about anything that might happen? I mean, really at peace—not just giving lip service to a concept that "God will take care of me"? If so, you have met a person who understands the divinity of NOW time. He/she understands that whatever might happen is well within the framework of their abilities, since they have in some way created the reality of it. How about that for an interdimensional concept?

The joke? Kryon says that we all have this potential, but that we have to "unlearn" what the duality of humanism gives to us. This, indeed, is all part of the test we have been participating in—that of climbing out of the 4D box we are in and getting a grip on our own lives.

Needless to say, it does not involve giving away our power to another Human, or any other entity of the universe. It's about self-enablement, self-discernment, self-responsibility, and yes, the development of self-worth. And that, friends (reading this book), is what the New Age is all about.

Example—Reality A: BOB. This person is constantly dragging up the past, which has shaped him into something he doesn't like. Therefore, he is in the NOW, not liking what he sees. In addition, that same person is apt to be fearful of the future, due to the experience he had in the past. So, he has created a NOW that is biased toward fear, victimization, and lack of self-worth.

Example—Reality B: BOB. This same person starts to understand how things work. He looks at the past and claims responsibility for it. Therefore, it existed with his permission, and it gave him value within the scope of his current experience. He feels far better about himself, and now he's confident that the future is filled with spiritual promise. This person (the same one) has created a NOW that is biased toward love, understanding, responsibility, and hope.

So . . . will the real BOB please stand up? Kryon says that Bob changed his reality. He didn't just change his outlook or projections—he didn't just start thinking positively. Bob changed his inner understanding, and even his time frame. For what Bob has now is far more aligned with the angel inside of him.

Human Reality

Okay, if the time and NOW discussion above was tough, this is even tougher, so I will make it brief. Reality—the stuff around you right now—the chair, the light, the smell of the air—all of it seems to be stable, and it's the stuff you can claim as REAL. What about discussions of multiple realities, or about changing our reality? What does that really mean? Personally, I have never actually watched the things in front of me dissolve into something else, so what does it mean? Well, Bob did it (last page), and his reality changed. He didn't seem to have multiple realities . . . or did he? I want to point something out about Bob: When he was in fear, he still had the potential of self-worth. Although he was participating in one reality, he had many to choose from!

Quite simply, it means that there are multiple realities for Earth and us, but only *one reality at a time*. Think of it as many different shelves within a vertical cabinet. We are sitting on one shelf called *our reality*, but there are also shelves above and below us that are real, and that also belong to us. Hey, it's our cabinet! As we manifest potentials in NOW time, we have the ability to change shelves—up or down. Later in this book, you will read the Kryon explanation of the wonderful story of Abraham and Isaac. It may give you pause for thought. Kryon tells us that through the understanding of who he was (and the message he received from God), Abraham changed the reality of his future during his journey to the top of the mountain, on his way to sacrifice his son. The whole parable takes on a different meaning about the ability of the Human to change his or her reality through choice. (You thought the story was about faith, didn't you?) As you read the metaphor of the train, coming up shortly in this discussion, all of this may make more sense to you.

Therefore, the stuff in front of you that seems real is indeed real. It's just that the *stuff* has many potentials, and you and everyone else are sitting in only one of them at a time. Like the multiple radio station programming flying by in the air, you can only tune to one of them at a time, but there are many available. To add to this puzzling discussion, many times the personal reality of your situation in life—perhaps of worry, concern, and what might happen to you, doesn't belong to everyone around you. It's related to your position in the NOW. Remember how we started with the discussion of time, and how it seems that clocks prove that it never changes, but it really *does,* according to science? I ask you this: In Einstein's "paradox of the clock," which was real—the time on Earth or the time for the traveler? The answer is "both." It's just that they had differing simultaneous realities.

***

I interrupt this discussion to give you a real-life example that happened just as I was typing this on my laptop on an airplane—one of my favorite places to write. Synchronicity is sometimes fun, and in this energy of the new millennium, I have never had faster validations and synchronistic lessons in my life.

It's February 20, 2000, and I'm on United Airlines flight 229 from Washington, D.C., to San Diego. I'm flying back home after a wonderful series of *Kryon at Home* meetings in some southern cities of the United States (Roswell, Georgia; and Spartanburg, South Carolina). I just finished typing the paragraph (two above this one), when we all felt a jolt on our Airbus—one that didn't feel like the typical turbulence that is common in flight.

A man sitting in row 12 on the right side of the aircraft (slightly aft of the wing) yelled that there was fire coming from the engine! The flight attendants ran to check it out, peering out the windows of various rows, while surprised passengers strained to get out of their way. Yep, there was fire! They ran back up the aisle, and a moment later, a number of things happened. First, they stopped the in-flight movie (I really wanted to see it, too!). Next, they dropped their smiles and became the most efficient team of no-nonsense instructors I have ever seen. Standing in the aisles, they waited for the captain to inform us that we had lost an engine (we suspected that), and that we were going to land at the first airport possible (which eventually became St. Louis). We were descending rapidly as well (my ears told me that, since it was dark outside and you couldn't see anything . . . except for flames coming out of an engine).

The next half hour was spent circling St. Louis while the pilots went through the standard checklists for emergencies like this, dumped fuel to reduce weight (allowing us to land safely), and the attendants turned on the lights and drilled us in the brace position. (I really would have preferred to see the movie.)

There were many who were very frightened. The man who had actually seen the fire was white with fear. He was glued to the window, waiting for more fire, even though the engine was turned off and cold (we were told). Others were starting to squirm, and you could actually see the fear spread over the group in this relatively small, vibrating, pressurized tube called an airliner that was quickly descending from 30,000 feet to slightly under 5,000. Other sounds that you normally don't hear while flying started to present themselves as the pilots tested systems, and the pumps continued to dump fuel. People were scared. The new sounds didn't help much, either.

I closed my laptop and looked around. This was real! Indeed, there is nothing like the feeling of a less-than-comforting reality. We were being drilled in preparation for crashing!

Now, stop the story . . .

Why was I there? What was the lesson? Kryon came to me (as he does all the time) and said, *Lee, are you afraid?* I said no. It was weird, but the answer was no. Everything seemed okay to me. He told me that I was in the right place at the right time, and that I should look around at the various realities that were happening on the plane.

Some were revisiting the recent West Coast Alaska Airlines crash in their minds as they felt the plane jerking around in a slower-than-normal circle around the St. Louis airport. This caused them great fear. Some were starting to panic. The man in row 12 was *expecting* to see more fire. The flight attendants knew this, so they came on the loudspeakers to reassure us all. The head flight attendant told us that she had done this before—etc., etc. (She had crashed before?) It helped some, but others were beginning to doubt that they were being told the truth. The plane didn't feel right. The unknown creates fear. Fear creates doubt and conspiracy theories—sounds like life to me.

The flight attendants also told the crowd that the plane could fly on one engine. (Then why was the plane designed with two, the crowd answered almost in unison.) In other words, no matter what was said, the individuals on the plane had a reality that was made up of what they had experienced, were experiencing, and potentially expected. Wow. What a nice lesson.

My reality? I saw myself on the ground in the air terminal in St. Louis typing this message to you and having a Coke (which is, of course, what happened). But for many, the reality was fear, panic, and no peace at all about this very REAL situation that was unfolding. I admit that I've had a lot of practice being in the NOW. It has tempered my reality, and I absolutely knew that all would be okay. I had no way of imparting that to anyone on the plane, but I felt in charge of what I had created, and I hadn't created a crash today with these folks. There were lots of different realities on that aircraft for that half hour. I got to watch them, and I realized why I was there.

Continuing the story . . .

We started our approach to the airport, and I was aware of the difficulty that the pilot must be having. The aircraft was *yawing* as we were on final approach. This meant that it seemed like the airplane wasn't able to stay pointed straight ahead. It was flying in a straight line, but the actual plane was pointed to the left, then the right, as the one engine on one wing was given more or less thrust as we approached the landing. With only that one engine to power the delicate landing process, the aircraft felt very different to all of us who fly frequently. I'm certain it did to the pilot, too!

At 500 feet, the pilot came on the intercom and sharply spoke the words, "Brace, brace." All passengers grabbed their ankles and put their heads between their knees. You know those emergency cards in the front pocket of your seats when you fly? We actually used them! I found myself, along with the others, closely inspecting my knees!

In a rehearsed scenario, the flight attendants chanted together in unison: "Stay down, don't get up; stay down, don't get up" as the plane approached the beginning of the runway. It was all very interesting, but I was peaceful. It seemed that at the last moment, the plane seemed to float above the runway and straighten out. We had what seemed to be a normal landing. The cabin broke out into applause as we slowed after touching down, and strangers who had shared various realities moments before were all sharing only one at that moment—the one of celebration!

We made our way to a spare gate at the St. Louis terminal that belonged to another airline, followed by at least eight emergency trucks—with lots of firefighters all eyeballing the right engine that had caught fire and had to be shut down. We all wanted to hug the pilots, but they scampered away—probably to do massive paperwork and get a debriefing about what happened before they forgot the details. I'm told that the tapes in the "black box" (which is orange) were also being downloaded to study the event for the FAA's safety board.

Right NOW my reality is the one I saw all along: I'm in St. Louis, on the ground, writing this to you. Kryon gave me a synchronicity—not to test my ability to sit in the *golden chair* (as some of you know about from previous books), but to look at how REALITY is very different from person to person even within the framework of sharing the same situation together.

Friend, how do you see your life? How about challenge in your life? Can you sit in peace and change your reality during some of the worst moments? If the answer is yes, then you truly understand your divinity. You are able to sit in the golden chair (Kryon book Six).

The Metaphor of the Train
(and dimensionality)

Kryon's metaphor of the train is alluded to in this book in several channellings, but I'm going to give you a more complete way so that you will understand it better when you read about it in the chapters coming up. This metaphor is about three things: (1) the explanation of dimensionality; (2) how prophets tell the future; and (3) a metaphoric example of what has happened in the last couple of decades to the reality of the planet.

Kryon tells us that we love to compartmentalize almost everything we can. We also have a desire to label or number almost everything—even concepts. Kryon told us that his/her family was that of Archangel Michael. I immediately wanted to know how that worked. What did the angel chart look like? The one of importance, command, and responsibility? That's when Kryon told me that there was no such *chart*. In fact, there was no hierarchy and no vertical organization! I wondered how this could be. I was used to vertical management organization, where there is a boss or commander, then subordinates, etc. How else would you know who did what? Kryon says that the family of Spirit is horizontal, interdimensionally! Go figure out what *that* means!

Imagine being in a corporate structure where you work with others and there are no managers at all—where all the employees somehow make decisions together about the direction of the team. This would require some kind of similar mass consciousness and common knowledge to work. Kryon says that's exactly what the spiritual family does!

Kryon also says that it's a silly thing for Humans to want to *number* dimensions. Here is what he tells us about dimensionality: (1) Dimensions are all related to each other and contain elements of each other. So how can you differentiate them? A "higher" one is often a combination of the lower ones and the higher one, but we want to give it a number and give it a level of importance. (2) Dimensions are all concepts, and never concrete things. Therefore, you can't even define them without somehow including the thing that they affect (they are relative to the thing they are describing).

For instance, Kryon says that we live in four dimensions (he doesn't like to even say that)! But for us, he says we are "4D." As I mentioned before, the dimensions are height, width, depth, and time. Each one is a concept, and you can't easily make sense of them unless you describe them relative to something they affect. Example: Pretend there is a square box on your lap. (If you are reading this standing up, then sit down.) The box has height, width, and depth, and it's in your time. There it sits with you in 4D. Now, along comes a friend who turns it over a few times and puts it back on your lap. Oops! The *height* of the box that your friend just turned over used to be the *depth* before he came along! *Which is it?* you might ask. The answer is that it depends on what *time* you looked at it!

Do you understand that all the dimensions—even our simple four—only exist as concepts that are waiting to manifest materially through our examination? In addition, they seem to be all one thing and relate to each other. Together, they create a wholeness, which we define as *our reality.* And like the box, it can change depending on circumstances we create.

Kryon tells me that together, the dimensionality of our existence is like a cake. When you cut into a cake (now I'm going to get hungry if I continue this), there are no pointers inside that are created with labels that say, "Here is number one, the sugar; here is number two, the salt; here is number three, the flower." No. These were ingredients that made up the whole cake. As you look at the cake or taste it, you are not aware of the parts. Instead, you enjoy and participate in the whole cake. This is as close to defining how dimensions relate to each other as I can get.

We are part of a 4D cake called *humanism,* which is a mixture. (No wonder Kryon doesn't like to number these things.) In addition, this 4D mixture sits in an infinite dimensional bowl—one we can't see, but one that contains ingredients that can be added to the cake to make it taste better. All it takes is for the cook (us) to decide we want more ingredients. Like a radio station that is not tuned to a station, unless we "tune in" to the other ingredients, we may not know that they even exist. Kryon says that it's this "tuning in" that is the subject of changing our reality.

The train: Kryon tells us that our Human 4D reality in linear time is like a train called *humanity.* It is moving along a track. You are aware of the motion of the train, which you call the passage of time. The track is your reality. As the train moves forward, you get your precious past, present, and future (which we like to pretend is there). The track represents everything that ever was (seemingly behind us) and everything that ever will be (seemingly in front of us). Before I give you the secret attribute of the track, I will let you in on some additional dimensions.

Again, this Human train is 4D (or three-plus-one, as the scientists like to say). It has height, width, depth, and time. Kryon says that there are a bunch more on our train that we are not aware of. We just haven't tuned into them yet. We also have dimensions five, six, seven (if we have to number them), and more lurking around, waiting to be activated.

Okay, Kryon, what is number five? Kryon says it's the ability to put *windows* in the train! What? Our train doesn't have windows? *Nope,* says Kryon. We feel the motion of time, but we have no idea either how fast we are going (by looking out the windows), or what is in front of the train (the ability to identify our potential future, or what energy we are headed into). I never thought about that. Now I better understand the process that visionaries with fifth-dimensional sight have!

Here is how Kryon says the metaphor of the train helps to create a specific reality that can be "seen" by those who have fifth-dimensional sight. To give you this, I should now reveal the secret attribute of the track that I mentioned before. When it came to thinking about our "reality" train, you might have visualized a perfectly straight track for this humanity train— one that disappears into infinity both in front of you and behind you. If you saw that, you were as fooled as I was. The track isn't straight at all. Instead, it's in a circle! The circle may really be big, but the track is a circular one. Does this remind you of NOW time yet? By the way, to the amusement of most mathematicians, Kryon also says that there is no such thing as a straight line in the Universe.

As our "humanity train" moves around the *track of reality*, energy packets are dropped at consistent intervals. (Remember, this is a metaphor, okay?) These energy packets are representative of the energy (consciousness and enlightenment) of humanity at the moment they are dropped. It's kind of like a time capsule that indicates who we are at the moment. As the train comes around again in a year or so (in its big circle), another packet is dropped in exactly the same place. If the spiritual energy of humanity is identical (as it has been for eons) to the first packet dropped earlier, then the combined energy of the two packets together amplifies itself on the track, and the potential on the track becomes bigger.

Soon, any visionary who has "fifth-dimensional sight" can see the energy packets coming from their window in front of the train. The packets are really big! Metaphorically, these packets represent our future *potential*, or what we are *creating together* for the future as we go around the track. Today's energy is tomorrow's potential (more NOW stuff). In addition, we have to mention the obvious. If the track is in a circle, then the past, present, and future are all part of the same straight linear time of the track. What then defines the difference between past, present, and future is our train's relative position on the track (even more NOW stuff). Did I tell you this would be fun?

Old prophets such as Nostradamus and those who wrote the scriptures; or new prophets such as the current Gordon-Michael Scallion, can use their gift of having a window in front of the train. They can look out on the track and identify the energy and see how big the packets are. They often give us a very accurate description of what we are creating for our future, and how long it will be before the packets are going to be converted into manifestation. As long as the energy of humanity stays the same, the predictions get easier and more accurate (since the packets get bigger each time around). Eventually we hit a very big energy packet, and it manifests itself into . . . (you guessed it) our present reality.

In my previous books, I told you that the entire purpose behind Kryon is to help us understand how this works so that we can understand how we've changed our future. But up until now, we've had a whole bunch of believable prophetic predictions about our end times that all seemed to "line up" (have validity, one with another)! This fact has scared a lot of people (kind of like being in an airplane with an engine on fire). If the stewardess and the pilots had told the passengers that they were going to crash, I think the reality would really have been far different. But look at this: On our earth, almost all the authorities (ones with the wisdom of prophecy) have told us that we were going to crash! Now if you noticed, when it came time to land on January 1, 2000, we made it. No crash.

So if you have to number them, the fifth dimension in our train is a dimensionality that gives us the ability to see out of the train. In addition to giving you a good idea of what is on the track in front of you, you also get to see the trees whiz by (metaphoric stuff again), so you can actually see how fast you are going.

Remember my discussion on the relativity of time? We really don't know how fast we are going. We don't even have windows! Our clocks all stay the same on our train, and we are aware of the motion of time. But are we moving faster on the track? Slower? This leads me to what Kryon calls the sixth dimension—the speed of the train! Like that cake we talked about a bit ago, these dimensions all have to fit each other, and none can stand alone. They all affect the "taste of the cake," or in our case, our "reality." The speed of our train (dimension six) is therefore relative to all the other dimensions around it, including the one coming up. I want you to remember something: No matter how fast we go on our track, the clocks still read the same (as I mentioned when we started). The relative time in the train is always constant. Even if we are really flying down the track, our clocks don't care.

The seventh dimension in our train metaphor is the *color* of the train. What does that mean? In metaphysics, color often represents the energy level of a certain vibration. So in this metaphor, the *color* means the *vibratory rate* of the train—or in this case, of humanity. Note that this is very much related to number four, time; and number six, speed. If this becomes confusing, just remember that Kryon told us not to number these things! He wants us to taste them so that we get an idea of the relative wholeness of the pieces.

So, now we have an explanation of seven dimensions: (1) height; (2) width; (3) depth; (4) time; (5) energy and time awareness; (6) speed awareness; and (7) vibratory rate awareness. Again, I'd like you to notice that there is no concrete, empirical meaning for any of these seven words. They all describe something else. That makes them conceptual in my opinion. Therefore, any discussion of dimensionality is going to be kind of difficult to grasp. (I'm still trying to figure out Einstein's time puzzle!)

Some books have recently informed us that we are now moving into ascension status, and that ascension status moves us into the fifth, sixth, and seventh dimensions. I agree! Take a look at how the metaphor of the train shows how humanity is starting to use number five, six, and seven. Now, do you understand it better? There's more here, and even another metaphor to explain it. Again, Kryon says that like a radio station, each dimension has to be "tuned in to" by the vibration radio of our cellular structure. If we are not tuned to the station, we won't be able to get the whole understanding.

Scientists have recently reported that the inside of the atom has multiple dimensions that we cannot see, and that we are going to have to develop a new kind of math to get a good picture of how things work. To me, this is like saying, "We can't tune in to them yet."

Okay, now we have a new cake. We have more ingredients than the basic ones we always used, and now it's time to add the chocolate or almonds or vanilla (I'm heading for the kitchen). The metaphor of the train isn't over. The best part is yet to come.

Changing tracks: In metaphysics, did you ever hear the phrase, "The only planet of free choice"? I always wondered what that meant. It seemed a bit grandiose to think that of all the planets that probably exhibit intelligent life, we are the only ones who could select eggs for breakfast (for instance). Well, this phrase is relative to the Human spirit, so it's not about breakfast or choosing what to wear or where to go. It's about spiritual choice.

If you read Kryon Book Seven, *Letters from Home*, you found a channelling called "The Meaning of Life" regarding our purpose for the Universe. I'm not going to rehash that now, but I point to it for help in understanding the meaning of our phrase, "The only planet of free choice." Humanity had made some kind of spiritual choice about itself. This changed the universe.

Kryon calls us *Angels, pretending to be Human.* Since 1989, and his arrival in my life, this has been his message to us. Remember the subject of Kryon Book One, *The End Times?* He told us that our future had changed, and that none of the doom-and-gloom prophecies were going to come true. Well . . . here we sit within the proof of that. Most of the times given for doom and gloom have passed. He also told us that we were members of a spiritual family that "always was" and "always will be" (more on that later). Evidently, this spiritual family called humanity had somehow made a choice to move itself from where it was to where it could be. The ability for this choice, therefore, was always there, but only recently realized and implemented. This earth is populated with a spiritual family that can change dimensionality. We can change our reality!

Back to the train: Our train of humanity has been in an existing circle for eons. The more we traveled the same track, the more energy packets we dropped. The more the packets were enhanced with a common energy, the more obvious it was that at the end of the test we had planned, a certain future would be manifested. Around and around we went. Prophets of old took a look out on the track and told us what was coming. So did the indigenous peoples of Earth, and most impressive, so did many of our living "seers."

But what happened? The quatrains of Nostradamus tell a story that simply didn't happen. Did the best Bible scholars on Earth who interpreted the time frames for the events of the book of Revelation all get it wrong? Many indigenous peoples of the planet, separated by thousands of years and thousands of miles, told a synchronous story . . . was *it* wrong, too? Go take a look. Don't just read this weird book and nod your head. It's everywhere to see! Something happened!

Kryon tells us that between 1963 and 1987, the "train of humanity" decided to *change tracks*! I don't know exactly when it happened, but according to recent channellings, the energy of the planet is measured (not tested) every 25 years. Do you remember the energy of the early '60s? There was a spiritual measurement in 1963. We were having race riots in America, Communism was threatening, we had war in Asia, and many of our leaders were being assassinated. We were right on the old track, and were headed for the energy packets that all the prophets had clearly seen.

When the earth was measured again in 1987 (the Harmonic Convergence), the energy had changed vastly. Most important, Kryon tells us that in that period of time, we used our free choice to change tracks. Although not entirely accurate for our metaphor, I love to visualize that we took a higher track, leaving the old one and all its old energy predictions behind.

What has happened since, including the energy we sit in, is an overview that should not be lost on any of you. Communism fell over by itself—ruining the old prophecies by removing one of the key players. The feared negative attributes of Y2K didn't happen (another spiritual metaphor God gave us for an unprepared genetic code for the year 2000). The celebration on January 1 of the new millennium was unmarred across the world by any old energy predictions, and here we are on a brand new track. In Israel, the prophesied flash point of the end times (according to most prophecies) didn't happen.

Ten to fifteen years ago, some current issues we now face would never have been issues at all. Politically, Americans almost impeached a president for what presidents and Congress (in general) had been doing for years. Morality issues and the elimination of the "good old boys club" is paramount in society. Look who quit Congress during all the fuss, and who didn't want to be examined (some fairly famous faces).

The greatest purpose in astronomy today (according to *Discover* magazine) is to find other life in the universe. Go figure! A few years ago, that would have been an "eye-roller." Now it's a mainstream goal. Every Mars probe from now on will contain an elegant life-detection kit. Many astronomers feel that a moon of Jupiter has an ocean under ice, and that life could exist there, too!

Instead of global conflict, we have tribal conflict (as Kryon told us might be the case at the United Nations channelling in 1996). The biggest conflicts we have on Earth are between ancient rivals. The biggest moral issue on Earth is genocide—the right of governments to kill their own people. This is something that has been with us forever, but now it's a very large issue. How large? Take a look at Kosovo, and the very unlikely coalition of governments that tried to bring an end to a dictator's chaos. (By the way, page 23 of Kryon Book One, *The End Times*, written in 1989, gives this exact potential.) It happened again in East Timor. There is finally an Earth consensus that the people of this planet won't sit back and just let it happen. That's new.

Today, much of our news is about the revelation of wrongdoing in the past, and also about (gulp) responsibility! Seen any police departments being called on the carpet today for what was "business as usual" for the last decade or so? Seen any investigations about past dictators, or the responsibility issue of past governments for what they did? Seen any scandals lately within formerly respectable institutions, such as banking or insurance? Call it what you want, but we are in a major housecleaning, and that requires a consciousness shift.

At a time when "everybody can talk to everybody" via the Internet, it's becoming more and more difficult for any government anywhere to conspire against its own citizenship (including the U.S.). As I write this, the headlines in the news today tell of our current Pope finally apologizing for the Spanish Inquisition! (I guess that's only proper, since last year he also apologized to Galileo's family for jailing him when Galileo said that the earth was not the center of the universe.) The Pope is also visiting Israel and is not afraid to say the name of the country! (The last Pope who visited Israel in the 1960s stayed only for a few hours, and would not say the word *Israel*.) This Pope is there celebrating with the Jews, and participating with them in ceremony. He has even openly asked forgiveness for the Church's past stand on the Holocaust. Things are changing!

Seen any reactions to intolerance lately? Many fundamentalist Christian organizations feel that more and more of the population is turning against them. They actually feel attacked. Actually, the issue is about Human intolerance, not about any belief system or doctrine. In an arena where almost everyone knows of Christ's admonition to "love one another," there are followers who are now being asked why they are not doing this. The question is a good one. The whole intolerance issue is kind of funny. Suddenly we have a general message of Human consciousness that "we won't tolerate intolerance"! Kryon has spoken of this many times as a potential for Earth shift.

In other words, we are looking at an entirely different Earth. The predicted problems are not the ones we are facing. Personally, nationally, internationally, scientifically, and medically, what we were told we would face is not at all what we are looking at. Instead, we have issues of morality, genocide, responsibility, intolerance, and ancient tribal differences coming to a head, and an awakening to many secrets of the past—ones that participants who are still alive can hardly wait to share. The beginning of an age of honesty and integrity? You can't help but wonder.

Also, take a look at what is happening regarding Kryon's suggestion at the United Nations in1996 about creating a Council of Indigenous Wisdom—a nonvoting council of wise indigenous tribal chiefs of the world, willing to be consulted about issues of importance to the U.N. Chapter 14 in this book details some of the work regarding this issue. It's starting to actually happen!

So, did we really change tracks? If we did, then those with fifth-dimensional sight should be seeing NO energy packets. Let's look at this. Years ago, Gordon-Michael Scallion gave us a frightening map, showing many of the populated coast-lines of the earth covered by water. I have spoken of this in my other books. In his first map, he dated events very clearly and published what he had "seen." Since *none* of the doom and gloom has happened as he predicted, and all the original dates on his map have passed, you might therefore say that Mr. Scallion was wrong. I say no! It takes a lot of courage to date these things within your own lifetime. I feel that Mr. Scallion saw what he saw, and came back from his visions to tell us about them. It was *real* as he looked at it since it was our collective reality that he saw at the time. He visited the window in the front of the train, saw the energy packets, and intuitively computed the time it would take to manifest what our train had been creating for eons. Knowing full well that if these things did not happen he would be ridiculed, he published it anyway. I celebrate his courage.

When the dates passed without incident, Mr. Scallion again went out to check his vision. Something had obviously changed, for he returned and published a new map with new dates! Somehow he felt that we had postponed the inevi-table.

When some of those dates also slipped by, he again used his gift of sight and decided to give us still another glimpse of the track before us. What we now have is his third map—without any dates! In addition, he has provided a printed "disclaimer" that voids the whole purpose of the map! It says (paraphrased): *Human consciousness can change any of this.*

Finally, I can now point to a current doom-and-gloom visionary who not only had his vision altered, but also accepts the fact that things have changed, and that *we* had something to do with it.

What's out there now on that track in front of us? Let me tell you what Kryon says: *There is nothing there!* Kryon even tells us that we are laying the track as we go, and that's called co-creation at its highest level. How's that for being interdimensional? I repeat something that Kryon told us very early on: *There is no entity on either side of the veil who can tell you your future!* You have discovered that you can change it through consciousness and intent, and the world will never be the same. The energy of today is not that of tomorrow. This is the attribute of an enlightened Earth—one that has changed its reality.

How is it different? What is the time line now? What are the potentials? That is the purpose of this book—to bring you the channellings of the past year, right before and right after the "passing of the marker," the entrance or gateway to the new millennium.

The Eternal Human Soul

I can't end this discussion without reminding the reader that according to my channellings, we are eternal. Some of you feel like you are "lab rats for God." I know, since I have spoken to thousands of you personally over the years. If you finally realize that you helped plan all this, executed it, and could hardly wait to return each time, it might help you realize that you are the *caretaker* of the test, not *the experiment.* As Kryon told you in the last book, the test is about *energy*, not about *us.* We are the testers, and energy measurement is the result.

I find the concept of being eternal one that I can't understand. Kryon says we are "eternal in both directions." Wow. That means that we had no beginning and will have no end. My brain can't go there. Everything has to have a beginning, right? Scientists have spent lifetimes pondering the beginning of the Universe—the beginning of time. You and I are born, and we see all around us with a beginning and an end. It's intuitive in our duality to search for a beginning for everything.

Kryon says that all this was presented as the illusion of linear time for the Human Being. Our discussion of the NOW in this section points out that we are circular. Kryon says that our inability to see this circle is duality at its best.

I have a funny thing to share with you, and it's about this very subject—the illogical nature of humanity in general to see our very spiritual nature—simply because the words *no beginning* do not compute!

Last year as we approached the new millennium, *Time* magazine, among my favorite sources for what's going on in the world, published several issues on religion. This was obviously due to the tremendous emphasis that old prophecy was having on people's fears and expectations. In one article I read, *Time* said that according to research, 85 percent of the earth's population believed in the concept of an "afterlife."

Wow! When you have that kind of consensus on the planet, I believe that it's more than wishful thinking. It spanned all religions and cultures, and even took in those tribes in the New Guinea jungles who had never seen a Westerner until three years ago. Most of them believed in an afterlife, also. When this happens, I believe that it's a cellular intuition, and most belief systems around God have this in common as well.

Here's the funny part. According to mainstream Human belief (85 percent), we don't die at Human death, but instead we go on to something more. We have souls that are interdimensional. But, according to most religions, none of this can happen until we are biologically born on Earth! See, although most of the planet believes in the afterlife, the majority *don't* believe in a "forelife"! You might be eternal now, but before you got here, you didn't exist? This really is a funny concept, and to me, it does not make spiritual sense at all and has no balance to it. Somehow our biological birth experience gives us an eternal soul? If so, where did it come from? I show this as an example of duality at work. It's illogical, but it is accepted as general thought.

Metaphysics is not the only philosophy that has the soul existing before it incarnates, but because we openly believe in past lives, we are the ones who are most often made fun of in the Western world. When you back up and look at a spiritual overview, to me it makes total sense that if we have a soul, it existed before we got here. Acknowledgment of that one fact will eventually open the door to the potential that maybe, just maybe, we might have been here many times—in the circle of the NOW—and that the family goes around and around, just like the train.

Enjoy this, Kryon's eighth channelled book.

—Lee Carroll

Live Channelling

"Time and Reality"
Part One

Channelled in
Indianapolis, IN — June 1999
Auckland, New Zealand — August 1999

Chapter Two

"Time and Reality — Part One"
Live Channelling
Indianapolis, IN — June 1999
Auckland, New Zealand — August 1999

*The live channeling that follows was transcribed
as a combination of two events on two different
continents . . . all with the same message . . .
given live. It has been edited with additional
words and thoughts to allow clarification and
better understanding of the written word.*

Greetings, dear ones. I AM Kryon of Magnetic Service. This is a precious reunion at this time, is it not? The feeling this fair day, as the entourage pours into this room—knowing who sits in these chairs—knowing the family and who is reading this, is one of precious family. It has an overview of sweetness. For reunions have that feeling—an attitude of overwhelming expectation and love.

We've said this before to so many of you who've come and gone, come and gone, spending so little time "at home": Here you sit in an age that is changing greatly, on a planet that resounds under your feet with vibrational shifts. The Human sits here and wonders if he is powerful, not understanding who he is. Humanity sits and fears the weather, never understanding or realizing that Earth is a partner with you. You are pieces of the whole! You are in control.

I will now reveal what the statement means that you have heard for so many years—the one I give when I come into your midst to greet you. I say, "I AM Kryon of Magnetic Service."

Perhaps you thought that I was identifying myself to you? If you did, you would be right. But there is far more than that, for in my identity greeting, there is a hidden statement. Within the statement "I AM" is a collective consciousness greeting. There is a transmission of energy in "I AM." When Kryon says, "I AM," it is the description of the connection to *you!* For the "AM" portion of the statement is "the family." When you put the words together into "I AM," it says this: The Kryon is part of the whole, and the "AM" is you, also part of the whole. So when you see a statement from another entity that has the "I AM" in it, you will understand, realize, and know that this is an acknowledgment of family. It is not just a greeting. It is a sacred greeting that speaks to the higher parts of your identity. Therefore, it is a family greeting!

It's those "higher parts" of you—the family—who sit with me today. In this sweet place, we will give you some information that you need to know. Perhaps you will understand more about what is being presented in this new energy when we're finished, but if I can continue with the "I AM" discussion, I will say this— there is more to that phrase than meets the eye. For there is an energy within that phrase that is untranslatable. When you see the phrase "I AM that I AM," it is the acknowledgment of the *"now."* For the "I AM that I AM" says that there is a circle within the phrase that continues to circle. The "AM" that is the circle, rotates, and the "I" that is in the middle, rotates. We are giving you symbols of "the now." We are giving you the geometry of a circle—unbroken—perfect in its base-12 geometry, because you need to hear this, dear ones. We have said to you over and over that we are in "the now." You, as the Human, are in linear time. This explanation is not just so many words. It means so much more to you in this new energy of expectation.

This is the subject for tonight, for it is time you started understanding the native attributes of your essence—that it is *not* a straight line—it is, instead, a circle. If you could see the miracle of the geometry of the family members who are assembled here with you (and for those reading this), you would see very few straight lines. The geometry is indeed made up of circles (and straight lines that create the symmetry and shape of circles), which almost always repeat upon themselves and close in their perfectness. In your natural, sacred state, you will never see a straight line that goes into infinity. That's not part of who you are as a "piece of God." Yet that is what a Human perceives, and it is one-dimensional and very linear. When you look backwards at your path, you add a dimension. That's two-dimensional. If you look upwards, that's three. If you look at the time it takes to go from one place to another on your path, that's four. And within those four dimensions, Human Beings operate about 90 percent of the time. Yet here we are asking you to be in five, six, and seven dimensions as you vibrate higher! When you place yourselves in the "now," you will accomplish this interdimensional shift.

As has already been stated, this is indeed the subject of this transmission—living beyond your apparent dimension—living in "the now." It has been discussed before that this "now" concept is a necessity for you to understand—as lightworkers— as ascended Human Beings. These things will help you bridge the transition into the new energy, an energy that is indeed upon you as we speak.

I am going to give you some attributes of the "now"— perhaps things you've never thought of. The reasons we take you on this informative journey is to show you that you'll need it to understand your new children. The Indigo Child comes to Earth with an aspect you did not have, and my partner (Lee) has mentioned this before. For the child looks around at the world, and within the cellular level, the child says, *"This is right; I deserve to be here."* Within the child's mind, there is a feeling of deserving and belonging—even of purpose. There is no confusion, and nothing is hiding. All is well. There is peace in the birthing process, and when they arrive, they realize that they "expected" to be here. When they open their eyes and look into those of their mothers and fathers, they see the spiritual family they expected to see. You wonder why they often act like "royalty"? Until you show them otherwise, they see the king and queen in you!

Is it no wonder that as soon as they can talk, children often speak of where they've been or who they "were" before this time around? You see, they think *you* are aware, too. They have no concept that you might not be. After all, you are the wise ones who birthed them! It is often in the devastating realization of your ignorance of understanding in this matter that they go into withdrawal and social isolation.

There is an aspect of these children that you've not recognized yet. It is not even in the publication that is here before you (speaking of the new *Indigo Children* book). You see, they have an attribute within their DNA imprint that you do not. They understand about "the now." How is it that a child could be so wise? How is it that a child seems to know a better way in which things could work than a system the adults give them? For that matter, how can a child understand a system that they've never seen before? The answer is that they *have* seen it before—in a circle, in "the now." They have an attribute of knowing, of having "been there and having done that." In the process of this "knowing" is also the attribute of them being seemingly difficult. Have you ever tried to tell a person something that they either already knew, or that perhaps they even knew better than you did? Think about it. It might not sit well coming from a child, but this is exactly what is taking place.

Let me tell you the difference between linear time and *now* time in a way that perhaps you've never thought of before. This *"now time"* is a spiritual way of being that you're going to have to get used to, and I'm going to take you through some attributes of humanness and show you how the linear versus *"now"* perception is needed information. It also will help you to understand why the Indigo is a peaceful being—one who understands balance. Dear ones, the Indigos only become unbalanced when the culture around them unbalances them. When you unbalance an Indigo, believe me, there is terrific imbalance. It's not marginal. When you unbalance a dynamo, it flies apart. The Indigos crave balance. It is their natural state. It belongs to the *"now."*

Human Beings see a path before them and a path behind them. Like an endless train track in which the engine of life moves, the Human Being can also understand infinity—something that never ends—a track that goes on forever. The Human Being cannot, however, understand something that has no beginning (infinity in the other direction)! There is a reason for this. It's because in your sacred state there is no such thing as a straight line that has no beginning. Indeed, it's very common for the family member who is hearing or reading this to say, *"I can't understand something that has no beginning."* I'll tell you why: because it's foreign to your cellular structure, a structure that exists in a circle!

If you could truly see the straight line as it disappears behind you and as it disappears into infinity in front of you, over the horizon, you would understand. Like a perfectly straight road on the earth, eventually it has to meet itself due to the fact that the earth is circular. And so, even the apparent one-dimensional straight line is, indeed, a circle. The "no beginning" that you cannot understand is what you're actually looking at in the future. If you stare long enough at it in the future—agonizing about what might be coming up—it comes around to hit you in the behind!

Now this may seen cryptic to you, but we hope it's going to be less so as we move forward in our explanation. What is the difference between the Human Being who walks in a straight line in linear time and the Human Being who understands standing in an open circle? Imagine yourself in life for a moment, walking a straight path. Some of you can actually visualize walking that path, and you feel that the straighter it is, the better! For, you might think, *Indeed, I am walking a "light" path—straight as an arrow, in spiritual awareness.* In humanism, there is always a horizon. You cannot see beyond it, so there is always something hiding. As long as there is something hiding, it fosters the parts of humanism that develop karma. We talk about fear and anxiety (parts of karma building). We talk about the synchronicity in making mistakes. We talk about self-worth. For you, there is always something hiding. It's just over the horizon, and you have no idea when it's coming or what it's going to be. This is a designed limitation in Human awareness and thinking, and very one-dimensional. It reflects an old energy way of life.

Now, Human—you who are in training, you who are spiritually awakening, you who realize that this is not the end of the test—and instead realize that it's the beginning of a new earth, it's time you took your place in the "now." What was once considered the end is now intermixing with a new beginning. Remember what we just said about that path that is a straight line? It indeed joins itself at some point over the horizon. What seemed to be an end is not. That is why the Indigo Children are here—they are here to meet you at the supposed end of the path on Earth, to guide you to the extension of the end . . . into a new beginning.

Envision this: Life is a circle. Stand in this small circle with me. See the path around you? You can see it all. Now, turn and look at it carefully. If you want to, turn backwards and look at what's behind you as it curves around and becomes your future. It's all there. No part of the path can hide, and all is seen. Blessed are the Indigo Children because they know it's all there. Do you want to know why the Indigo child knows about your systems? Do you want to know why this child has a better way of doing things? Because the child is in a life circle and knows it. It belongs to humanity, but it recognizes the wisdom of what "has been." It has intuition that you did not—about being in the *now*. When you ask Indigo Children to do something new, they will often leap to the challenge. And when you see them "learning," you might note that they are really "reacquainting" themselves with something they were already familiar with. It's not really new!

Let me tell you the basic difference between the current Indigo Child's DNA and yours. Here we are talking about biology again, and some of this is metaphoric, and some of it is actual. We have spoken of a sheath that covers the DNA. This is metaphoric. The sheath is there, but you cannot see it with your instruments. The metaphor is the fact that the sheath is crystalline. Within the word *crystalline* in English is an understanding of "remembrance of energy." Those of you who have used the crystalline energy, perhaps manifested into stones and gems or perhaps used in an astral way, received the same kind of energy—a remembrance of an "imprint." And within the crystalline structure of anything is "memory." Within the crystalline structure are instruction sets waiting to be delivered. I don't expect you to understand this, not all at once. There is a mechanical description coming that you may wish to revisit later, as your science catches up to what is being stated here. The kind of information that is being passed to the DNA is the consciousness of awareness in a "now" state, rather than a linear state. It's spiritual, and it is also biological.

The crystalline sheath around the DNA contains all the memory of a perfect genetic code. A perfect genetic code not only contains seeds of a 950-year life span, but the consciousness of shamanism. We've told you this before. Do you want to know where miraculous healing comes from? When the miracles occur, they come from inside—via your own divine process. There is a divine entity in you called the Higher Self. It's not just angelic or spiritual energy, but rather, it joins with your biology. It's a divine family member, and the actual physics and chemistry of what is going on within any miracle is that the crystalline memory slowly imparts to the DNA the instructions of becoming more perfect, for the sheath knows the perfection of the code. It is the sheath, therefore, that controls Human evolution spiritually.

What activates the sheath? you might ask. How can you get access to the sheath? That, dear ones, is tied in with information that says you are "the only planet of free choice," and may choose at any time to activate it. It is the intent of the individual in pureness, who discovers their divinity and says to their own biology, *"It's time to change the sheath, to impart another bit of DNA, another bit of memory to make it more perfect."* This process actually changes the planet itself!

Some ask, *"How does that work?"* There's always the scientist who wants to know about the exact process. How does the sheath "talk" to the DNA? I'll give you some hints. Magnetism! The magnetism isn't what does the changing, but rather, it is only the medium of transfer. For the instructions go from the sheath to the DNA, using magnetics, with a code-set that talks to the DNA. The instructions say, "It's time for your genetic and biological processes to work better. Let's have better balance awareness of the cells. Let's communicate better." That's what's contained in the sheath. How does it work? Magnetism!

We'll give you another hint. It is the same process, dear ones, that is in the cellular matter of your brains. The synapse that you call intelligence and consciousness is a wiring system that never touches. Did you know that? The biological parts come close, but they do not touch. How can messages be transferred from one place to another at incredible speed when the "wires" don't even touch? Seemingly, it's a mystery. Yet that's the transfer method you have going on right now in your own minds and brains. It allows you to think, and have Human consciousness. It's also a process that you fully understand in your science when it comes to magnetism, electricity, and current flow—and it's called *inductance*.

Here is information we have never shared before. It isn't a prediction, but rather a statement of how your internal biology works. Someday your science will admit it, and you can remember that you heard and read it here first. Recently your science discovered that DNA was not a strand, but rather a loop! That means that it closes upon itself and is in a circle [surprised? See page 360]. What has also just been discovered is that DNA transmits electricity with the same attributes of a highly cooled wire. That is to say, your science now has also found that DNA is a super conductor of current! [See page 359.]

Here is a scenario for you to ponder. DNA consists of loops of code with a consistent but often unique current flowing through each. The current sets up a small magnetic field, which allows for the transfer of information through magnetism. Scientists, did you ever wonder why the DNA ladder twists? Part of (but not all) of the answer is that it is magnetic, therefore polarized. The polarized proteins in their coded stranded groups of 12 move in a symmetry that twists in reaction to the attraction and repulsion of their magnetic polarization.

The magnetic system of the earth (the magnetic grid) postures the ability of the sheath to work its miracles. As we told you in 1989, we are here to move the grid. Now you know why! Not only does the grid change affect your spirituality, it allows for new health empowerment at a cellular level! When this information started coming in, your science denied that the grid system of the earth had any effect at all on your biology. Today, ten years later, they know better, and are discovering that the effect of magnetics is indeed profound and diverse in all living creatures, and at the cellular level of all living matter.

So, the earth's grid allows for the sheath to do its work of transferring new information to the DNA. What do you suppose is the catalyst that allows for the sheath's instructions to the DNA to be transferred? It's a profound energy that can change matter, and it's called the Human consciousness of *intent*.

When intent is given, the sheath releases its magnetic information that intersects the magnetic fields of the closed DNA loops, and through a process you call inductance, the information goes into the polarity structure of your cellular makeup.

Most of this cellular makeup is already in place with the Indigos. What you are having to work for, they have naturally. There has been more transferred to their DNA in the way of core informational memory than you came in with. You are now catching up to what they were born with—an ability to understand and work with a "now" concept. This is why we call the Indigos "the next spiritual evolvement of humanity."

How can you be in "the now"? What does it mean? How is it different from a straight line? How can you place this into practical use? Let's talk about it—about why fear and anxiety and synchronicity and even self-worth are so difficult for the linear Human Being. It's because you are living in a straight line. What's the difference between the enlightened Human Being, standing in the middle of the circle, and the one who stands in the straight line? I'll tell you. First, let's talk about fear. We have spoken about fear over and over, and now it's time to give the information to you in another way.

What is fear about? Fear is generated because something is "hiding." Would you have fear if your future were in the open? What's going to happen next? How are things going to work out? If you knew all of those items, would you be frightened? If you knew all of those things, would you be anxious? The answer is, of course not! The one who stands in the circle, however, sees the bigger picture—the complete picture. Nothing's hiding! It's a spiritual wisdom, and that person is peaceful and without fear.

You might say, *"Oh, Kryon, there's something missing here! We live in a linear time frame. You can't change that. There was yesterday, there's now, there's tomorrow, and unless that changes, Kryon, I don't know what's going to happen tomorrow. In fact, Kryon, you have told us that nobody can tell you about tomorrow because we're changing the energy as we go."*

True. So, what do you do with a "circular Human Being" in a linear time frame? How does that work? Let me give you a hint. There is a Human Being who stands on a straight line in linear time who wrings his hands, who fears the future, who doesn't know what's going to happen tomorrow. Take that Human Being and put him in the circle of the *now*. Does he know what's going to happen tomorrow? No, so where is the difference? Listen to this, for this is the key: The one who claims the divinity inside and therefore co-creates his own reality actually controls what he does not understand and what is seemingly hiding. The one who sits in the circle of his own creation is the one who is peaceful. How can you fear what you create? Think of that. For what is created, belongs to the creator! The creator is *you*.

Let me give you another example, old, fearful, anxious one. You worry about synchronicity, don't you? Some might say, *"Kryon, talk to me about synchronicity; I don't understand synchronicity. What if I miss it? What happens?"* Again, visualize your path right now. Most Humans will again see the road that goes into infinity—over the horizon—straight as an arrow. That's not the path at all! Start visualizing a path that is circular. You might say, *"Kryon, that means that I'm going around in circles!"* That's right! You got it! [laughter]

What does that tell you? It tells you that old ground is covered over and over! There's nothing really new! That's right! How is it that the enlightened worker can face a situation that to others would be devastating? How does the lightworker have peace over it? What is it that the guru knows that you don't?

What is it with the ones who sit in perfect contentment with chaos all around them? What do they know that you don't know? The answer: They are not fearing and tormenting something they created and control. There is no fear about what they have created. There is no fear with the familiarity of it all. Instead, there is peace, for they sit in the circle creating their own reality. Although they might have the feeling of not being able to see over the horizon, they have the spiritual assurance of what is there. They are aware that the future is also the past, and that nothing is really unknown.

"Kryon, what happens if I make a mistake and miss my synchronicity?" You might also say, *"Sometimes I'm stuck—just standing there—and I can't move forward or backward."* Let me tell you what happens when you think you're stuck. I started by telling you that you are in a circle. Well, guess where the family is? It's between you and the center. Now, quite often you are moving one way and the family is moving the other way. If you understand concentrics, you can visualize this. Whereas your circle might be on the outside, moving in a clockwise fashion, quite often the family is moving in a counter-clockwise fashion. If you happen to stop, they don't! Don't be surprised if you think you're stuck, only to find out in retrospect that we stopped you so that the synchronicity could catch up! And while you're wringing your hands wondering what's going on, praying to move forward, Spirit has held a giant "stop sign" that says, "Please wait." The Human view during this process is often, *"What is wrong with me?"* The ones in the "now" understand that there's nothing wrong. They celebrate! For they realize that the stop is to allow what they asked for to manifest.

The circle is a divine one. Sometimes it moves at fantastic speeds, and sometimes it is still. Sometimes the center moves faster than the outside, and synchronicity sometimes will come and meet you even if you're "stopped and waiting." Sometimes it even hits you in the rear! I would like to give a name for that process: love, caring, and protection. We, your family, are not in a vacuum as we support you. What were the first messages of Kryon in 1989? You have "guides." You are never alone. We know who you are and what you've been through. That has never changed! Here you are in 1999, with an entourage around you that you've had for life. Each of you has an entourage that you're unaware of. You call them maybe two or three guides. What you don't see are the "oversouls," the inner connections, and what you don't understand is the support group behind each and every single family member in the chair or reading this. It doesn't matter who you are or how old you are. That support, dear ones, is activated with your pure intent.

Fear, anxiety, and lack of self-worth have to disappear when you're creating your own future and changing your reality. Let me tell you what happens when you do. The one who decides to try to understand the interdimensionality of their essence is the one who puts one foot into the *now*. That's intent. For years we have spoken to you about feeling peace about things that seem to be chaotic—tolerance in the face of the intolerable. We have told you about the potential of the future. Time after time, we have given you directions about how to be more peaceful and how to chase fear away. We have given this information every time in pure love, and now we are starting to give you the mechanics behind it. It goes like this: You are beginning to have the power, literally, to be closer to the attributes of the entity that you really are in the now. "Vibrating higher," dear ones, are not just words. It's not even a concept. It's real. The person—the Human, who vibrates at a higher level, is the one who has chosen to move up. You could call that whatever you want to, but that is *ascension*, and I will tell you that the secrets of it are now being revealed on this planet!

The Masters gave you the examples. Take a look at the avatars all over the planet as they showed you that   they could create matter out of conscious intent. They showed you peace in death. They emanated love. Dig as deep as you can and find whatever scriptures you wish, and when you get to the core of the original ones, the ones that were written by the pens of those who were enlightened, you will discover that their channellings were about a humanity that can change itself. Change is the norm, and that is the gift. Move in a straight line, but be in the circle. And when you do, peace will be in the circle with you! Come join us there, Human Being. Live a long time, and *create* tomorrow; don't fear it.

Let me give you a potential. There is a consciousness shift on this planet, and you're starting to see it everywhere. Whoever thought it would penetrate your own politics! Now you are going to start seeing it penetrate your religions all over the world. Watch for this. You will have religious leaders decide to change doctrines. I want you to think about that for a moment. For those who would say to Kryon, *"Wait a minute, religious doctrines all over the world are unchangeable. They are based upon tablets and scrolls and sacred elements that were given to Humans to tell them about the way God works."* You're right.

Let me give you an analogy. There's a sleeping Human in a bed, in a room. Now the "sleeping Human" is a metaphor for the duality. The part that is sleeping is the awareness that the Human is also spiritual and powerful, and it's asleep—unknown. Through the years, a methodology—a protocol of caring for the sleeping Human in the room—has been developed for all of humanity to see and use. These have become spiritual instructions for the sleeping Human. The Human is cared for. Bodily functions are cared for. Ingestion is cared for. Peace is cared for. Warmth is cared for. There are ways of controlling temperature and creating health, and the Human is honored and well kept. The procedures for this care are all written down in books, tablets, and scrolls. Many of these instructions were discovered in caves and in the seas long dead. The methods are absolute. They always work, and the sleeping Human is cared for spiritually within the duality he sleeps in.

Now, let me ask you this. When the Human wakes up, what are you going to do with the instructions for a sleeping Human? They don't work anymore. *"Kryon, what are you saying?"* I'm saying there's going to be a consciousness of shamans who are going to change the rules of spiritual caregiving because the population is waking up! The divine aspects of who individual Human Beings really are, are going to change! The gifts, the tools, the power, the enlightenment—even the light itself—is changing on this great planet of free choice. And when it gets down to changes in religious doctrine, you will know and feel and see it for yourself. Watch for it. It is inevitable and has to be. You cannot have a divine doctrine work for servicing a sleeping Human, when the Human has awakened and left the room!

Do you understand this analogy? Even some of your finest spiritual books are no longer going to serve you as they used to. They were well written and channelled, but for a different Human than you, or the children you are now bringing into the world. You are going to have to rewrite the books. And when you do, call them the "now" scriptures—the "circular" scriptures—instructions for the "Now Age" Human Being.

How about *you?* Where do you see yourself in all of this? Are you walking the straight line, worrying about your lone walk, or do you see yourself in the room with us? Let me tell you what the reality is right now, here in the room with us and for those reading this: Where is your reality? You think that perhaps you're in a meeting room on three-dimensional earth, or sitting alone reading something? Our reality? The family is here! If you haven't felt them yet, perhaps now is the time. If you give permission, they will manifest themselves to you physically. You will then know that this day you were hugged from beyond the veil, and you even had your feet washed! The reality? It's that you are not alone, and that you are indeed here with us. All else is an illusion. As you respond to this, the linearity of your life will slowly bend, and it will join the other parts that always are, and were, in a circle. You will slowly become the circular being that has the sacred attribute of creating where they are going!

There is so much love here. Do you understand the honor we have for you? Do you understand what happens when part of the family leaves and accomplishes greatness? Do you know what it's like for a part of the group to go and visit the family when it's in the field doing its work? Well, we do! This group has come to visit you today because you are doing the work. And this group is the one who washes your feet and hugs you from behind the veil and says, "We love you."

Some of you will be able to sit again in front of this entourage. It is not the last time we are here. When you do, we want you to remember the greeting from now on and what it means. We want you to understand what the "I AM" is. We want you to see the circle every time you hear, "Greetings. I AM Kryon of Magnetic Service." We want you to understand that family has visited you today.

We have said that this is the hard part. How do you take family members and split them apart? We know there are never any real good-byes in a circle, because we're always there. But this reunion is about ready to close. My partner has asked that the energy of this love be transmitted this day so many would receive it. There is more here than meets the eye. Let me tell you, things are not always what they seem. Seeds have been planted here this very afternoon among family members who walk this planet, who sit in these chairs, who read these words. We want to tell you that we know why you came. You're going to walk from this room carrying the energy you've asked for. Do you think we could ignore your requests? Do you think Spirit delights in your puzzle? Spirit delights to see you enjoying "the now"!

And so, dear family, it is with some sorrow that we retreat from this room and from the area where you are reading. Again, we tell you this: You are never alone! The energy you have felt today may visit you anytime you want it. You can join us in that circular place. Feel stuck on your path? Celebrate it while the synchronicity moves toward you. Feeling stopped with no apparent direction? Celebrate the knowledge that all is relative and that you are stopped so that others may catch up or come from the front or the side or even from behind (the past) in their time. Celebrate the fact that all is in motion, but that your linearity simply looks like a halt. Actually, the family is in motion around you all the time—just like the incredible love that we have for you is never still.

And so it is.

Kryon

Live Channelling

"Time and Reality"
Part Two

Channelled in
Nancy, France — May 1999
Sante Fe, NM — July 1999
Melbourne, Australia — September 1999

Chapter Three

"Time and Reality — Part Two"
Live Channelling
Nancy, France — May 1999
Sante Fe, NM — July 1999
Melbourne, Australia — September 1999

The live channelling that follows was transcribed as a combination of three events on three different continents . . . all with the same message . . . given live. It has been edited with additional words and thoughts to allow clarification and better understanding of the written word.

Greeting, dear ones. I AM Kryon of Magnetic Service. Let's take a moment while a very special family floods into this area—a precious moment—while the room is being prepared to match the hearts of those who've come to hear and read. We use the word *precious* quite often now. Rather than just being information to be shared during a time that some may call academic, this channelling experience has become a reunion of the first degree.

Oh, there are those here who would say, *"This cannot be happening. It is indeed a product of a fertile imagination on the part of all those attending."* You are hearing a Human voice, yet we say to you, "Let divine energy in this room be the proof of what is really taking place." You can't have angels standing in the aisles and behind your chairs and kneeling in

front of you without feeling it! You can't have those whom you've known in Human form, some small and some large, revisiting you now and tapping you on the shoulder and hugging you from behind and not feel it! You wonder why you came? You wonder why you read these words? Oh, dear family member, I know you so well! Some have come as a gift for those next to them. Some of those might be saying, *"I won't be affected by this spiritual talk. This energy won't touch me."* I say to you, "You don't have to be affected. Why don't you just sit and be loved?" If this is as good as it gets, it will be better than when you arrived, won't it? Sit and feel the love of the family!

We spend time with this group—this family—as we are complete with those who are going to come in and visit from the other side of the veil. There are so many more of us than there are of you, walking among the chairs, re-greeting you after all of this time, asking you to recognize the energy. Do you feel it? Reader, do you feel it? There will be some of you who don't need to hear any of the words in English that are going to be spoken during this time. Some of you hearing this will be removed from consciousness during this time so that you can simply be loved— to float and enjoy. Then there will be some of you who will need to hear, read, and understand what is said, for it is specifically for you.

The message is for all of you. It is a continuation of the last time there was a channelling on this subject. For, awhile ago, we spent time with the family, much like this, in a room similar to this one. In that session, we had a discourse about "now" time, and the discourse had many metaphors and much teaching. It explained the difference between the linear time of the Human Being and the spiritual divine "now" time of the anointed energy that is inside you, called the "Higher Self." What is going to be presented now will simply be a continuation of that study.

We are going to give it a different name this time. This second part has literally nothing to do with linear and circular time, as the first one did. This lesson will be named "Changing Reality." It's time you heard it and understood it better. For of all of the concepts that the Human Being must grasp in ascension status, this one is the hardest. But we're not ready to begin yet. [Lee laughs]

Don't you think we know your name? You think you could be some kind of generic Human and just sit there? Do this: Examine all of the things you've arranged this day that allow you to "sit in the chair" right now. It's a finite group, the pieces of God that are here hearing and reading. It's a finite group that I know and you have known for eons. You have known them intimately as your family. Many times you have watched each other coming and going. Lemurian that you are, shaman that you are, divine one that you are! What do you think of the attributes of those waking up right now? Why *you?* What brings you to this place of hearing and reading? Why do you brave the storms and the verbal arrows of those who would look at you and say that you've gone off the deep end listening to a channeller? [Laughter]

It's the awakening of the divine being inside you that is starting to understand how things work. You, dear ones, are starting to change the very fabric of reality in your life. We use words such as *co-creation* and *contract*, yet a Human Being still does not understand "changing reality." And so as we continue here, I want you to understand that we know who you are. You are sitting exactly where we expected you to sit. Did you know that? Otherwise, we wouldn't know who to send around to hug you. [Laughter] We just want you to understand that the pairs of eyes and ears looking at this page right now and hearing these words are the eyes and ears of family members, known to us, loved by us.

Reality

What is reality to the Human Being? It's an unchanging attribute that is a postulate of existence. Go ahead and ask any Human Being—not necessarily one that is versed in spirituality, either. Ask: "What is reality?" They might say something like this: *"It's what I can count on. It's what never changes. It's the wood in my chair—the dirt that I walk on—the air that I breathe. It's always constant and always the same, I can count on what's real to me because I can reach out and touch it and feel it. My senses always react to it in the same way. It's real stuff, my reality. It's physics. It's biology. It's the way things work. It's life on planet Earth."*

I'm going to give you an example of your reality that you might not have thought of, and I'm going to give you a reminder about it. Is time part of your reality? The way it moves by, the way it works in your life? Well, our lesson is that *reality* is as relative as time is. We have given you example after example (along with some of your scientists) of the variability of this constant that you thought never changed—that of time. If time is relative, then why does it *seem* to be such a constant? The reason? Because humanity is couched within it. When it changes, all changes together, and no one notices. The only one who might know it changed would be the observer who stands aside and is not part of humanity and is not affected by the shift in time. An interdimensional being would also be aware of it, since the other dimensions reveal it. Remember the physics, however? Time is relative to speed.

Question: What if humanity and the Earth were vibrating faster than the rate of 50 years ago? What if the actual atoms were all vibrating faster on Earth, the solar system, and all the things in your area? What if this "speed change" of vibration changed how fast time went? You would never know it! Since you are all in the "lifeboat" called Earth, it continues to look the same to you. Only the Universe around you would know, as your "reality" changed but seemed to stay the same to you.

Here is another question: What if you were on a train with no windows, heading toward a destination that was also unknown (like life, for instance). You are aware of the motion, and the fact that you are moving ahead—but nothing else, however. While you are riding the train, it changes tracks, moving itself subtly in another direction, and therefore another destination. To you, who could not see this, it would seem like nothing happened. The train is still moving forward, and seemingly nothing has changed—but it has! You are now heading somewhere else. This is the relativity of your reality! Therefore, we bring you news that REALITY is also variable.

The Circle of Energy—a Metaphor

Picture for a moment, a circle of energy. Go ahead and make it a doughnut if you like, so it has a height dimension. In the circle of energy, there is a force. Make this a "life force," and let it flow around and around within the doughnut structure with a speed that never changes. It is the life force of humanity. It also represents the reality of humanity. Consider this visualization your *reality*—an unchanging energy, one that is indeed circular. It goes on forever.

Some have likened this metaphor to the train we mentioned that is riding on a track, around and around. It never changes. It's always the same train and always the same speed. Although this train has many dimensions, the Human only sees four: height, depth, length, and time. Other dimensions that the Human does not see on the train are: (1) the ability to look out the window of the train and see things passing by; (2) controlling the speed of the engine; (3) the ability to look at the track in front of you; and (4) the makeup of the train. There are others as well, but these represent a metaphor of four more dimensions that are present but which you cannot see.

In the last channelling, we mentioned the fact that all things are circular, and that even the paths that you think go into infinity, such as your life, are also circular. We told you that there are no straight lines. The lines that seem to be straight simply curve to meet themselves eventually. Therefore, time and reality are circular. That is why the potentials of your future can be measured, and prophecies can be developed—because potentials in a circle return constantly as items that have familiarity within the constant. And so, instead of a future that disappears over the horizon as an unknown mystery, your future is a large circle that comes back around and around. It's part of the "now" time we talked about in the last channelling. It's why potentials can turn into manifestation, as the circle returns to the energy that created the potential. Those who are able to prophesize have an interdimensional gift. They are able to dimly see through a window in the front of the train. Therefore, they can see what is on the track directly in front of the train, and they can give you ideas of what might happen.

Since we have told you that the train circles, the potentials of energy are seen, and they are later turned into reality when the train passes over them again. The difficulty for those who prophesize is this question: How many times will the train circle over the potential before it becomes reality? Therefore, even a good prophet may miss the date, but the event is still a potential that might indeed happen.

This life force train, the "circle of energy," never seems to change to you. The energy is rock solid. You can reach out and touch it. That train is "Reality-A." On it goes for eons and eons, and the prophets use it to generate the potentials we just spoke of. As the circle continues in "Reality-A," the potentials slowly turn into manifestations of their own creation, and the circle creates a matching reality that the prophets foretold. Think of your reality on Earth. It seems to be unchanging, going on forever. It's something you can count on—something you can reach out and touch. To some it's the grounding energy of the life force of existence. Some of you may wish to call it the attributes of the Cosmic Lattice, which we have discussed. It's always constant, always powerful, always there. You are indeed used to it.

The Divine Catalyst

Now, I want to throw a "curve" into this unchanging cycle of existence. Enter into the circle something that has never been there before. Here it comes! It kind of looks like an elongated crystal. Some would say it's a "wand," perhaps. It has polarity. It is another force! It's not a Human life force, but it has a Human characteristic. Look at where it's going! It's headed for the middle of the circle! It has power to do this by itself, since it's called "divinity," or "God." We are going to call this new independent power, "the divine catalyst." As this crystalline, wand-like divinity enters into the field of the life force, it affects its own potential. It shifts the potential and allows it to change. It changes the constant attributes by letting the force change direction. The Human life force becomes more powerful in the process, like the engine of a train that can climb uphill. Suddenly, as this train changes tracks and begins to climb uphill to a higher track, this unchanging circular energy called "Reality-A" becomes "Reality-B"—another track. (By the way, Spirit calls all realities simple "reality.")

What has happened and what has changed? More important, who knew it? Reality is still reality. The train is still surging around in a circle, but it now has different subtle attributes—those that are not necessarily apparent to everyone. Look at what happened: The train just changed tracks to a higher track. To most, nothing seemed to change, but the truth is that the whole train (life on Earth) has a different destination. It can now be called "Reality-B," or track B, if you wish. The Human, who can only sense four dimensions still sees an unchanged four: height, depth, length, and time, and they still look the same! The train is still the same train, and it is still on a track going the same speed. What the Human does not realize is that it is now on a much higher and different track.

Look how it got changed: It changed because of a divine catalyst that intersected the old constant life force called "Reality-A." The intersection of the divine wand, therefore, created a new potential—a track change—yet most of humanity never felt it.

I have just given you the picture, dear ones, of what the *new* enlightened Human does as he/she walks the planet. For that divine wand—that crystalline piece—is *you*. This is the metaphor of how one in ascension status changes the planet and how the old reality of past prophecies gets voided out. You sit on a planet that has had its reality changed—absolutely shifted— and *you* have done it! You see, when you sit in the middle of the life force that changes, you're not aware of "A," "B," "C," or "D." It's just reality, yet the train of reality switched tracks! Therefore, the circle you are in is now on another plane. Think of this as circles above and below each other, and even though you just switched tracks to another higher circle, your train still moves along, and you are not aware of the new circle.

"Kryon," you might ask, *"is this a personal reality or a planetary reality?"* You cannot separate the two. It all started at a personal level, and tens of thousands of Humans began to change. The consciousness of humanity reached a point where the Earth had to change due to what the Humans on it were doing, and the result was a change of reality personally and planetwide. Most of this shift happened between 1962 and 1987—and what a change it was!

"Kryon, are you saying that there are multiple realities, and that we just move from one to the other? Perhaps there are multiple Earths?"

No. There's only "one reality" and one Earth. There are multiple "potentials," however. The only "reality" is the one your Human train is on. There might be hundreds of tracks, but they are only potential tracks for your train. When your train isn't on them, they manifest nothing. The train is the energy of life. When it's on an energy track, it responds to the potentials of the new track. Do you understand? The reality, the thing that you can touch, is the track your train is on! The change of tracks, however, is often invisible to you. Therefore, you might look around to see some of the things that are showing you that, indeed, your reality has changed.

"Okay," you might say, *"but how can we see this? What good does it do to talk about something we can't even discern?"* The thing that gives all of this away is that the prophecies were for the lower track. Therefore, they won't happen now, since you moved from the track called "Reality-A" to the new higher circular track called "Reality-B." There can be no manifestation of a former potential when the old potential was created in a lower energy. The circle of Human life force is now in a higher one. The old potentials that the prophets saw were a view of the old track, not the new one! This may seem cryptic to you, but it is the way your dimension works.

Although you might not have felt a reality change, you can observe it easily within the life around you on the planet. None of the prophecies have come about, did you notice? We're going to remind you about some other items and get right down to the Human element of them so that you truly understand the scope of what a changing Earth reality means.

Seven Attributes of Your Reality

Let's begin with the big, then go to the little. There are seven attributes we wish to speak of.

Political: Look at your planet right now. Oh, dear ones, there is an area of your Earth that is politically not even close to what its old reality said it would be. We have mentioned this for the last seven years. We've gone to the grand assemblies, and we've mentioned it there [speaking of the three visits to the United Nations to channel]. Yet, because you floated through it seemingly on a gentle wave, you don't understand how many reality shifts you have had.

I speak now of Israel and the Middle East. Do you know what that area represents? First of all, I'd like to tell you who is there—family! Don't ever isolate yourself because of geographic position or language. Don't ever isolate yourselves from the family due to culture. You have been many cultures in the past; your current reality simply is the one you chose this time around. That is family over there in the Middle East, and like you, that family sits in 1999 having expected something at the cellular level far different from what they're actually going through.

Let me tell you about the reality that is Israel. Israel is about ready to experience the potential of the third Exodus. The first Exodus was that of moving from the tribes of slavery out of Egypt. The second Exodus was from the nonpersona group to that with a country in a place that had its energy of birth. The third Exodus, and most profound of all, is the one that will bring in the New Jerusalem that must start right in Israel.

This third Exodus is the one of "consciousness"—going from the old consciousness of warring, to the enlightened one of peace. The divine miracle is that on the old "Reality-A" track, there was no third Exodus. The prophecies were clear, and the destination of the train was heading to a potential that did not include anything but the manifestation of the creation of self-fulfillment of prophecy. When the train changed tracks between 1962 and 1987, you didn't notice it. Gone was the old circle where you would meet up with the manifestation of the old. It was replaced with a new track—a new destination—and the potential of a third Exodus into a humanity that is changing energy.

I want you to look at what is happening right now in that land. There is a new leader in that country, one who has been elected by his people, and they elected their greatest warrior! His past is well known, and his deeds are, too. He has come out of an energy where Israel said to the rest of the world, *"We deserve to be here. They (the enemy around them) cannot have our land. We're going to take it back at all costs. This Holy War is centuries old, and it is not finished!"* Do you remember that energy? It wasn't that long ago! Now, I want you to listen to what the new warrior-leader is saying, the one elected by the consciousness of the people of Israel.

This former warrior now says, *"How can we make peace, and what must we compromise to make this work? How can we have four or more major belief systems sharing the same Holy places that we also call sacred? How can we co-exist together without terrorism? How can we create this? How can we do it without negativity or blame? Let's get started!"*

Welcome to "Reality-B"! Is this what was prophesied? Is it in the time frame looked for? The answer is NO! The new reality track has a new destination—peace. The old one is gone. Right in the center of the place, right now in 1999, was supposed to be the crux of termination and horror! Instead, the new leadership asks, *"How can we make peace?"* Tell me about the *reality* of that—about a reality you can touch! What were the potentials of that? Yours is the planet of free choice. The *choice* we talk about is the choice you have to change the fabric of reality within this planet—the only planet like this in the universe.

Earth changes: Here's another attribute. What about Earth changes? What about the physics of Earth? I don't have to sit here and tell you that there has been a grand acceleration in Earth changes. You are all looking at an acceleration of Earth geological evolution—almost as if the years are going by faster than before. You are seeing changes that perhaps you would not have seen for decades, yet they're happening *now*. And you wonder why the oceans warm and the earth shakes! That is because the land that had an old consciousness is reacting to a reality shift. When your train of reality changed tracks, the Earth came with it. That's reality shift! Oh, but there's more. What about the upcoming event [referring to the channelling given in July '99 in Santa Fe]. You know, the fearful one? Oh, dear ones, they are all fearful ones now, aren't they? What about August 11, 1999? Some predicted this date to be ominous—an alignment— an energy like no other. *"What are we going to do?"* Humans have said, *"It's not good. Something's happening."*

Let me tell you about an old reality that used to go in a circle. Many of the things that have come your way in the last years since 1987 had different potentials and energies since the track became new. These physical events have new realities. Instead of termination, you now have "celebration," and this date was one of them. I challenge all of you. Think about that day and remember these words, "I want you to celebrate." Do the numerology first of all: 8, 11, 1, 9, 9, 9. And the sum is "11." [Remember in numerology to consider identical double digits as a final number, such as 11.]

What is the energy of the Kryon? Remember the original teaching I gave in 1989? It is the energy of "11." This has been known to you now for almost ten years. We have also told you about the energy of the "9." It represents completion, and therefore, the "9" and the "11" are the Kryon attributes! How many of you have ever thought to multiply these together, for you'll find the year that you sit in is right now— "99." This is the shining hour! This is the message of the Kryon and entourage that has a profundity as never before, because you're sitting in the changes of reality that you've made—changes that we told you about years ago. Now you are sitting in them! That was number two.

Spirituality: What about spirituality on the planet? This is a review, and we'll make it brief. There are some of you who say, *"Okay, I can buy into reality shifts in politics and reality shifts in Earth changes, but there's one thing that will never change, and that's God. God is the same yesterday, today, and forever."* You are correct, but the God/Human relationship is not the same! It has changed, and the instruction sets for humanity have changed!

Go back and review what was given to you in Part I of this channelling. Remember the metaphor of the sleeping Human? Thousands of books were written about how to take care of the sleeping Human, then suddenly he wakes up. What do you do with the books? They are no longer valid. So many of you are awakening into a new paradigm of spirituality. Do you feel anxious? Do you feel that your spiritual connection has been severed, or at least altered? Congratulations on your awakening. The old "sleeping" ways no longer work!

There is going to be an awakening of spirituality on this planet that goes far beyond anything you have seen. *"Kryon, does that mean that everyone will be metaphysical?"* No. As we have told you before, that will never happen, and it should not. We are speaking of a wisdom overlay that will be for all doctrines and cultures. Watch for this. Many beliefs that seem to be absolutely rock solid in their old energy proclamations will change them to adjust to planetary issues such as overpopulation, trade, and tolerance of former enemies. Never will there have been such a spiritual shift. Look to the new Pope for profound change. He will go against much of what has been, and will change the very fiber of his followers' beliefs. In this process, he will be controversial. Look to the nation of Islam to move toward tolerance of others and to bring themselves to a modern understanding of how best to honor their beliefs, yet stay within the new energy of general Human rights and empowerment for women. They will lift themselves out of an old paradigm of worship into a new one, and never diminish their great lineage or their devotion to God. There is much more, and you will see it before your eyes, including the changing of a government that encompasses more than one-fourth of Earth's population as it changes and bends due to the spirituality of its people.

Does this sound like the old reality? What kind of power is that? What is happening that would allow for such a change? A reality shift, perhaps?

Matter: Matter is also variable, and is as relative to reality as time. Oh, there are rules around it—you just don't know them all yet. It has been discussed by Kryon that matter is also in a circle. Let me define that now for you: It is not in a circle. Matter and biology, consciousness and life force, are in a loop. *"What is the difference, Kryon, between a circle and a loop?"* Here is the difference: A circle has no source point. It always moves equally with energy. There is no bias. A loop would indicate, however (in English), a return to a source. Therefore, we are here to tell you that your scientists will eventually discover loops in everything in the basic elements of matter. The smallest particles they can imagine will have loops. It will answer some of the most profound questions about why there is so much space between the nucleus and the electron haze. Look for the loops!

In biology, you've already found some of them, and that's just the beginning. What did you think when your scientists discovered that DNA was not just a strand [information brought to you in Part I of this series]? What does that now tell you about DNA? It's a loop! Why do you think it has to be a loop? It's because it must carry current! DNA is, therefore, a small electrical engine. This engine is sensitive to magnetic influences since the current carried in a loop creates its own magnetic field. Now do you understand how the crystalline sheath can magnetically alter DNA with "awakening" lines of intersecting flux [a technical discussion that Kryon gave in Part I of this series]? Is this starting to fit together? Your new reality is giving you the power over your own DNA! Remember that consciousness can change matter. Ask the quantum physicists about that. And while you're at it, remember also that INTENT is consciousness.

"Well, Kryon, matter is matter to me. It always behaves the same, and it is constant. I can't really relate to all this scientific stuff." Good, because now we'll give you an example of those on the planet who can change it at will, right before your eyes! Real enough for you? We speak now about the avatars who are here—the ones who can take INTENT and create and change matter seemingly from nothing. We speak of the avatar Sai Baba, and others you don't know of, who have these same attributes. If you could see this, you would be amazed. Those of you who want to see, feel, touch, and know that matter exists will have to "re-think" the reality of matter.

Years ago, we told you that you had profound abilities over matter. Dear ones, you don't have to be an avatar. Let me ask you this: "What do you think happens when you have a healing miracle in your lives?" It doesn't matter what spiritual group you're in, or what the name is on the door of the building you're in. You see, all these groups have the divine Human family inside. When they call upon the love of God, when they give pure "intent," there will be miracles. And when the bones snap back into place, and tissue is placed where it never was before, and tumors are taken away, what is happening, do you think? That is "intent" and "consciousness" and "divinity" coming in as a crystalline wand into that circle of life and moving it to another reality! When that happens, you get a miracle. When that happens, you get a change in matter and biology! The ones who sat there deformed and are now able to walk miraculously with bone they never had before had matter altered! That is divine, and that is a miracle! It comes right from the divinity inside the Human Being, and it changes reality.

Spiritual path: I want to speak again about your spiritual path, as we did in Part I of this series. Every Human in the room and reading these words sees their path as a straight line going into oblivion. They can't see where it's going since it disappears over the horizon. "Have faith," you're told—last-minute solutions, you're told. Still, you all see yourselves marching along to unknowns in the future, and some of you are afraid. This feels far different from what you have felt as a spiritual path in the past.

We told you that your path is not a straight line, but instead, it's a circle. It's exactly like the reality train that we have discussed. Your personal path covers "old ground" over and over. Now you find yourselves on a new track, but some of you feel anxious as a result. We discussed why many of you feel stopped in your tracks, and what it means. We gave you instructions about what to do about it, too: "Sit down and celebrate," we said. Celebrate the fact that your circle in that concentric puzzle has simply stopped for a while. Do you know why it stopped? Because you gave "intent" for the ascension status.

This is how powerful you are! Your spiritual path is actually waiting for the elements of co-creation that we have just discussed at the beginning of this channelling. It is waiting for the divine catalyst of your new empowerment to create new potentials on the new track of life. Much is different about how your spiritual path works, and so many Humans are afraid because it feels so strange.

Celebrate it! Is this not additional proof that your reality has changed? When did you feel like this before in the past? This is new, and it is part of your new vibrational shift.

Human nature: Did you ever think that you would see Human evolution in your lifetime? What kind of a reality is it that brings in children who are so different that you'll need to relearn how to raise them [speaking of the Indigo Children]? How many years have Human Beings been having children? This group is suddenly different.

Dear ones, the children who are being born right now represent a new type of Human. You can call this phenomenon anything you want to, but I'm going to label it: It's a change in "Human nature."

There are those who will say, *"Human nature will always seek power and greed, and that is our undoing as Humans. No matter how good you think it's going to get, that is going to sink Humans every time."* There's a new reality afoot. The children who are coming in now do not represent the old Human nature paradigm. Oh, they'll have Human traits that will be very common to what you've known and seen. But watch these children (as well as the children of these children), for these children are looking around and saying, "Why are things the way they are?" And at the cellular level, they have the wisdom, the knowledge, and the profound ability to create a world where peace is the main goal. The task of humanity is how to put a world population together and have it work—one that trades together, tolerates one another, and has free boundaries.

Many have said that humanity has eons of history to prove that it can't happen. *"Basic Human nature will take that hope away, eventually,"* it is often said by those who only see doom. Well, Human nature no longer exists in the way you thought it did. By the time the second generation comes in, you're going to see a new kind of leadership. You're going to see integrity within the seeds of the individual overpower the old nature seeds that only sought power and greed. You're going to see the desire to better humanity, and not what you used to call "Reality A." These children are different, and they are going to give you a different planet if you let them. Have you noticed them? How is that for a change of reality? Do you think you would be seeing this if your train had not changed tracks? Does this give you hope for the future? It should.

These are the potentials that you sit within, dear ones, as you move this grand train called humanity from track "A" to track "B" to track "C" to track "D." When you look into the eyes of these children, you'll see it—the "old souls" are here. You know what their attributes are? They're not from any other place but Earth. Start looking in their eyes, and see if you recognize them as family. They have a purpose like no other Human Being that has ever come in to this planet of choice. They have a great purpose, and there is a grand difference between the way it used to be when you came in and the way it is now. You see, their purpose is collective, but their contract is singular. You never had a collective purpose. It wasn't possible for that overlay to ever be within your spiritual structure. Suddenly, you will see it in the children. It is all part of the new track that your train took.

The last item is a parable that has been channelled five times. The first time it was transcribed it was in another language on another continent. This channelling is to be given in English on this, and one more continent. Therefore, it will be the last transcription, and it will have been presented on three separate continents. It is given here for the very reason that we have waited for the channelling or reality shift to present it. We want to show you through a parable that you are very familiar with so that you can know what changing reality really means. I started the channelling today with the greeting I always give. I said to you, "Greetings, dear ones. I AM Kryon of Magnetic Service." Do you remember what we said in Part I of this series? The I AM greeting is a sacred identifier of family origin. It is not a name identifier. Therefore, "I AM Kryon" means "I AM of the family of God" and so are you. As you might recall, the "AM" is you. My name is Kryon. The "I AM THAT I AM" is a circle of language that means that you and I are eternal in both directions—forever a universal entity. It is a sacred greeting. Remember this as you hear and read something you might have felt you already knew about. What follows might change your reality of understanding.

The parable of reality: It was a hot day when God came to Abraham with the news. Abraham never saw it coming. When God had made known the request that Abraham was to sacrifice his only precious son, Isaac, to the altar at the top of the mountain, he was laid flat emotionally. He couldn't believe it. It was the beginning of a beautiful lesson for Abraham—one that we can reveal now as something far more than a parable of obedience to God.

Abraham's obedience was not blind. Abraham had the "mantle of wisdom" that we speak about, which allowed him to understand that there was sacredness in this test. Not for a moment did he doubt that he would do it, but it wasn't blind obedience. Abraham "felt" the importance of this challenge, and he immediately began praying for his lesson to be removed from him. Even as he prepared the porters for the trip up the mountain and informed his son of the journey, he prayed to have the lesson removed from him. He told no one in the entourage what the real purpose was of the climb. Instead, only Abraham knew it, and only Abraham bore the burden of the reality that was to come.

It was a three-day journey to where the sacrifice would take place. The spot they were headed for was sacred, where many lambs had been sacrificed before as an honoring to Spirit in the ways of the day. This time would be different, and Abraham began to look into the future to a reality that was revolting to him—a reality that had him murdering his precious son—the son he had called "his miracle from God." This miracle was given to him very late in life from his wife, a woman who wasn't able to bear children again due to her age—yet she did.

Abraham hadn't slept the night before, and he took up his position in the rear of the troop. This wasn't like him to be last, but this time he did it for a reason—he didn't want anyone to see him weeping. His son asked many questions, but Abraham held steadfast in his truthful description of a sacrifice at the top of the mountain—a special one that they would all remember for a lifetime. Abraham was at the lowest ebb of his life, but he tried to hold it together as they spent the first day on the rugged pathway—one they had done many times before.

When it was time to camp the first of the two nights, Abraham literally fell into a heap away from the campsite, and he began sobbing while praying to his loving, fair God. "Dear God, please take this anchor from me!" he prayed. "Dear God, there is nothing you cannot do. Take this burden from me now that you know I will indeed do the deed. Help me to understand all this. Please!"

In the stillness, exhausted and half sleep, Abraham clearly heard the voice of God.

"Abraham, be still and know that I AM God," came the reply.

Abraham didn't know what to do with that answer. "Dear Spirit, how can I be still? My heart is broken, and my soul is flat. I keep feeling that I am dreaming all this. It is a nightmare to my existence. It is a horrific reality. Where is the stillness in this? Where is the peace in this? You ask me to be still? How?" Abraham slumped in desperate fatigue and defeat. Again he heard the answer.

"Abraham, be still and know that I AM God," came the reply.

Abraham drifted in and out of sleep. Each time he awoke, the same prayer was on his lips. He was in the dirt, prone before God, pleading and begging for more of an answer than he had been given. His dreams presented him with a reality that was abhorrent to him: There was Isaac on the altar, the dagger of sacrifice about to be plunged into his heart by his own father. Abraham felt himself grip the hilt of the weapon as he began the downward stroke. He awoke.

Again the troop started its uphill climb, and again Abraham was in the rear. He felt that he had not slept, and that he was a zombie to the task, simply placing one foot before the other. All day the sun beat upon him and his men, and Abraham couldn't take his eyes off his boy—his precious boy. Each time a rest period was called, Abraham asked Isaac to be at his side so he could admire his youth, and love him for the few moments left in his life. The greatest fear of any parent was that they would outlive their own children. Now here he was, about ready to ensure this fateful reality.

Again, nightfall came. This was the last night, and tomorrow would bring the third and last trek to the summit where the "deed" would be accomplished. Abraham again found a spot alone and apart from the group. He built an altar of his own, and he begged God to let him be the sacrifice—right then and there. He tried to communicate with God, but seemingly received nothing. When he felt God was no longer there, he again heard the reply. This time it was slightly different.

"Abraham, listen!" came the words.

"Listen—be still, Abraham," said the voice. "Know that I AM God."

Abraham picked up his head. Was this an answer, or just God being God? It sounded like there was a message in this statement—one that had some kind of hope within it. Why would God do this? He remembered his teachings—something that Spirit had said to him once. He remembered that he was told that God does not delight in the suffering of any Human. He remembered that God had told him that all lessons were about solutions, not just obedience. Abraham knew that there was something different in the air. He began to understand. At first just a glimpse of what the meaning was came to him; then he began to get the whole picture.

Abraham understood that to create peace and stillness, he would have to change his vision, or his reality of what was going to take place at the top of the mountain. He started to visualize himself with his son having a picnic at the top. They would all eat a feast, celebrating the love of God, and his son would be the guest of honor. Abraham held this vision and believed it with all his heart. This was the only way he could create the stillness that was being instructed. When his heart began to calm, and his well-being started to return, the rest of the message was given to him.

The I AM was a signal? Perhaps a message? It wasn't a reference at all to who God was. It was a message within a message, just like the scriptures had been written. Abraham knew and understood how those of the time had used the *pesher* method of writing scripture. This might be the same kind of metaphor. What could "Know that I AM God," mean? Then Abraham had the revelation. The I AM was him! It was the circle of divinity that he knew was his mantle of Spirit. The message was this: "Abraham, be peaceful in the knowledge that we are God!"

Abraham couldn't believe it. He shouted with joy. He had been prone on his nose for hours and hours praying that "God could do anything." "God could take this burden away." "God could change reality." Now he realized the message. He was a part of God! Abraham was about to change his reality with the absolute power within him to do so. Abraham was already celebrating as he took the lead up the mountain, his son on his shoulders. He was going to do the very thing he had asked God to do. The message was clear, and Abraham was empowered to make the change himself.

You know how the story ends. Abraham had a picnic with his son at the top of the mountain! Not quite the moral you remembered? Not quite the lesson you were taught about this story? It's about changing reality. It's about the power of the Human Being to create visual solutions to the most horrific lessons possible. It's about victory over fear, and it's about peace.

Ask yourself right now as you sit there, "What part of the mountain am I on? Am I doing the *woe is me* part? Am I begging Spirit for help? Or . . . am I celebrating a vision of a final solution that I couldn't possibly know how to make happen?"

What is your reality, dear one? Are you going into fear with a reality that has doom, gloom, and lack of hope? That's the old track! Why not create the new one? You are absolutely empowered to do so. The entire meaning of today's message is this: YOU ARE ABLE TO CHANGE YOUR REALITY. THERE-FORE, DO IT! Start with the visualization of hope. Try to create peace over the problem, no matter what it is. Understand it within the grand scheme, and be part of the overview. Then, like Abraham, with pure intent, begin to change the fabric of reality around you. It will happen!

We give you this message in love. We remove ourselves from the place where you have been listening and reading, but we have some sadness that the time spent hasn't been longer. We didn't get to hug you long enough. We didn't get to tell you the other stories—countless ones of Human empowerment, joy, revelation, and reality change. History is filled with them!

We will, though—when you allow us to return and love you again in this fashion.

And so it is!

Kryon

Live Channelling

"Packing for the New Millennium"

Channelled in
Portland, Oregon
August 1999

Chapter Four

"Packing for the New Millennium"
Live Channelling
Portland, Oregon
August 1999

*This live channelling has been edited with additional
words and thoughts to allow clarification and better
understanding of the written word.*

Greetings, dear ones. I AM Kryon of Magnetic Service. We hold the energy to be dear among us, as the entourage pours into this place, because you have asked it to be so. There is an energy that can only be felt through the intent of Human Beings at a time like this. There is a process of love that flows into your body that can only be felt through the pure intent of the Human Being to have it so.

Oh, there are those here who say that such a thing could not be so—stepping across the veil to hear the voice through a Human Being—the voice of an entity who does not live on the Earth—who claims to be family. Let the proof of this be in the love that flows into this room right now. It doesn't matter if you are hearing in the NOW or reading in the NOW; it is all the same time to us. Let the proof of this phenomenon be in the thickness of love that my partner has spoken about, which can press upon this room and the area around your chair. Some of you will know it from the pressure you feel.

Some in this very room and reading this will begin to get the message of why they came in the first place.

This is the energy you expected. For it is so. There is a loving entity and an entourage that pours in here who knows you by name. This entourage knows you by a name that can never be spoken in English. This entourage that now walks in the aisles between you, in back of you, in front of you, and next to the reader's chair has expected you to sit exactly where you're sitting and has been here for days in anticipation of the potential of this moment! The only reason this group is here is to experience this with you—this reunion—because of the honor of your intent. The intent of the Human Being is the energy that has caused this meeting. It is the "engine" that lets something like this happen. The intent of the Human Being is the energy that allows the love of God to flow in here and touch you personally, to wrap its arms around you and say, "Do you remember us? Do you remember this feeling of Home?" That's the energy that flows into this room now.

And so, as many who wish to receive this energy, let it be so. For those of you who have come this night or are reading this, hoping this will make a difference for you, perhaps you are indeed in the right place at the right time. Perhaps you need to hear and read these words. We know what you've gone through— about all the upset and all of the changes. Don't you think we've been standing here the whole time? There has been much celebration the whole time, even when you were on the floor in your sorrow! Don't you think that the entourage was there? You see, you can never have a situation where we're not there, dear family. Dear Human Being, you're part of a group. Dear Human Being, the duality wants you to believe that you are singular, living in a straight line, but that is not so. You're part of a group, and this group, like your life, is in a circle. This group is always with you, and we're going to discuss that a little more now.

There are some of you in this assemblage hearing this who do not need to hear any more. The parable that follows may not be for you, so let it be known that there will be other things given to you in these next few moments that you will need more than the parable to come. This is the individual channelling that we talk about that is disguised as "The Third Language." It is available only to those in this room at this time.

For the rest of you? The energy that will pour into your body now will only be the energy that you've asked for, and no more. For the ones who have come for the healing? Let it begin now. Do you think we don't know who's here? Do you think we don't know whose eyes are falling on this message? For the upcoming situation that you are uncertain about, it's time to have peace, is it not? In these next few moments, do something for us. Do something for yourself: It's time to throw on the floor those things that would keep you out of full realization. It is time to put away those things that would get in the way of an enlightened Human Being, and you know what they are. For it will not damage you at all to leave those things down low, while you rise above them and feel the energy that is being presented here.

The entourage is here, and it's complete. This entourage sits with you, stands with you, and hugs you in these next minutes as we walk through a parable. Let it be known that this message is to be transcribed. It is in the style of the NOW energy. This NOW energy of the channelling of Kryon is what we speak about to the *readers* of the transcription right NOW. For we know who you are as well. All of the potentials of the eyes reading the words that are now being spoken, as well as the ears hearing this, are known to us. Dear family hearing these words, as you listen to this parable, understand that there is also a group that has their eyes upon the very words you are now hearing. For this is the reality of Spirit, that all of the potentials of divine realization, of the recognition of the divinity within, is together in one place. It's in the center, and we see it as a revelation within you, within the readers, and within those who will go on to read even more later. To us, it is happening together. To us, it is an energy stamp of this Earth that makes it so different from when you started it all, dear ones. When you started this, we could not speak to you in this fashion. We could not have had nearly the energy pouring into a room like this! Things were different then. You had only just begun to wake up.

We have some in this room, right now, who are just beginning to fear that the energy is real, but rather than fear, there is love here! The love you feel could be branded as anything you want it to be, but it's the love of God, and it comes from *home* and represents a family that's here with you. We want you to know that even after you get up and leave this place where you're hearing or reading, there's a family that will walk with you tonight. It's there as often as you wish to acknowledge it, for you are indeed the honored ones.

The Parable of Wo and the Suitcase

We bring you a parable. And within this parable, indeed there will be fun, but there will be teaching as well. This is why we ask for this message to be transcribed. For within parables there are always meanings within meanings, and there are meanings even deeper than those that the ears will hear or the eyes will see. Within this parable we are going to again introduce the character we have used in the past. This character is called *Wo*. Now, Wo is not a man or a woman. We're going to call Wo a *he* in the parable, but you see, Wo is really a "wo-man."

***

We find Wo standing before us with many suitcases. He's ready for the millennium shift, and he is ready to cross that bridge from the old energy to the new. Wo is considered to be an enlightened Human Being on an ascension path. That is to say, the attribute in Wo's life that is *ascending* is his "vibratory intent." So, Wo considers himself a lightworker, and he's packed his bags, ready to move over that bridge. Wo's intent is to become a Human Being who is going to change his life. He's going to move into a new energy and become something different from what he is now. Wo is in transformation and rejuvenation, and he knows this. He is "under renovation," and he feels it!

Ah, but there's one more step, you see. He has his bags packed, and he's ready to go, but Wo must visit an angel before he moves over the bridge of intent into this new energy he desires. It's a beautiful angel whom he's going to meet, and to make the parable more fun, we shall tell you that he's going to meet the "Packing Angel." This is the angel who is going to inspect Wo's bags!

Now, Wo is intelligent. He is a spiritual Human Being, and he feels prepared to travel. He has packed many things in his bags that he knows he is going to need to move into this new, uncharted area in his life. And so he greets the great Packing Angel who's going to give him advice on what to expect, and what he should take with him or *not* take with him. Wo feels absolutely certain that he has done everything properly and correctly, and he feels that his bags have been "spiritually assembled" very well. He has reasons for everything he is bringing. He is ready!

Wo greets the Packing Angel with a wonderful, loving hug.

"Nice to see you," Wo tells the great Packing Angel.

"And you, too," says the angel. "You have been expected."

"I am ready to go, and this is the last stop before I move into an ascension status. My intent is beginning to take me on a new path." Wo swells up with expectation. "Please inspect my belongings."

The Suitcase of Clothes—Preparedness

"Let's look at the first bag, Wo," the angel says with a smile.

Wo opens the first bag, and out spills clothing—not just some, but a lot! There is clothing for all types of weather, and in no certain order. The great angel doesn't say anything to Wo about the fact that nothing matches.

"Wo, what is all of this clothing?" asks the great Packing Angel.

"I wish to be very prepared," says Wo, "and I'm moving into areas where even Spirit has admitted that no one knows what is going to happen. I don't know what the weather will be, so I brought everything I might need. Being prepared is a virtue." Wo smiles, but is horrified moments later as the Packing Angel begins to take out all of the clothes and gently places them on the floor.

"I don't think you're going to need any of these things, Wo," says the Packing Angel, as he goes on to teach. "Blessed is the Human Being who understands that as they walk into the new energy, even though they do not know what to expect, they have an entourage around them that does. Blessed is the Human Being who trusts and loves his entourage! The only thing that the Human Being will need are the clothes, literally, on his back." And that is a metaphor that means that Humans are *complete as they are.* Honoring the uncertainty is the metaphor. The angel continues: "Blessed are the Human Beings who understand that the uncertainty will be taken care of as they walk the path—that the preparation they have done before is not necessary now. They don't have to bring the clothing for the changes, because metaphorically, all of the changes will be recognized and solved as they are presented."

***

This angel was delivering a profound message to Wo, dear ones. Understand that this Human Being, the one who sits and hears or reads right now with pure intent to move into the new energy, doesn't have to worry about preparing for the unknown. Remember what I told you? There is an entourage around you. You are never alone! Dear ones, stand tall. You don't need all that baggage. Preparation may be a virtue of the old energy. Knowledge and peace of the unknown and the ability to deal with it are the virtues of the new.

The Suitcase of Books—Spiritual Reference

The angel opens the next bag. It is the heaviest of them all, and in it are books. He looks at Wo and again questions him.

"Wo, what are you going to do with all of these books?"

"Well, now, beautiful Packing Angel, these are my *spiritual books*. I'm going to need to refer to them on my spiritual path. If you'll notice, every single one of them has to do with God. I'm going to need to keep these books because they are filled with spiritual information. They make me feel good, and I couldn't possibly remember all the contents, so I'm going to need to take them and refer to them in my new spiritual life." The angel looks at the books, turns to Wo, and smiles—then looks back at the books. Again, Wo is surprised when the angel begins unloading the books, placing them on the floor with the clothes.

"You're not going to need these either," he says. Wo is disappointed and confused. The angel explains.

"Wo, take the highest spiritual book in this suitcase, and let's take a look at it." Wo reaches down and finds what he considers to be the highest spiritual book and holds it out with reverence.

"This is it," says Wo to the angel. The angel recognizes it.

"Wo, it's obsolete! Let me ask you this: Would you bring a scientific notebook with you that was 150 years old, or a textbook that was more than 2,000 years old that had to do with science?"

"Of course not!" exclaims Wo. "Because we keep making new discoveries about how things work."

"Exactly," says the angel. "Spiritually, Earth is changing grandly and greatly. What you could not do yesterday, you *can* do today. What was the spiritual paradigm for yesterday is not the spiritual paradigm for tomorrow. What you were told as a shaman about spiritual energy that worked yesterday is not going to work tomorrow, because the energy is shifting and being refined. You are standing in the shift, and you must go with the flow of new empowerment. Wo, you'll be writing your own book as you go, and it's the only one you will need."

"With all due respect, Mr. Packing Angel" (Wo was getting ready to make a point), "what happened to the phrase *the same yesterday, today, and forever?* Isn't that a phrase about the consistency of God? How is that obsolete?"

"Indeed, it is about God," answers the angel. "But it tells you about the attributes of God, not about the Human's relationship to God. All your books are instruction sets written by Humans about how to communicate, draw closer, and move through life dealing with God. God is always the same. Family is always the same. The Human is the one who is changing, and the books are about the Human's relationship to God. Therefore, the book is obsolete."

Wo understands now. Of course! Why didn't he observe that before? He is a complete piece of divinity. He has all of the messages and teachings inside. If he needs information, the entourage and his Higher Self will have them instantly. In addition, Wo is very aware that things are changing greatly in a spiritual way. After all, that is why he is standing here. Indeed, his relationship with God is very different!

"I don't need these books!" Wo exclaims. "What is wrong with me? I'm so thankful you're here, dear Packing Angel. Thank you for revealing this to me. Can I go now?"

"Not quite yet," says the angel with a wink. "What is this hiding down here next? It appears to be a map." The angel draws out a long tube of parchment from under the books he is unloading.

The Map—Direction

"Naturally, I must have a map to know where I'm going! This map was given to me by a spiritual leader, so that qualifies for its inclusion in this spiritual suitcase. It was given to me by a shaman of the highest order." This seems logical. Certainly the angel will grant him a map to go into a new land—especially a spiritual one.

"We shall see," remarks the angel. "Let's look at this map, Wo."

Wo takes the map from the angel with a flourish. He is proud of this acquisition, and he feels that he is on solid ground in his request to bring it along. He unfurls it and lays it on the floor in all its grandness for the angel to see. The map is completely and totally blank! The angel smiles. Wo is in shock.

"Ah, yes, I think I know this shaman," muses the angel. "He is indeed a wise one. Put the map away, Wo. You won't be needing it." Wo doesn't understand.

"Why would a shaman give me a blank map when he knows I am going into seemingly uncharted territory?" Wo asks. "A territory where only a shaman would be able to guide me."

***

Let us stop the story for a moment. I think some of you here listening and reading already know the answer to this profound question. The teaching is as follows, dear ones. The map is a metaphor of your path. Visualize your path for me. As we have said before, you see it stretch in front of you in a straight, narrow line, seemingly into infinity. And as we have informed you before, your path is not the mystery that you think it is. Your path does not stretch into infinity—it is a loop, a circle. We have spoken to you about the synchronistic events on your path being a circle. Many pieces of the other family members are also walking their paths in pure intent, in concentric circles both above and below you. Some are inside your circle, and some are beyond it—all circles turning in different directions. This is the complexity of co-creation and synchronicity. We have talked to you about the path being an enclosed one. We've talked about the honor and the love that goes into this. You see, this spiritual path is far shorter than you think, and you keep covering the same ground. That's why it begins to feel comfortable and familiar to those wise in enlightenment. The path is not a mystery, and the map is not necessary. For you keep moving over the same spiritual ground, but it's ground that is only obvious to those vibrating high. That's where the peace comes from, don't you understand? Familiarity says, *I've been here before. I've done this before, and it feels familiar and good, and I know what to do.*

In Wo's own words, he says, "Why would a shaman give me a blank map when he knows I am going into seemingly uncharted territory? A territory where only a shaman will be able to guide me?" The new shaman with the perfect internal map is Wo! He is right. Only a shaman can guide him, and he has been anointed and ordained by his pure intent to move into his perfect spiritual self. Wo is now his own advisor. He is his own map.

The Suitcase of Tools—Fear

"What is this very heavy and oddly shaped suitcase, Wo?"
The angel is lifting the case to open it. "What's in here?"

"Well, Mr. Angel, those are my tools." Wo is beginning to
feel a bit sheepish about almost everything he has brought, but
he has to go through the whole set of bags with the angel, and he
knows it. It is turning out to be some kind of customs inspection
to a brand new land.

"Your tools?" inquires the angel.

"Yes," Wo says timidly." Out of the bag that the angel has
opened clanks a huge shovel.

"Wo, what are you going to use this shovel for?" The angel
waits while Wo composes himself and tries to explain.

"Well . . ." Wo knows he is in trouble on this one, but he
clears his throat and continues. "I, uh—I know about the Earth
changes coming up, and I want to be able to dig myself out." He
looks at the angel as a child would who has been caught with his
hand in the cookie jar. He continues. "There's a big Earth
change coming up next week [speaking of the 8/11/99 eclipse].
I don't know what's going to happen, but people say that the
earth is going to shake, and I need to be prepared with my shovel
and other tools. Now, can you blame a guy for that? These are
spiritual happenings on the earth, so I need my shovel!"

Wo knows that his discussion isn't being well received, but
the angel simply nods at Wo and unloads the shovel and the
remaining heavy tools—ones that would have been good for
digging out of a burial. Wo doesn't say anything. He knows that
the angel is right. It has to do with fear, and that is *not* an attribute
of the ascending Human Being.

***

Let's stop the story again for a moment . . .

Dear ones, let's talk about what's going to happen next week, and let's celebrate this window! The window begins on 8-11-1999. What do you know about the numerology of the window? Let us speak about what you may not have thought of. What is the energy of Kryon? What is the number that was given to you ten years ago? It's good news, this energy about completion, about love, and a message for all humanity. The energy that has been identified to you as a "master number of Kryon is 11." It also responds and relates to what your 11:11 was for. That was the time when you were asked as Humans if it was now appropriate on Earth to allow for an evolution of your Human DNA— something that had not changed for eons. If you think about your new promise, it has the master number 11 all through it. That is why my number corresponds to your 11:11 permission.

Now, I want you to take a close look at something. The beginning window starts with an eclipse on 8-11-1999, seen in a different part of the world than this [not America, where the channelling is being done]. This eclipse has a marvelous energy within it, which also begins a window of alignment of the planets. Let's look at the window's alignment numerologically. The sun is in an 11-year cycle. Did you know that? Ask your scientists. It is an 11-year cycle that has to do with radiance and luminance, and it is at its height in brilliance right now. The energy is at its peak only every 11 years. That's the first 11.

It's going to happen on the 11th day of this month. That's the second 11. Now, we challenge you to add the numerology of the date fully, and remember that when you add these things, never add a master number together. Add 1-9-9-9 + (11) + 8, and when you reduce these to their common number (from 47), it is an 11! There are three 11's aligning in a row, and you ought to be celebrating! No shovels should be out now! Instead, it's time for celebration!

It's time for a new energy to be delivered to the planet. The last time this took place was when the comet Hale-Bopp came by. The computed numerology of the date of its nearest approach to Earth came to a sacred 7, yet there were many who feared, trembled, and headed for the hills. It is the same here. Wo does not need that shovel, and neither do you! Celebrate the astronomy! Celebrate the alignments—even the ones with a fearful prophecy attached to them! Not all is what it seems.

As to the energy that is to be delivered on 8-11-99? It will be the beginning of a delivery of feminine energy, which the planet needs desperately now to balance those here, and to energize those children whose very nature includes the attributes of Human spiritual evolution—attributes you gave permission for on the 11:11.

***

The Suitcase of Gifts—Agenda

"What's in the next suitcase?" The Packing Angel is now on a roll, so to speak. Wo needs a break from the obvious soft beating he is receiving by having all his objects rejected. This case is different, however, and he feels it will be okay. The things in this case show his love for others, at least that's what he believes.

"This suitcase is an honored one." Wo feels justified. "It contains gifts for my friends—those I will meet who will become my friends in this NOW time frame that you keep speaking of. I am therefore preparing to GIVE to others." Wo feels good, but not for long.

"Wo," the Packing Angel speaks slowly. "Do you think if you give them gifts they'll treat you better?" Wo feels the hammer of guilt coming.

"Well, yes," says Wo. "It has always worked that way. I mean, uh..." Wo is losing this argument, too, and knows it. "It's kind of a protocol to give gifts. It's a sign of respect, and people treat you better if you do."

"I think we'd better abandon the gifts here," says the angel as they add to the increasing pile on the floor. Wo watches as the pile grows larger, and the angel grows increasingly amused.

***

Dear ones, the gifts that are in Wo's suitcase have to do with agenda. You have lived all of your lives in a way where you expect Humans to react in a certain way. Sometimes the culture bias gets in the way of spiritual purpose, yet you cling to it just the same. If you give this, they'll do that. This is agenda. Blessed are the ascended Human Beings who understand that the highest gifts that they could carry into any situation are honesty, integrity, and holding their spiritual light! There are no gifts higher than those from one Human Being to another. Without agendas—without gifts that are physical—the enlightened Human gives the highest gift of all, which is unconditional love. Wo does not need the suitcase of trinkets, for where he goes, he stands tall. He has blessed divinity–a spark of God that has an immense light in it. That is his gift, and he doesn't need to carry it in a bag.

The Small Technical Suitcase—Security

The angel is getting to the last cases, and Wo is glad. The Packing Angel picks up a very small case and says, "Wo, this next suitcase is very small and has something technical in it. What is this?"

"Well, sir, that's my telephone." All is quiet while the angel looks intensely at Wo, and Wo looks back. A full minute passes, and then the angel can't withhold his mirth. How he loves this Human before him!

"Wo, why do you need a telephone?" asks the very loving and gentle angel. Wo knows that this explanation is going to sound odd, but he launches into it anyway.

"You know that sometimes there is trouble on the road. You have said yourself, angel, that in the spiritual realm, all things are not going to be wonderful. I'm going to have challenge. Isn't that right?" Wo sits back, happy to have the angel answering for a change.

"Yes, you are, Wo," answers the angel. There is an awkward pause.

"Well, during times of need, I need my phone to call people and get help! Would you deny me the potential of getting help when I need it?" The angel gently lifts the small package and places it with the clothing, books, map, tools, and gifts. Wo knows he is saying good-bye to his false security.

"Wo, it's time to leave the telephone out of your baggage," says the angel as he faces Wo seriously and gives him the reasons. "Blessed is the Human Being on the path to ascension," the angel continues. "For he knows that he is NEVER ALONE!" The angel pauses to see if Wo is really *getting it* this time. "The Human who vibrates in a high manner has the security of an army—a legion of angels called *family*. This family is better than a phone, for it's always in reach, never in a dead spot, never needs a number to contact, and is awake even when the Human is not. More than that, they are family. That means they love *you*, Wo!"

Wo is starting to feel good about this experience. He has learned much from this Packing Angel, and he knows there is more to come. The angel turns to one more suitcase. It sits alone among the discarded baggage and personal items that Wo is about to leave behind. He wonders if this one will survive.

The Suitcase of Vitamins—Health

"What is in this suitcase that rattles when I pick it up?" asks the angel.

"Dear Packing Angel, these are my vitamins and herbs. I need them to stay healthy and balanced on my trip into the new energy. I feel fragile sometimes, and since you know all about me, you know that I am sensitive to certain substances and foods. So, I need these herbs and vitamins to sustain me and keep me strong on this trip."

Wo feels that he has represented himself well on this matter, and feels nervous that the angel will take these, too. He feels that he needs them. There is a pause.

"Are you going to take my vitamins and herbs?" Wo looks at the angel with his hurt puppy-dog expression.

"No, Wo, I'm not going to throw them out," replies the angel. "But *you* will, eventually. As you walk the walk and realize your potential as an ascended Human, you will slowly understand that your DNA is being changed. Your immune system is being altered and bolstered up with energy from the stars. Messages and instruction sets will be delivered to your cells from the very crystalline structure of the Earth, and you will absolutely know that these supplements, although valuable to you now, will drop away as you gain your well-being. No Earthly energy or attribute will be able to wear you down. No substance or food will affect you in the same way. Rather than becoming more sensitive with enlightenment, you will instead have a bolstering of your system so that nothing will be able to penetrate the light you carry. Slowly you will be able to drop any seeming dependence on the chemistry you travel with. Instead, you will find new supplements, new energies and facilitations, and new ways of gaining the nutrition that your body needs. Don't be surprised when you find that your *new* body and biology needs new balance. No, Wo. You can keep your vitamins and herbs, but there will come a day when your body will no longer desire them. Then you will know of what I speak."

This is a victory for Wo. Not only does he get to keep something (finally), but it is also the last suitcase. He is happy, and he is ready to move through the door into a new world—one where life is more in the NOW—a life where he can carry his light, and mean something to Earth and the humanity around him. He is very excited.

"Dear angel, thank you for all your help," Wo declares as he shuts the case.

"We are not finished, Wo," says the angel as he opens the case again.

"What do you mean?" asks Wo nervously. The angel reaches his hand down and moves it around a bit. Wo knows what he is doing.

"There is something hiding down here, Wo." The angel brings up a black zippered compartment that has been cleverly hiding in the lining of the vitamin and herb suitcase.

The Secret Compartment—Drama

Wo is shaking. He casts his eyes downward. He doesn't want to be standing there, and he doesn't want what is in the zippered compartment revealed or unzipped. The angel respects this, and simply stands there with the small, unopened bag in his large hand. He waits for Wo to speak.

"Please don't," says Wo in a pleading manner.

"I won't open it," says the angel, "because I love you, Wo, and would never willingly make you uncomfortable . . . but you can't take this with you either, and you know it."

***

Now, dear ones, what do you think was in this small black package? We stop the story again to develop this metaphor fully for you. The answer is the one you are going to give to me in your mind as I ask you, the listener, and you, the reader, this question: *Who is it that you won't speak to in your life? Who is it, dear ascension candidate, who you will not forgive in this lifetime? Who is it whom you have drama with, who cannot gain your love again? Who has betrayed you? Who is blacklisted in your Human mind?*

That is the energy in the black bag that the angel holds. It's ugly. It does not fare well with a higher vibration. It does not mix with the pure intent of an individual who is about to start a new path of higher vibration, and it cannot remain a secret. We will speak more about this exact thing after the passing of the marker.

Does this fit you? If it does, let me give you what is in another secret compartment called the divine Human soul. It is the power and strength to get beyond the drama that is being held in the darkest corners of your mind. It is LIGHT that can shine upon any situation. It is the essence of forgiveness, of maturity, and of wisdom. It personifies the anointing of the new Human. It's the realization that you are a piece of God, and the family around you has done its part as well as pieces of God. Whatever they did, whoever they are, and wherever they are (even in death), they are now seen as equal players in a grand play that you both helped to create. Can you see the overview? Can you see how it has taken TWO to create the energy that you hold in the black bag? Can you forgive and love them? You can! That's the miracle of the new Human-evolved consciousness that is yours for the asking. That is the power of the ascended Human Being!

***

"Please take the bag," Wo says with tears in his eyes. "Put it with the others on the floor where it belongs."

"What bag?" asks the delighted angel. "It disappeared a moment ago with your intent for forgiveness and with the wisdom that you carry, my beloved Human. Congratulations on your understanding. Congratulations on your graduation. Congratulations, Wo, on vibrating to a higher level."

Wo says good-bye to the angel and hugs him again. With one small bag, he disappears through the door that is the metaphor for the Human Being's desire to cross into a land where nothing is the same as it used to be—a land with promise and love, and also a land of great spiritual challenge. Wo joins a land of lightworkers who hold the energy of a new Earth in its genesis configuration.

Wo feels light, peaceful, and very loved as he moves out of sight.

***

Dear ones, this parable is about *you*. What is your perception of vibrating higher and carrying an ascension energy? Is it something you do between lunch and errands? If so, you don't understand what it is. This is not something you *do*. It is something you *live*.

What is before you is the most profound and altering spiritual energy of any in all Human history. What is before you is your ability to change the very essence of your existence—to live longer lives, have a more peaceful and joyful fulfillment, and the power to change the very earth under your feet. In the process, you get to learn, learn, and learn. And also in the process, you get to be loved without measure, and begin to feel the *family*—as it is one step closer to you spiritually than ever before. These are *not* the end times. This is, instead, a new beginning.

There is a family that is beside your chair. And in that family is the Kryon, whose existence for eons now has been to love and inform you ... never asking ... no agenda ... never demanding. I remain as your friend and family. I remain in love watching you do something no one expected—changing the Universe itself. I remain on Earth until it is over. And that, my dear family, will be a long time from now.

We leave with the same love we came with, and, indeed, we will be back. Let the listener and the reader alike know that this day they are dearly loved!

Let the new Earth begin with those who are awakening to their power—those who hear and read these words. You.

In love,

Kryon

No Actual Heaven or Hell?

Regarding Heaven
Written by Pope John Paul II — July 1999

"In the context of Revelation, we know that the 'heaven' or 'happiness' in which we will find ourselves is neither an abstraction nor a physical place in the clouds, but a living, personal relationship with the Holy Trinity. It is our meeting with the Father which takes place in the risen Christ through the communion of the Holy Spirit. It is always necessary to maintain a certain restraint in describing these 'ultimate realities' since their depiction is always unsatisfactory. Today's personalist language is better suited to describing the state of happiness and peace we will enjoy in our definitive communion with God." [1]

Regarding Hell
Written by Pope John Paul II — August 1999

"The images of hell that Sacred Scripture presents to us must be correctly interpreted. They show the complete frustration and emptiness of life without God. ... More than a place, hell indicates the state of those who freely and definitively separate themselves from God. Hell is not punishment imposed externally by God, but the condition resulting from attitudes and actions which people adopt in this life. Scripture uses many images to describe the pain, frustration and emptiness of life without God. More than a physical place, hell is the state of those who freely and definitively separate themselves from God, the source of all life and joy. So eternal damnation is not God's work but is actually our own doing." [2]

[1] *L'Osservatore Romano;* "Heaven is Fullness of Communication with God"; Editorial and Management Offices; Via del Pellegrino, 00120, Vatican City, Europe; July 28, 1999; Spoken by the Pope in general audience on July 21, 1999; Full article may be seen at [www.vatican.va].

[2] *L'Osservatore Romano;* "Hell is the State of Those who Reject God"; Editorial and Management Offices; Via del Pellegrino, 00120, Vatican City, Europe; August 4, 1999; Spoken by the Pope in general audience on July 28, 1999. Full article may be seen at [www.vatican.va]

Live Channelling

"Five Spiritual Millennium Energy Changes"

Channelled in
Cleveland, Ohio — October 1999
Singapore — October 1999

Chapter Five

"Five Spiritual Millennium Changes"
Live Channelling
Cleveland, Ohio
Singapore

*The live channelling that follows was transcribed
as a combination of two events on two different
continents . . . all with the same message . . .
given live. It has been edited with additional
words and thoughts to allow clarification and
better understanding of the written word.*

Greetings, dear ones. I AM Kryon of Magnetic Service. This is a precious time for us as our entourage moves into this room. Oh, dear ones, this special time is due to what this particular group, whom we call *family*, has done—not only on this planet and for the Universe, but for those of us called the Kryon entourage who flood into this place. Indeed, there are far more of you who are awakening than you think. Even some who are here wondering what this is about have come due to the calling in their spiritual hearts. If this fits the reader or the listener, now is the time for you to feel what this new millennium is about.

Sit patiently in the chair until the energy flows to you now. For this meeting, dear ones, is about the love of family . . . for family. It is about the fact that so many of you, angels each one, are pieces of God, disguised as Humans. You come and you go so quickly, and you are missed so! This particular precious time that you have asked for

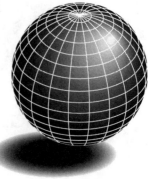

allows us to flow from our side of the veil to yours. We're not going to wait a moment more! We flow into this place en masse, pressing upon you the love of Spirit and family.

We move through the aisles—alongside the chairs—and we pause and hesitate. Each part of the entourage assigned to a Human, no matter where they are in this room, is filled with the profound knowledge that they are brother and sister to those who sit here hearing and reading. They take the time to wash your feet lovingly, and there's only one reason they would do this, because this reunion is real and conveys the feeling of uniqueness to all of us. There are so many words to describe the reality of what is taking place right now—among them: *honor*, *love, congratulations*, and *appropriateness.*

There are not many weeks left before a marker is approached—a marker that will turn around the planet itself. Here we all sit, seemingly moments from the change to your new millennium. Many in the Universe never would have accepted that this particular group of angels called Humans could have made such a shift on this planet of energy testing. Yet as we all sit here, there is celebration that indeed you have already made a huge change.

We all wait for the marker—seemingly for that clock to run down and begin the energy of the year 2000, and the new millennium moving forward to the year 2012. This will be a period of time where much can be changed—a 12-year period allowing some of the new children to grow up, some of those in this room to change profoundly, and the provision for energy on this planet that was never ever conceived of before.

We have said this to other groups before. It's core information, and it goes like this: There has never been a time in Human history when the energy will descend upon the planet like it is scheduled to now! There has never been a time in Human history when humanity has awakened to the degree it has now!

And so we say to you and family, "Blessed are you, shamans each one, who elected to come to Earth yet again and play out that finality of this lifetime and the finality of Earth's plan." Some of you may elect for this to be the last time. All in this room have had a driving passion at a spiritual level to make sure that this test was played to the end—and here you sit doing just that.

I sit in front of those who started it all! I sit in front of those who helped the Kryon before humanity existed, setting the energy of the grid system in a way that would foster humanity and its spiritual attributes so that the duality would be strong. In the last years, you have changed all of it. Some have said this: *"Oh, dear Kryon, if this is indeed true that you knew where we would sit and you knew our names, then what are they? Kryon, perhaps in this period of time, you would give us our spiritual names?"*

I'm going to tell you the truth. This entity called Kryon cannot do that. There is no way we can express the grandeur of your real name with the limited resources we have within the language of the Human who sits here. You have chosen limited dimensionality on this planet. Perhaps you would understand a little more when I tell you what it's like when we "feel" your name on the other side? For there will come a time, dear ones, when you will see me again. And in those moments when we recognize one another on my side of the veil, you will again approach me and SING your name to me with LIGHT! How am I going to give you that name as you sit in Human form—pieces of God—divine, each one? How can I give you that glorious experience within the small dimensionality you currently possess? I can't.

It is time that your thinking encompassed the reality of who you are, for this is the forerunner group who sits and reads and listens to this message about the coming days. The ones awakening now are the ones who are going to make a difference on this planet. We can hardly wait to have you back, dear family!

We can hardly wait to give you the message that says, "Not only were you on Earth for eons, but you changed the very fabric of the Universe! The energy of the reality on my side of the veil has been changed because of what you have done on Earth! Did you know that? And you wonder why the entourage loves you so? You wonder why we come to you with such a profound feeling of family? You wonder why we wish to spend this time with you now? Oh, dear ones, some of you have come to sit in these chairs and begin a healing that is long overdue. You sit reading this and hearing this, and perhaps you don't think we know who you are? We know who sits in front of us, we know your names, and we know of your eternalness. You are sister. You are brother. And so we say to you in the energy that is here before us all, "Let the healing begin."

We say to those of you who have come to sit in this energy of love, "Let the light changes begin and pour forth to this group—the essence of self-worth that so many have come here for." Let it be known that when we are finished this day, this family can stand up from the chairs where they sit and leave feeling different from when they came in. And the difference will be that a spiritual healing has been received!

The millennium is going to change many things on your planet. The marker that is going to take place at the year 2000 is a "permission" marker. Many of the things that have been withheld have been waiting to be delivered, should you make it to this marker . . . and you're going to make it. The withholding has been on purpose, for the energies are correct and proper and the astronomy is correct and proper to move this planet from the old energy to the new energy. Now, so many of you will feel nothing—no grand changes—but the marker will have been passed. Like a train that passes the green light that was never there before, the energies will come pouring into the planet in the next 12 years to make humanity aware. This energy will touch the Human race in a way you never thought it could, and you wonder why we get excited!

Five Spiritual Millennium Energy Changes

We would like to address some issues about the coming millennium energies. We would like to give you five attributes of the new millennium energies, some of which consist of core information, and some which have not been heard before. We are going to begin with the one that is the most profound: the changes in the DNA of Human Beings.

DNA

Some will say, *"Kryon, you've been saying for a long time that the DNA is changing in Humans. Will we ever be able to verify this?"* Dear ones, in the next two generations of humanity, scientists will begin to be able to look into their microscopes and see differences at the cellular level between older Humans and newer ones. We speak now of the two strands (or loops, as we call them) of the physical DNA that are responsible for the chemical name given to it—the strands that you can see and study. One of the revelations of the current study of the Human genome will be that it changes! There will be no better measure of Human evolution than when this study is complete, for you will then be able to compare the total code itself (understood or not) to a comparison of the codes within new children over the next two generations. We have told you before: As your science increases, so will your discoveries of some of the strangest attributes we have given you about Human existence. Again we say, today's New Age oddities will be tomorrow's science.

Not just your DNA will be changing, though. The Human body's chemistry will change in the area of immunity. The immune system is the first to shift, as it should be, but there will be more. At the cellular level, you will see anomalies that you never saw before—strengths that you never saw before. Even the cells will divide differently. The Human will be changing, and "cellular awareness" will be changed. Many will wonder if it was always there but never seen before, but this is not the case, for what you eventually perceive as a different kind of biology will be starting to sweep the planet. Some will call it the beginning of "intelligent cells." Some biologists will wonder why they never saw some of the intelligent processes at the cellular level that will make themselves known. Some will understand that they are new, and others will puzzle at how the processes could have changed the way they did, with essentially the same chemistry as before. What many will miss is what we will call an enabled DNA—the next step in Human evolution.

Let me tell you where this evolution begins. Many think it begins with the Indigo Children who are being born now. You may think that to have evolved DNA, you must be born with it, but you do not! Cellular shift begins with PURE SPIRITUAL INTENT. *"Kryon, do you mean that with intent we can actually change our cellular structure?"* Yes, you can! Again I tell you that the grandest miracles that have ever been reported on this planet have come from "the inside out." That is to say, the divinity in the Human Being actually created the changes in the cellular structure that was able to create matter out of consciousness.

There are avatars on the planet right now who create matter out of consciousness! If that is the truth, then isn't the next logical step for the advanced Human Being to do the same? That's what a miracle is, and it can be generated in your body just as the avatar does it, for the principles are identical. As you begin to see who you really are and you start to see that spiritual "family member" inside you, you change. What does a grand avatar have that you seem not to? The answer to that question is: COMPLETE SELF-AWARENESS. When you discover the divinity inside, your DNA changes to accommodate the reality of your discovery. This is also called "creating your own reality," a subject we have explored before.

Your DNA is perfect, but you have allowed restrictors to be placed in your body that provide for short lifetimes, disease, and imbalance. With intent, these restrictors are lessened and the DNA is allowed to become closer to what it was designed to be. All of this was created by you and for you. Now you are being enabled to bring the DNA into a state that will respond to your consciousness.

There is another attribute we have talked about regarding DNA. It is the birth of the new children called "Indigo." This is a planetary attribute, dear ones. It is not sequestered to a single culture or continent. The arrival of these new children is a direct result of permission you gave spiritually on the 11:11, seven years ago. These are the Humans we speak of who carry the seeds of Human evolution within them, and it's important that you realize that this DNA discussion is about ALL the loops, not just the ones you might examine under the microscope. (Kryon often speaks of the 12 strands of DNA, many of which are not chemical and therefore not seen.)

How appropriate! The 11:11 was the window of permission given at the highest level of Human consciousness in the early '90s. The question was asked of all Humans on the planet: "Do you give permission to allow a change in the DNA to the extent that those born after you will carry a consciousness that you did not?" The answer given in this 11:11 window was uniformly YES.

The message of Kryon from the beginning has been that not only did you live through the parts of life when the "doom-and-gloom" prophecy was absolutely certain to come about, but through your conscious effort, you changed it. It's important to realize that Kryon had nothing to do with this permission window, or the work you have done on the planet. Instead, this good news has to do with the human/angel walking this planet— YOU! It has to do with an empowered Human race. Altogether, your planet has gradually chosen to understand that things could be different and that humanity had the ability to change it. Finally, you understood a code that we had given you over and over—that you had the ability to change the course of time, change prophecy, and create a new future. And you did!

The grandest attribute of Human change in the new millennium is the DNA shift, and the pieces and the parts of it you cannot measure will be the first to change. These parts you cannot measure are those that are magnetically influenced. These magnetically influenced parts are designed to awaken pieces of chemistry in you. Many will think that this is miraculous—the ability to have life extension, the ability to have peace in the midst of turmoil, the ability to have the love in your heart you asked for, or to have the anxiety levels greatly calmed. The shift also allows you to finally glimpse the piece of God that you are. All of this begins at the cellular level, for within the cells of the Human Being is the blueprint of a spiritual and physical life. It represents all that you have ever been and the reason you are here; the karmic attributes carried from the past (what we call the "recipe" and setup for your life) are represented in this DNA blueprint.

The Path—Motion

As you pass that demarcation point called the millennium, you can expect some changes in the second issue: PATH. Some of you have felt "stopped" within your spiritual growth. You have felt a seeming halt in what, in the past, has at least given you a feeling of "forward motion." Now, even that is gone. Human Being, lightworker, healer, family member: Do you really think you've come though the ages only to have a 1999 "stop"? How's that for the new energy? [Laughter]

Let me tell you what is happening. You have the ability to sense motion in a linear fashion that my partner described to you [earlier in the seminar] and what you call your REALITY. Even in a spiritual way, you feel spiritual motion in a linear fashion. It takes you from one place to another on the spiritual path. Now it's time to let that perception change. Earlier, my partner [Lee] described a train in motion on a track as a metaphor of your life force in the old energy. Let me ask you this interdimensional question: What would happen to that metaphor of the train on the track traveling in a circle if we told you that *the train was in the same place, but the track was still moving?*

The question for you is this: Is the train still in motion? For that matter, are you traveling anywhere? The answer to both is an interdimensional YES, but in your 4D, you might question it. This is because your "motion detection" system has now been drawn into the NOW time frame. The reason why you feel stopped is often because in the NOW (a higher vibration), you receive an interdimensional motion that feels nothing like what you have spiritually felt before. It is out of the normal Human 4D. The track is moving, and the wheels are still going and going, yet you might say, "I'm stopped." You ARE NOT stopped. The track still moves under you, so the engine is still engaged and running well, but the perception is now less linear. It's more relative to what is around you, and you feel stopped from an OLD energy paradigm of understanding.

For those who can't understand this, we give you a joyful vision to help with your patience. Pretend you're spiritually paused, and simply waiting for something wonderful to catch up with you! The feeling of motion is completely and totally different spiritually than it ever was before. In addition, you have often measured motion by the synchronicity that takes place within your lives. Not only that, healers and lightworkers, you also tend to measure motion and spirituality by how well things are working within your facilitation. Do you know what happens to a factory when it shuts down for renovation or retooling? It stops. Do you know what happens to the employees when they get laid off for two weeks WITH pay? They celebrate! [Laughter] And so, we must ask the obvious: If you are stopped, why not join the party? For those of you who felt stopped by challenge during this renovation time, why are you not awakening in the morning feeling elation during the time off?

The first thing in the morning, do you wake up and remind yourselves that you are on a planet that you've changed? Do you celebrate? Your first thoughts upon awakening could be this: *Thank you, family. I'm grateful that I am never alone; thank you, family, for this opportunity of challenge on this planet of free choice; thank you, family, for allowing me to be a part of this grand experience.* Instead of pulling yourself up in the morning and bemoaning life, try saying to yourself, *"I'm going to celebrate this day, no matter what it brings!"* Maybe that's a bit different from what you do now, but you see, things are not always as they seem.

The Path—Time Acceleration

Speaking of the spiritual path that you are on, you should know that another attribute of the new energy will be *time acceleration.* It is what you have asked for in the vibrational shift of both spirituality and physics. In essence, you, by choice, have caused the very atomic structure of this particular part of the universe to vibrate faster. Your time is speeding up! What you are seeing in your Earth geology is also an accelerated time frame. Geologists will tell you that the Earth changes that are taking place now are not changes that they expected to see for 20 to 30 years, yet they are here on your doorstep now. *"But Kryon,"* you might say, *"why are all the clocks the same if time is speeding up? Wouldn't they go faster?"* Not according to your own science, they wouldn't! Remember the scientific relativity puzzle called "the paradox of the clock"? Two clocks are compared. One is with Humans on Earth, the other with a traveler who is moving away from Earth at a very fast rate. The clocks seem to be reading exactly as they should to each group, but when the traveler returns, he finds that the earth has aged, and he has not! Yet his clock seemed to be normal in every way as he was traveling. His speed changed his time frame, but his clock seemed normal. It was only when he compared it relative to home that it was shown that time had somehow changed.

In the next years, your astronomers and your physicists may begin to put together the anomaly of relative time, and your part in it. You are changing time in your area, but you have no other time frame to compare it to. Therefore, time appears to be the same, but at the cellular level, most of you are aware of the acceleration that is going on. Although this may not make sense to you, there will come a time when science will look at the Universe around you and say that it is "slowing down." The reality is that *you are speeding up!* Watch for it. It has to do with the relativity of time, this planet, and what you have done. Some of you can already sense this and say, *"Of course, time is speeding up. We can feel it!"* Some of you wake up early in the morning with anxiety because your cells feel it. You are absolutely right if you have wondered if time is accelerating. Welcome to the beginning of a dimensionality that you did not have yesterday!

The Path—Finally, the Relaxation

Finally, regarding paths, we will say this: As you move into the marker, past the millennium shift, there will be a promise of relaxation. That is to say, you will sit in a groove that you'll understand you belong in, and it will settle in. The anxiety will start to dissipate. At the cellular level, you will begin to feel comfortable, start to understand the "gifts," and begin using them in a fashion you never understood before. The renovated factory will reopen, and the new tools will be presented for you to begin to learn with as you continue work. So we say to you: Patience, dear ones, patience—for the marker is at hand.

Challenge, and a New Tool

The third attribute that is going to change greatly is the attribute of challenge. We want you to know what the mechanics of challenge are, which we have not yet discussed before in a group of this nature. You have been told that challenge is about raising the vibration of the planet. Indeed, it is. A lightworker uses challenge to work through current lessons of his own creation in real time. Dear ones, that's all part of raising the spiritual vibration of the planet, as measured every 25 years. The next-to-the-last measurement was in 1987, and the last measurement of this complete and total test of energy will be in 2012. From that point on, the planet will never be measured again, but it will continue to exist with a new paradigm.

For you are entering into a new energy—a new humanity, a new Earth purpose—and you stand on the cusp of the marker for all of that. You may wonder again why the entities in this room could hardly wait to pour in here or around your chair and wash your feet? "Pride of family" is a love attribute that has nothing to do with ego, and from this side of the veil, we feel the "pride of family" with you! You think you came here to see us [speaking of those who have come to the seminar]? We've been here for days in anticipation of seeing and loving you once again! This time together is for us as much as you.

Challenge has another attribute that you should know about. Challenges in life, when solved with the wisdom of the spirit of love, are also going to do something completely different in addition to changing the vibration of the earth. The wise solution to challenge is going to change the very essence of your *duality*. Here is what we mean: For years you have had a duality that presses upon you and that questions your every spiritual move. This is as it should be, for Human duality is the great balancing force. It has allowed for the unbiased testing.

It is the duality that awakens you at 3:00 in the morning and says, "You're nothing, you know. You don't deserve to be here." It is the duality that taps you on the shoulder and says, "All of this spiritual stuff is nonsense." It's the duality that wakes you up and says, "Let's worry about something!" [Laughter] There are those of you who struggle with duality daily. It is responsible for so much of what you feel is holding you back, and now we have new information about it. Human duality is going to start to distance itself from the Higher Self. For the first time in Human spiritual history, the actual duality balance of Humans will change. It must, to allow for the ascension process that we have been speaking of so often.

Human duality is the part of you that you have elected to come in with, which is of a lower vibration than the angel inside you. It is designed to temper all of the spirituality that you have. It is the *doubting Thomas*. It is the part of you that questions all things spiritual, and it is appropriate and balanced. As we have discussed before, the magnetic grid of planet Earth helps to support Human duality to the degree that it has been for eons of time.

Now we are telling you that the balance of this duality can and will change as you move through challenge. Do you know where fear, anxiety, and doubt come from? It comes from that piece of you called *duality*. As you solve problems, the duality will be pushed away and will change its balance within your spiritual structure. Do you know what a Human Being is going to be like when he pushes that away? It's called ascension! It's the beginning of a new kind of era. Do you know where you're going to see it first? In the children. They have something you don't have. They have the ability to push the duality away. It is one of the attributes they have arrived with spiritually, since they come in with the knowledge of "deserving to be here." Some of them will tell you who they've been and why they are here! Not all will become spiritual giants. They will still act as children, with Human choice.

There is truly something different about this Human breed, however, and the biggest difference is that the essence of their passion for the planet is not power, not greed, and not jealousy. Therefore, what many have called basic Human nature is different with these children. These small Human Beings whose very world is shaken because their parents might argue and shout, will not leave the room as they're told to, not go and hide under the bed. Instead, they will cling to one leg of a parent and beg for them to resolve the argument!

This child comes in to this planet with a passion for peaceful existence. Watch for it. It's already here. The children of the children will be even more obviously different, and by the time you experience the third generation, they will be demanding peace on this planet to a degree that has never been seen before. And the things that you have seen regarding this planet's immediate past history will become ancient history . . . almost a DARK AGE. These new Humans will not have the attributes of any kind of Human you've ever seen. Watch for it. Oh, it will take some time as the old moves on and new comes in, but the posturing of this new generation is far different because they will be demanding tolerance within your individual relation-ships—then country to country, and religion to religion. They will say, *"There is a way to unify this planet, even though people and cultures are very different."* They will begin to work on some of the most exasperating problems humanity was never able to solve. And you will see solutions to the world's problems come right out of the little ones, and the children of the little ones.

The Final Split

Where are you going spiritually? What's going to happen next with the New Age philosophy? We're going to give you an expression for those left in the old energy after the millennium marker comes. The expression in the year 2000 is that "the train has left the station." Those in the old energy who have refused to accept any of the new gifts and have stayed with the old ways, now have a final invitation to come on-board this new millennium train. The steps have been small over these last years since 1987, and many could have moved from the old to the new energy slowly, incorporating their knowledge and enhancing their lives. Some of them have refused, however, and stick to the old ways.

Whereas the transition from old to new could have been made gradually, it will now be a giant leap for them. So there will be those who will stay in the old energy, calling themselves lightworkers and calling you "wrong." They will not understand ascension status nor see the gifts that are available. They will tell you that they have earned their knowledge with their experience and that you could not have these new things without "paying your dues" as they have. Many of them will say good-bye to you, and there will be a split. This is Human nature, is it not? But this is what was foretold and expected of such a dramatic shift.

The differences between the two of you will be obvious to anyone looking in from the outside. Those in the old energy who call themselves lightworkers will have lists of things that a person must do, and procedures and agendas in order for anyone to have an enlightened energy within. The NEW energy features Human enablement and power. There will be very little structure and no ego developed around any Human hierarchy that must be adhered to. It will be obvious who is the OLD and who is the NEW energy to anyone who compares them.

Those in the new energy will have attributes that you can also easily recognize. There will be "the four attributes of love" represented in their work (given so many times in the Kryon channellings). There will be no agenda within their work and attitudes. They will be quiet about their gifts, and not act in ego. They will not be puffed up with their own accomplishments, and there will be wisdom in their words. The mark of the new energy lightworker is the one who is in the NOW. When you ask them what's going to happen tomorrow, they will look at you and say, *"No one knows that."* They will act confident and with love about the future—without anxiety, because when it arrives, it will be co-created appropriately as it should be. And that, dear ones, is *opposite* the old Human nature. The OLD way fears the future and has no confidence in the ability to create reality! The NEW way fully understands that the future is exactly what the Human makes it to be. You don't fear what you can create.

Support and Special Delivery

Number five is going to be called *support*, and we speak now of the guides and angels with you. When you pass the marker, dear ones, you're going to experience spiritual changes. Think about this: If you are going to force the duality into a new separation, if you are going to create a new spiritual Human Being, if you are going to change the DNA, if you are going to start seeing miracles in your lives, if you are going to have peace in areas that were troublesome before, then there's going to have to be a spiritual entourage with you . . . more than just three guides!

There will be overguides that are oversouls—ones that you have known but don't recognize. These entities are inter-dimensional, and difficult to explain, but they FEEL like family and are poised and ready to share this new energy with you. Some are in this very room where you sit! They are simply waiting for the marker and your *intent* to say, "Let it be so."

This is core information, and we have mentioned it before: There are Human Beings whose greatest setup is loneliness. [A setup is a contract or karmic attribute.] It is an attribute some arrived with, and something they don't always have a grip on. It's part of the lesson of this current life. Long after this meeting is completed, some of you may go home and get into the closet, and in that closet, you may pretend to be alone. We say to you, "Go ahead and turn out the light, and pretend all you want to that you are alone . . . and while you are pretending that nobody in the Universe knows who you really are, or knows about your life, there's going to be a crowd in there all having a party!" YOU ARE NEVER ALONE! That closet will be bursting with entities who know your life attribute, your name, your oversoul, your contract, your potential, your self-worth, your angelic magnitude, your memory, and your potential future! Difficult to comprehend, I know, but the fact is that there is a support group that is ALWAYS with you, and it's about to increase with your permission!

Blessed are the Human Beings who go into their closets, turn off the lights, and participate in the party! [Laughter] What we are saying to you, dear ones, is this: Past the millennium marker, you can expect new energies around you. Many of you are waiting for the new energy processes. Have patience, for finally it is at hand, and the new family will deliver them to you.

Much new energy will have to be delivered to this planet in the next 12 years. Special astronomical alignments will be the key. Remember that your spiritual factory is being retooled. Join with the others in the celebration of this until the tooling is over. The beginning of the marker of the year 2000 will give permission for these new energies that are being developed to be delivered to you slowly over time as you need them. The new millennium has an energy about it that has the potential to be far different from anything you have experienced before. Much will be said and done in humanity about the crossover of walking that bridge between the millenniums. But you will know, as the core group, what it really means. That is why you are here today, reading and hearing this.

Many will fear the planetary alignments or astronomical anomalies that will occur very soon. For you, remember what has been said this day. Stand in the middle of the fear of others, and instead, celebrate the alignments! Bask in the energy of new promise for the planet, and receive the balance that is coming. Much feminine energy will be delivered to this planet in the next 12 years. This is not a gender issue, but a balance issue for Earth. The delivery of the feminine energy will enhance humanity as a whole and bring the earth into a more gentle consciousness, away from the OLD.

We waited a long time to be invited into this room where you sit and read or listen. The potential was there all along that allowed for this entourage to love you. This kind of meeting could not have existed ten years ago. Did you know that? This kind of energy could not have been delivered to you ten years ago. That is how much you have changed this planet spiritually.

We invite you to experience love at the cellular level. Right now, pause, and feel the love of the family, for we are about to depart. After the information has been delivered and congratulations are given, this family leaves. Yet the bowls of our tears of joy, as we washed your feet, will be ready to be used again when you wish to rekindle this love through your intent.

It's the hardest thing we do when we leave you after having been allowed to hug you as we have done. There will never be another meeting exactly like this with a family assembled just like this one, and we know this. But on we will go, meeting you one on one. You don't need to attend a meeting like this to have this love experience. You don't need to come to a Kryon channelling ever again, if you choose not to. You don't have to read another Kryon communication to have this love, either. Let this message show that there is no agenda around Kryon for you. All by yourself, you can have ALL the energy that was generated here today. How? Try walking into that closet again. This time, join the party! You can create all this energy of family love by yourself on a daily basis in that closet... go ahead, just try to "be alone." [Laughter] This communication is not about Kryon. It's about FAMILY!

Walk from this place carrying a life force so strong that anytime you wish to, through intent, you can create this kind of energy and love. Have your own "family reunion" anytime you wish. It is so. That is the power you have!

And so it is that this Kryon entourage retreats from this room. We say thank you for what you have done for the Universe—for you have no idea how your actions have changed us all.

And when we see you again, we can all say,

"Let the celebration begin. Let the party begin."

And so it is.

Kryon

Live Channelling

"Passing the Marker"

Channelled in
New Hampshire
November 1999

Chapter Six

"Passing the Marker"
Live Channelling
New Hampshire

This live channelling has been edited with additional words and thoughts to allow clarification and better understanding of the written word.

Greetings, dear ones. I AM Kryon of Magnetic Service. It is the family that we greet again in this place that is familiar to us [speaking of the meeting room in New Hampshire where 400 are gathered]. It is the spiritual family and the entourage we talk about, which pours in here by the invitation of the angels who sit in the chairs, pretending to be Human. It is with the invitation of the one pair of eyes, leading to thousands of pairs that fall upon the transcription of what is being said right now. I speak in the *now* to the one who is reading this. As difficult as it may be for you hearing this to understand, in this *now* reality there are thousands of those touching the words on the page, which is being generated for you in an auditory fashion.

Odd as it might seem, we know who they are and where they're going to sit as they read, just as we know who you are and where you would sit today—for the potentials of enlightenment are in a circle and we see them all. There is no linear time on this side of the veil; therefore, we see the potentials of the ones reading and hearing all at the same time. This is the way we also see Earth, and the potentials of what you can do.

We're going to say something to you that we have said to the last five groups. *You are eternal!* You are eternal in both directions! The circle that is the spiritual life force in you is permanent! It always *was* and will always *be*. As far back as you can even conceive of a past, there was "you." If you could see it in the circle that we do, you would understand that as far back as you could go in linear time, you could meet the future of what you have become. So what we are saying is that you were the same yesterday, and you will be the same tomorrow—a piece of the divine, a piece of the whole, a piece of God. Whereas some of you may have felt from the depths of your awareness that God is an all-powerful being and oversees all things in the Universe, you are only partially correct. "All-powerful" is correct, but God is literally made up of a collective of trillions and trillions of family members, each one known by name. Each is known to the other. Difficult as it may be for you to understand, the names of each of you are known by all.

Oh, anointed one, oh, shaman, as you sit in the chair right now reading this or hearing this, lifetimes of monkdom press upon you. For lifetimes you groveled on the floor in ritual and worship, not understanding that *you* were God! Even though you knew the words I AM, they never seemed to fit the "I" in your I-dentity. You never thought it was you! Finally, right before the marker comes [the year 2000], you are beginning to understand that *you* are a piece of the whole, and that *you* are divine. But on this planet and your 4D existence, there is no way I can give you your real name. You cannot hear or see the things that can be heard and seen on the other side of the veil. Here [Earth], there is no concept of what your name is, yet as I see you here, I can still see your incredible grandeur. You think I come here with this entourage and just perceive a vast sea of faces? I just told you that there are trillions of pieces of God, we know each of you intimately, and we are always connected with one another. We know who you are!

And so as the entourage pours in here—with the love energy that has your real name on it—we prepare to hug you from behind and touch you on the shoulders and place our energy upon your heads. We will even wash your feet! Listener, reader, we say we "know" who we sit in front of. If you think you came here to see us, it's not that way at all. There are far more of us here than of you! Make no mistake who came to see who. Oh, there's such an outpouring of love for this family who sits here. We invite you at this time to begin to feel the energy we are delivering.

Dear ones, in these next moments, there's going to be new information about the upcoming millennium, and there's going to be a discussion of science, physics, biology, and much more. In these next few minutes, we're going to open up the veil and give you potentials for the planet. But while we do that, even though the information may flow to you, there's even more going on where you sit. This is about a reunion with the family. We have said so many times that you have no idea of the power this year that is different from last year. And it's because you have allowed for such a thing—actually created it with your intent. You have no idea what you are capable of, and even before the information begins, we say to you, don't you think we know why you're here?

Dear one, and you know of whom I speak, it is time. Let the healing begin! Celebrate it right now with us. There would be infinite joy for all of us if you were to leave the chair where you sit, different from when you originally sat down. Dear one, let your life's purpose begin tonight. As the sun goes down in this place, let the energy shift, and let a new Human Being emerge from the chair—a very different one from the one who came in. Let an awareness of being eternal surge through your body. When you eventually leave this planet, there will be a transformation of your being into a piece of God that is divine and angelic.

We could bask in the energy of this reunion and remain quiet—just hugging you. We could be still and just let you participate in the incredible love we wish to pass to you through your heart chakra, letting it permeate your being. Not one of you would miss the fact that you were visited today by a sister/ brother group that is profoundly yours. Each time we are invited into your midst, we are tempted to just be still and let you feel.

There are potentials as you pass the marker (the year 2000), dear ones, that we cannot begin to explain. Many of you are so aware, as this marker comes upon you, that the last millennium change was very different from this one, or of the ones before it. Oh, there is always energy around the changing of a millennium date. There are always those who would be the soothsayers of doom and gloom who might say, "This is the last one!" The irony is that, indeed, this *was* going to be the last one! By your design and with your permission, and through all of the planning that went into it by the angels that you are, the Human existence calendar was pieced together to make this the final millennium shift for humanity. This means that most of the prophecies about these end times were correct!

In 2012, the last measurement will be taken of the planet for the test at hand. Whatever that measurement turns out to be will be the end of the test. This test of energy level—the test of vibratory shift for the planet—is already at an all-time high. The marker is being passed right now that is going to demarcate permission to change the planet. Think of this marker as a green light that is being passed by a train that is on a track that has been tentative—almost a mystery. Think of the track as being one that is dangerous, and that has no assurance that another train might be coming the other way at you! Suddenly you see and pass something that gives you tremendous relief—a green light, a signal from the track controller that indicates, "We know you are here, and the track ahead is clear."

Many of you have felt stuck in these past years. Get ready for the release. For when you pass the marker, you have passed the point at which permission has been given for a clearer journey. You, dear ones, as the frontrunners of this age that we wish to call the "now age," will begin to totally release the OLD and build the NEW. For, those who will give permission for such a thing are creating more green lights for the rest of you. Through the intent of the Human Being, you will change the planet on that new track with the green light. It's a virgin track—not traveled upon—ever. There is going to be a train called humanity, and it has the potential of creating itself as it goes. Think of it—a train that lays its own track before it! Therefore, nothing can be placed on it in advance to derail the train. There can be no foretelling of a future that has no existing track path. The potentials are finally in the *NOW*. They are created as the train moves forward, laying the track directly in front of it rail by rail.

You might ask, *"Dear Kryon, what's going to happen next in this world?"* Let me give you our perception of some of the potentials. Let me describe the next two generations—past 2012, and what this group of angelic beings sees for humanity [the Kryon entourage in the room]. The question has been asked, *"What are we going to do about the obvious problem—-too many humans on the planet? What are we going to do about our planets' greatest problems that exist this day?"*

Dear Human Being, we cannot give you the future, for you are laying the track. The shift of energy has been placed into your laps completely regarding what is going to happen with your most pressing issues. If the Human Being is going to live a great deal longer, what are you going to do with all of them on the earth? How will you feed yourselves? What will you do about the warming of the planet due to the energy you use? There is not one entity on or off this planet who can give you the answer to that!

But let me tell you this. There is going to be a change of consciousness that is going to allow for the answers to come far easier and grander and in a quicker time frame. These problems that have been with you for decades will suddenly see a greater wisdom and consensus. No longer will some of the obvious issues fall on deaf ears. The Human Being who is the angel in disguise, who sits in this room or reads these words, will also be able to contribute to the visualization of solutions to these challenges simply by visualizing all together. The solutions are there before you, and the wisdom of humanity will prevail with solutions far before the emergency point occurs, should you allow for such a thing.

In the past, often the engine had to break down before the problem was realized. Suddenly we are telling you that the engineers are beginning to gain the wisdom that the engine can be serviced as it rolls, eliminating the emergency stop. The operative word therefore, is *wisdom*, and this wisdom comes from the *mantle of Spirit*, which many of you have decided through ascension status to apply to your lives through intent. When you say to Spirit, *"Dear God, I finally understand that I am a piece of the whole and know I am here on earth temporarily. I know I shine a grand and great light for the planet; therefore, I will stand before Spirit and say, 'Tell me what it is I should know. Tell me what it is I should do.' I shall be quiet and silent and listen for answers. I will respect and honor synchronicity. I am a piece of the whole, and I AM."* And that, dear ones, is different from how it was ten years ago. That, dear ones, is going to create a race of Human Beings who are going to study the answers to your greatest problems and gracefully solve many of them with cooperation from the majority. This can only happen if there is a critical mass of evolved Humans on Earth—and now there is. Although this sounds like a fantasy to you now, just watch it evolve.

I have nine points of this communication I wish to enumerate and explain. They are about the potentials of the planet. These sections are categories, and we use nine of them because nine stands for completion. Although they are potentials, they become reality when Humans lay the track for it.

World Energy

Some have asked, *"Kryon, what about the world environment? What are we supposed to do for energy in the future that won't deplete our resources, or spoil our delicate environmental balance?"*

Dear ones, we are going to reiterate something we've said before, for there is a potential at hand for you to use energy resources that we have asked you to investigate many times before in the past ten years. You have not done so yet, for the wisdom marker was not yet passed, and there didn't seem to be an emergency. Now you will begin to understand the wisdom in these words.

There are two sources that we will give you again, and they represent the answers to creating much of the energy production on Earth. Both of the sources are abundant. Both of them are free, and neither of them will deplete any resource anywhere on the globe. They have been with you from the beginning and have been given to you for your discovery. Yet they have not been developed and used even though they are both obvious and are with you all the time.

The first and grandest one is the gift of your moon, and what it does to your oceans. Most of the population of the earth lives near coastlines on the various continents. The majority of the population is grouped in cities around the coastlines. Right where you need the greatest creation of electrical power, there happens to be tons and tons of push/pull energy that comes and goes on a schedule that is well understood and is consistent. This vast energy pushes and pulls and begs you to use it to create the hydroelectric conversion for clean production of electricity. Compared to the technology you have elected to use for nuclear power, this one is technically easy.

Physically, you've had the mechanical inventions for this conversion for a very long time. Basic physics can be applied to take the push and pull of the wave actions and tides and turn the wheels for the generators. The biggest wheels you can conceive of can be turned with the tons of pressure available to you at the shoreline. And you can count on that push-pull action to the end of time! What a resource, yet development is in its infancy. It's free and never becomes exhausted. It does not deplete a natural resource, and it's been placed where you need it the most. Many think that the moon was given for Humans to gaze at by those in love. [Laughter] Listen! You needed it to create the tides for a moment like this! That was the intent all along. Let the inventions begin that will harness it.

Here's another one: Think of the time and expense on your planet that has been spent on creating heat for steam—steam that spins electric generators. We speak now about your work with nuclear energy. Think of the resources it has taken, the risk, and the problems you now have as a result of what you've done. Think of the time expended to create just one of these energy-producing facilities. Think of the short time it can be in service, and then compare it to the disappointment that you can never again use that land for anything! What does one of those facilities actually do? It creates heat for steam. That's all it does.

We have given you the answer to heat generation before. If you want to create steam—lots of it—there is an engine that will be around long after humanity is gone. It's an engine that is producing heat for this planet, and all you have to do is dig! Dig far enough down and you'll find it. For the promise is this: No matter where you dig on Earth, if you dig far enough, you will find heat! Why not take some of the resources that it took to build the atomic engines and instead research solutions to the difficulties extracting heat from the depths of the ground and converting it to steam? How long is the heat going to last? Forever! And it's been there as long as Earth has, and will remain there as long as Earth does, and it's for you. Use the heat engine that we gave you!

We give you these two examples and again invite you to develop them. This is the answer to energy for the planet! It will not deplete any part of nature, will not change the temperature of the earth, nor put anything into the air. It's free, clean, and it's from your partner, the planet Earth. You wonder about your partnership with the planet? Take a good look. It sits there waiting for you to discover and develop it.

World Politics

"Kryon, what is going to happen politically on the planet regarding world politics?" We'll say something to you here that we said a few weeks ago to a group on another continent [China]. Governments, listen to this. If you do not give choice to your people, you will not exist long. The new consciousness of all citizens of all countries has already begun to change with respect to what they expect in leadership. This is not a statement to any specific government saying that you're going to lose power. Instead, it is an invitation for governments to change in order to satisfy something that is brewing within the populations, and that is the need for choice. Blessed is the government on this planet that has integrity for each citizen it controls, for this is the government that will shine above all of the others. Blessed is the government on the planet that understands that there is a spiritual awakening within its citizens and keeps that attribute separate from governing. Two pillars can support and enhance any house of power. They should stand separate, but hold up the house together. They are (1) choice of spiritual growth, and

(2) government. When either one tries to mingle with the other, the house will fall. Take a look at your history for confirmation of this.

"Kryon, will Earth ever see one world government?" Dear ones, there will never be a reason for that. It is not something that is at hand. There is honor in the existence of many cultures. This has been placed on purpose for diversity. These diverse cultures even provide for the karmic interaction of contracts, and they teach tolerance. What we are saying is that there is the awesome potential that eventually all governments on the planet will feature choice for their people. If they do not, then the people will cast them out. And if you doubt what we are saying, then look at what is beginning to happen as people rise up in your current times, tribe by tribe, and throw out those in charge.

In the old energy, a dictator could say, *"If we have enough power, we can control the masses."* This is now changing and is different. The invitation is out for even the oldest governments to recognize that a Human change is taking place. Humanity will choose who governs them, and you are beginning to see this even before the marker. That, dear ones, is the potential of the planet in these next 24 years. Continent after continent and tribe after tribe will determine their own fates, and consistently overthrow the tyrants and dictators who do not give choice to their citizens in the matters of morality, spirituality, and personal worship.

Ah, but there's more. We haven't gotten to number nine, yet, and this is only number two!

World Monetary System

"Kryon, what is going to happen to money?" We'll give you a potential that some of you are already realizing. We have said to you before that the planet is going to have to agree on what

things are worth, and there's going to have to be a consensus among nations on this. To put it in monetary language, we will say this: There will come a time when there's no such thing as an "exchange rate" between nations. In addition, to decide what things are worth, there must be a decision on what the Human work ethic shall be and what Human work is worth as well.

Dear ones, for those of you who are astute in these things and sit in a most affluent country [America], you will understand something that we are telling you. There will come a day when the government that you sit under will have to devaluate its own currency in order for the rest of the world to come up to a consensus. In order to facilitate this, you will witness the beginnings of common trading currency around the globe, which is exchanged in commerce without any value adjustment. The beginning of this is already happening on another continent, and you are witnessing countries gathered together to create one kind of trading currency. This process will not be easy, and may take two full generations to accomplish, but the potential is that you WILL accomplish it. It will not come easy, however.*

Watch for this, also: There may be an interim currency used by bankers only, and only for commerce between nations. This monetary attribute may eventually expand to the very money you carry in your pockets. And when you look at it all, it does not represent a one-world government. Instead, it represents tolerance and agreement on what the other culture's goods are worth. Dear ones, I'll tell you where things are going for the potential for this: The planet Earth must do this because there will come a time when you'll have to barter with those you have yet to meet! When this occurs, a universal valuation of planetary resources will be necessary.

* [*Note:* As this channelling was being delivered, Seattle was erupting with dissension at the World Trade Conference. This is exactly what Kryon was speaking of.]

World Religion

"Kryon, what is going to happen with religion? What are we going to do about diverse spiritual doctrinal issues around the planet that are so different? How are we ever going to agree on anything when one religious group says that the other group is wrong? One calls the other 'infidel,' and the other answers back, 'heathen'! Several groups claim they each have the only true answer to life, and they are each exclusionary to all other systems! How are we going to deal with that?"

The answer to the problem has already begun. There is a spiritual leader in your country who has been severely critical of those who come in to this planet with the heavy karmic attribute of a gender shift—a planned challenge—and some of you know what I mean. In the past, this religious leader called this group "sodomites"! The leader went on record as being against anyone who came in with this gender issue, and he told his following in the past that these family members were "hated by God"!

Not long ago, this particular religious leader met face-to-face with those whom he had berated, and he called them "loved Human family." Oh, he still didn't agree with what they represented or what they did, but something inside gave testimony to the fact that he LOVED THEM! And he spoke publicly to his following that God loved them, too!

Dear ones, what happened to shift that man's mind? Why, now? Indeed, it was the love of Spirit! It has to do with his realization at the cellular level that he would have to preach and practice tolerance even if he didn't agree with them. He would have to meet face to face with his "enemy," the ones he had called sinners, who he had told his flock didn't even deserve to be here. Even though he disagreed with them, they loved one another face-to-face before all to see. He also acknowledged their right to worship the same God he does. Do you find the timing of this interesting? Do you find it profound?

We mention this, for it is a model for you to see as an example of the possibilities for those who never before could tolerate each other. Watch changes like this worldwide. Watch for those to change who you never thought would change. Watch for the great Islamic mass to change attitude, and tolerate those who do not believe as they do. Don't be shocked, but their doctrine teaches morality and love, also.

"Kryon, will there ever be a time that there is one religion on Earth?" No, It was not designed that way, and it is very impractical to think that this could ever be. The potential is this, dear ones: There may come a time when there is, instead, religious tolerance and doctrinal wisdom. My partner spoke earlier of the "wicked Pope" [a prophetic subject related to the fact that according to the Dead Sea Scrolls, the Essenes called Christ the "wicked priest." He was called that because he gave away the secrets of the temple and promoted Human spiritual enablement]. Do you know why there is this prediction, and do you know what the potentials are for the "wicked Pope"? I'll tell you.

This man may not be very popular in his castle, for he will say the following thing: "It's time for family planning! [Laughter] It's time for the feminine gender to be honored as priests!" He'd better have protection! [Laughter] And whether this is the potential of the next Pope or the one beyond that, it will have to do with the contracts that are accepted or rejected in that religious hierarchy. You see, even Spirit cannot give you information about which one it is going to be, for it has to do with how humanity unfolds itself within the reality it creates. We cannot tell you who that's going to be. There is also the potential for a short-term Pope, in-between this one and the next. We cannot tell you which one it's going to be—the one to be called the wicked Pope. But when it happens, dear ones, I want you to remember where you heard about it! [Laughter]

Science—Astronomy

The fifth potential is about astronomy. The potentials are unlimited. The grandest one is attitude, and it has already begun. It is diametrically opposed to the attitude of your astronomers 10 to 15 years ago. Dear ones, there is going to be an acknowledgment that life exists in the Universe other than on the planet Earth. There will be an acknowledgment that the universe is made for life! It will be an acknowledgment due to overwhelming odds from all sources examined that the Universe is teaming with the potential of what happened right here on planet Earth!

The better the scientific instrument becomes, the more you will discover other planets with the same chemical potential as what happened to create original life on Earth. Science will begin to understand that the Universe is seeded with life, and eventually perhaps even postulate that the life seeds of what happened here [Earth] were carried from someplace else! Whereas in the past this was nonsense, tomorrow it may be accepted science.

Also, in astronomy, there will begin to be the acknowledgment of what we have called "different time frames." It must be, for it will eventually become obvious that this is the only physical model that will fit the "impossible physics" that is being recorded all over the Universe [see Physics, page 150]. Eventually there will also be an acknowledgment—a profound move off that peg of misunderstanding—called "the big bang." As you realize that the universe is self-creating, you will understand that it actually "bangs" all the time! [Laughter]

Health

Number six is health. Dear ones, you are at the edge of a revelation and a revolution called Human life extension. We've spoken of this so many times, and we've talked about Human DNA a great deal. Let me tell you this again: The next 24 years hold a potential of doubling your life span as a Human. And isn't it odd that these things would be presented only about now—not available ten years ago or ten years before that? The timing is perfect, you see, for it is you who have brought yourselves over the marker and have allowed for such a thing! In the new energy, Human termination, short life spans, and old karmic attributes and lessons are a thing of the past. It is the end of an old paradigm. The new way of being speaks of the "New Jerusalem." This metaphor means a new beginning and a peaceful existence. This new energy gives the potential of a peaceful planet. It speaks of Humans living here a very long time for purposes other than the one they came in for in the last millennium—and that's the truth. Isn't it odd that instead of doom-and-gloom termination and nuclear war, at the cusp of the new millennium, you have discoveries that will increase your life span?

But that's not all. There are those right now who are mapping the Human genes. There are billions of elements in the Human gene system that make up the entire Human Being. It is the Human blueprint, or at least as much of it as you can chemically look at. And when it is fully mapped to the extent where all is known and seen as a whole, there will be the potential for grand revelation! For then and only then will science begin to see the overview of that blueprint. They will see "the loop" that has been hiding. In addition, they will see a coding that will astound them! This coding will absolutely shout to them that it could have never happened on its own!

Think of this: Let us say you visit another planet. Standing there is the biggest supercomputer you've ever seen—gleaming, and doing wonderful calculations. It's smart and self-sustaining. You might look at it and say, *"This is astonishing. What a machine this is!"* The first thing the Human is going to ask at that point is,

"Who made it?" Immediately the Human will try to find the master builder, for there would be an attitude that the machine could never have built itself.

You've never had Human life presented to you in the way that the Human genome is going to. When the project is finished, and after much analysis, the results will demand an answer: Who made it? It could never have made itself, because it is far too grand to have come from the accepted workings of evolution on Earth. Instead, the codes tell a story of logic and creation, and the geometry tells a story, too—the base-12 story that we have alluded to so often!

There is more. Information is being given to you here that no one has given to you before. When the scientists begin to marvel at the overview of what the coding is telling them, when they feed the information into the grand computers and come back with patterns that mean something, that's when it will occur to them that they have something extraordinary! Not only will they see something that could never have created itself within the framework of the evolutionary process that they know and have taken for granted, they will also see the code of a puzzle! Stand by for wonderful revelations about life extension, for the code will tell the story of how the Human was designed for short lifetimes, and chemistry that actually defeats itself. When these are understood, then the limiting factors can be removed. [We will have more on this later in this channelling.] There is also the potential for much misunderstanding, much fear, and even some religious reevaluations—all because of chemistry.

Biology

Number seven is biology, and although it may sound like health, we have things to tell you that are new. Sometime ago we mentioned something to you that we have never discussed again until now. There is the potential for you to discover life on Earth in another dimension. It will shake to the core the beliefs of those biologists who have defined life as this or that, only to find that it exists also in another form, in another way. Seemingly intelligent, seemingly having developed, seemingly to have evolved in a whole different dimension—life you can't quite touch, but life you can see.

We told you to look for this on your planet about a year ago, and now it's at hand. We tell you that the potential is grand, for you are on the cusp of a discovery of this new life! And when you make this discovery, again I want you to remember that "the family" told you about it here first. Why do we say that? It's so the other things that are happening here will be believable, also—like the healings that are taking place now in those who are hearing and reading this, or the ones who are being touched by Spirit, or the fact that somebody is channelling from the other side of the veil! When you hear the scientific validations, you'll remember that you heard it in that weird channelling meeting! *"That was real,"* you might then exclaim! Maybe your 4-D will then catch up with the multiple-D of the potentials you are creating?

There is more. You're going to begin to unravel the puzzle of deliberate blockages in the chemistry in the Human Being, as we have just discussed in the health issue a moment ago. Your bodies are designed to rejuvenate perfectly. You were designed to last 950 years, and yet you don't. You gave permission for short lifetimes so many eons ago, and those attributes are now part of a closing age. When the final measurement is taken, there will be new potentials for humanity, and you're going to need the science tools that will facilitate those potentials. We have said this before: Human Being, you are designed to rejuvenate, and yet, when you lose a limb, it does not grow back! What's going on with your chemistry? Why is it that the basic vertebrae animals on your planet who you were supposed to have evolved from can grow back limbs, but you—the top of the evolutionary ladder—cannot? Have you ever thought about it?

Why is it that when nerves are severed in the spinal cord, the Human Being spends the rest of his life in a life lesson called the wheelchair, unable to feel any part of his body? Why? Why is it, biologically, that when the Human was designed to rejuvenate every part, it does not? Here is an odd fact: There are growth inhibitors that awaken and race up to mask and block the healing and reconnection of injured or severed nerves. Did you know that? You might think that's a poor design for biology, and you would be correct! But it's by your design, because those in wheelchairs have lessons to learn by being there. You are looking at spiritual intervention of natural evolution, and that, my dear Human Being, is part of what is changing! Sometime ago, we told you that the nerve tissues in your body all have addresses (they have chemistry that codes them). We told you that even if they are severed, they will still "know" who they each belong to! You haven't seen it yet, because they haven't been allowed to grow together. Watch this change. You are on the cusp of discovering where the blocks and growth inhibitors are in the Human body. When you find them, watch for miracles to happen as the body's nerves reconnect.

When you finally see these miracles happen, perhaps you will also begin to understand that the miracles that you've seen in the old energy were simply "awakened DNA"—an awakening that came from the power inside the Human instead of from above. It's the God force *inside* the Human, and not some mysterious energy from above that makes the miracle happen. Watch for it! It's going to be great, and when you see it, celebrate it, dear Human Being. It would never have happened on this side of the marker, but on the other side of the marker, after the year 2000, there is much yet to be delivered to you in knowledge!

Physics

Number eight is physics. We're going to cover this as simply as we can, and we're going to give you two attributes to ponder. The potential now, however, is that neither will be understood. [Laughter] You have yet to develop THE formula of physics. It is not here yet, and we're going to give you the three attributes of the formula, but without the formula. [More laughter] These attributes are related, but the way they relate is misunderstood. Your science is just now beginning to see the shadows of them, however.

The first attribute of the formula is the ability to understand the DENSITY OF MASS. Why is the electron haze so far from the nucleus? We have told you that you can change this distance, and in doing so, the density will change in the mass that is defined by the atoms being shifted. The electron haze will have to vibrate faster, the closer it is to the nucleus. When the electron haze vibrates faster, that means that its TIME FRAME will shift. Therefore, the second attribute of the formula is a time shift, and they go together. Also, be aware that you make an erroneous assumption that the actual speed of electron HAZE must always be the same no matter what its distance. This is not understood yet either. There is a difference between speed and vibratory rate, and it has to do with the actual physical definition of the ELECTRON HAZE.

Mass discrimination is the ability to control the density of mass. With a density shift will come a time shift, and with a time shift will absolutely come a third attribute that you will not understand at all! We will call that the REALITY OF LOCA-TION, or where the matter is . . . in which dimensional reality it goes to when it is shifted. Here is an axiom: Shifts in dimensionality when matter is changed in this fashion create a reality WHERE the matter HAS to be to exist in its new form. It might be inches from where you changed it, or miles. That depends on how much it got changed. The difficult thing to explain to you is a concept that has not been recognized . . . that matter has a reality index, and that its core attributes are linked to where it exists in time and space. Therefore, the three attributes that must work together are DENSITY, TIME FRAME, and LOCATION.

When you look out into space and you see physical attributes going on that shout that you are seeing a different time frame (what we call "impossible physics"), it's also going to tell you about mass, and the dimensionality (location index) of what you're looking at. This particular formula is profound. It is the basis of all universal physics, yet you don't know it yet.

Let us discuss massless objects, something we've spoken of before. Already your science knows about the kind of a concentration of mass where one spoonful of it creates something as heavy as your planet! What's really happening there? What could the attributes of that mass be? What is the actual size of it? Look at the gravity it creates! Did you know that this kind of condition can only exist at certain realities . . . or areas of space? The density and time frame dictate exactly where it has to be.

Now, what if you had something huge that had almost no weight at all? What would be the gravity aspects of that? The relative aspects, therefore, are not necessarily size. They are density and time frame. When that density is changed, then the time frame around it changes, also. If science would apply this model to what happens in a black hole, they might understand the "impossible physics" they see around it. You want to know about anti-gravity? There is no such thing. Instead, look for the secret of creating variable mass. And when you do, watch for the other two variables that come along with it in one profound formula of regular relationship.

The other potential discovery we're going to give you is this: We cannot close the physics discussion without speaking of the

Cosmic Lattice one more time, for the information of the lattice was given right here [New Hampshire], two years in a row. There's something we are going to call APD, Atomic Phasic Displacement. That is a term that is going to refer to the ability for you to eventually tap the lattice for unlimited energy. When you understand how to tap the lattice, you will have infinite free energy without drilling into the earth, without capturing the waves, or without atomic power.

Here's what going to happen, and here's the promise of what's hiding behind APD. We have spoken of the lattice before, and now we wish to give you a metaphor of a huge spider web, as big as you've ever seen. What happens at any location of a giant spider web when something is in motion in another part of it? The answer is that it is felt as vibration. The whole web vibrates due to the way it is constructed when one part is touched. We're here to tell you something profound: When you tap the lattice for energy, the entire lattice feels it. The energy will rush in to fill the void that you have opened with APD, but this flow will be felt all over the lattice.

We have given you some of the communication aspects of the lattice before. We have discussed how fast the communication is to the whole universe (the entire lattice). Here is something you didn't know: At whatever time you are able to figure out how to tap the lattice for energy using APD, everyone else that has that ability (APD) will know it! There will be other life forms farther away than you can even imagine who will know it instantly! And what does that tell you about the potential for communication in the universe? How about modulating signals upon the lattice itself? How about communicating with specks of light you can't even see with your telescopes? When you can tap the lattice, you can communicate with the whole thing. Beyond your understanding? Yes, today. But when it takes place, you'll remember that you heard it right here from a family member—one who knows the incredible potentials of your Human future.

The Children

Ah, we have waited for number nine, and we're almost done. The best one of all! The most powerful potential ever. A new energy is on the planet—an energy that has never been here before—potential peace on Earth! And it revolves around an angel who pretends to be Human, a change in DNA that facilitates evolutionary Human change. This new energy changes Human consciousness, and it is already beginning with the children.

Some of you are confused by who the Indigo Children are, so let me just tell you in a couple of sentences. These children represent a new Human consciousness. They represent Humans who will be more interested in creating peace in their family and peace on their planet than they will be in what you have called old "Human nature." Power, greed, jealousy, and all the other Human attributes that you have witnessed in the old energy for eons are part of a darker duality than Humans are currently being given at birth.

Oh, dear ones, if you could see the duality balance shift, you would understand. If you think the children are something, watch the children of the children! We have told you not only of a consciousness shift, but we have labeled them as the peacemakers! We have told you that biologists will be able to look at their genome and see that it has changed from the ones they just completed mapping! [Laughter] Science will discover an increase in the power of the immune system in the children of the children. They will find that the children of the children do not and cannot acquire the diseases you easily get now, and you'll wonder where that ability came from. I'll tell you where it came from: It came from *you!* It came from what happened between 1962 and 1987 on "your watch." It's due to what you did, and it enabled the potentials we have been speaking of this very afternoon. It is why you are loved so much. It is why this entourage that we call family is right now washing your feet, dear ones. Whereas the promise of Earth change resides in the children of the children, make no mistake that the core issue of their evolution was started by YOU!

Kryon and the entourage come into a place like this and want to remain in front of you, in back of you, beside you, but it can't be so. As you read these words, there is activity around you, and we know that some of you have felt it. We wish to remain and have you celebrate with us the potentials that we have spoken of. You have no idea how much love we have for you. So many of you think you're alone when you leave this place and you go home. So many think that when you put down your reading, the energy is broken. You are not alone! The energy stays with YOU as long as you carry it. Try to be alone, and you cannot be. We've told you again and again that you are never alone. You may wish to get into that closet of self-denial—the closet that we call the "woe is me closet." You may shut the door and turn off the light and think you're alone. In your own creation, you begin to weep within your loneliness, never being aware of the party that's going on around you! Oh, there are so many of us in there with you! [Laughter]

The invitation is this: Don't turn on the light bulb in the closet to see if anyone is there. Instead, turn on the light that's inside you, and watch us celebrate your life! Turn on the divine light that exposes family energy, and feel the love flow in from all of us. Then know that you're never alone.

Kryon and the entourage will retreat now, and we say this every time: This is the hardest thing we do. We flood in here with joy and excitement in love for you, and retreat with sorrow in our missing you. Who wishes to end this reunion? Not us. Yet it must be, for dear ones, there is still work to do within the duality and the lives of all humanity.

We celebrate the energy of the family.

We celebrate the new marker.

We celebrate YOU.

And so it is . . .

Kryon

Kryon's Advice Validated?

"... in regard to computer technology, you are missing the most obvious thing imaginable! When you see the Earth's most amazing computer operating in biological beings all around you, why haven't you emulated it? . . . The electrochemical computing machine is the way of the universe. It is the way of your own biology and your own brain. When will you start investigating merging the two together?"

Kryon — Kryon Book 2 — *Don't Think Like a Human;* page 222; July 1994.

In Kryon Book Three, *Alchemy of the Human Spirit*, page 248, we showed that *Scientific American* magazine reported that scientific research was looking into protein-based computers. Now look where it has gone!

DNA Computer is Created and Does Complex Calculations

Scientists have created a DNA computer from strands of synthetic DNA they coaxed into solving relatively complex calculations. . . . Conventional computing is driven by computer chips, but that technology is fast approaching the limits of miniaturization. Scientists dream of using the vast storage capacity that enables DNA and its chemical cousin, RNA, to hold the complex blueprints of living organisms. . . . After years of work, Dr. [Lloyd] Smith and his colleagues made several of the computers, each composed of about 100 trillion synthetic DNA strands that repeatedly solved the problem, though with Human help.

The New York Times; By the Associated Press; Thursday, January 13, 2000; "DNA Computer is Created and Does Complex Calculations." Entire article not shown.

Live Channelling

"The End of the Old . . . the Setup Revealed"

Channelled in
Buena Park, California
December 1999

Chapter Seven

"The End of the Old . . . the Setup Revealed"
Live Channelling
Buena Park, California

*This live channelling has been edited with additional
words and thoughts to allow clarification and better
understanding of the written word.*

G reetings, dear ones. I AM Kryon of Magnetic Service.
We would like to take a moment to celebrate what is
taking place here in this room. For those of you who can
feel energy and see the colors—who wish to know who visits you
this day, you should know that there is a grand entourage filling
this place. It is an entourage with graduates and recently de-
ceased humans. An entire family group pours in here right now
because of your requests. They wish to fill this room and the
aisles between the seats in the back. There are more here than
have ever visited any assemblage like this—ever.

For those of you who feel energy, you will begin to feel the
presence of Spirit here. We say to you as we have said so many
times before: Let the proof of the reality
of what is taking place right now
happen because of the energy that
fills you up. We speak here, not
simply to Human Beings or to some
foreign entities as perceived from
our side of the veil to you. No.
Instead, we speak to FAMILY. And
again we will tell you this, angels pretending to be Humans.
Listen: You are just like we
are! The only difference

between us is that you are here doing the work, and we are in support of you.

Dear family members, like us, you are eternal in *both* directions. There was no beginning of your existence, and there will be no end. The divine spark that is inside of you knows this so well! There will come a time for each of you, where at the end of this existence in this incarnation, you will have the chance to feel the fear of what you call death. Yet so many in this room will wink at it and recognize it as something they have been through before for eons and eons of time. There is no sting in death. It is simply a transmutation of energy—one energy to another. When you feel it again, you will know in an instant that it will be a "welcome home." We tell you this, family members, because we want you to understand how profound your work is on this planet.

We have given you much information over these last 11 years. We've wrapped it up several times, representing several subjects. Tonight, again, we wish to impart to you not just instruction sets or potentials, but truly a celebration of completion. For each of you, even those who are here disbelieving that this message could be from the other side of the veil, are playing a part as a family member in the consciousness shift of the planet Earth. This is the last time in this millennium that this entity called Kryon will address a crowd of this kind. You might ask, *"What is it Kryon wishes to say to you?"* I would say, "Thank you!" Thank you for letting the divinity inside of you increase to the degree where it changed the vibratory level of your very being. Thank you, healer, for letting the energy flow through you and for giving intent to let it spill out into humanity. Thank you, lightworker, for listening to the words from the other side of the veil, and recognizing the FAMILY. Thank you, lightworker, for channelling the truth of LOVE. Thank you, angel, called Human, for enhancing the earth!

Some of you might say, *"I don't fashion myself as a healer or even a lightworker. I don't know what I do for the planet."* I'll tell you what you do. You carry a light that is so bright that we can see it from our side of the veil! Every Human Being who has given intent to find the spark of divinity inside has created a spiritual light. Sometimes you might ask for intent to find your light, and then sit and wonder if you got it. Let there be no greater proof of what you've asked for than the difficulties that come racing in after your intent! You want to know if it "took" yet? Yes, it took! [laughter] Sometimes you might ask, *"Why is it that I have to go through these trials?"* Dear ones, we have some words for you, and we hope you understand the metaphor: *"Iron sharpens iron."* If you're going to stand tall and hold that light, you're going to have to go through the forge. Some of you have different degrees of trials in different areas, and every time you go through them, we say to you: You are not alone! And in the process of going through them, you have raised your own vibration.

Do you know how much celebration there is in this room right now? Some of you will feel these family members around or behind you during this time. Reader, do you think you are left out of this process? This entire message is for the NOW of transcription as well. Therefore, this celebration is for ALL who hear and read it in the NOW time in which it is being presented.

Some of you will know that you've had your feet washed before you leave here, or rise from the place where you are reading. This entity group you call Kryon, who is in love with you, carries no agenda. We do not ask you to do anything. We just want you to sit there and be appreciated. We want you to sit there and be honored. We want you to understand our love for you, for what you have done for your planet.

We never expected it, you know—the way it has turned out. For eons of time, humanity has been here, and the potentials for the end of the test seemed set by your energy. Nothing ever changed, and the experiment with energy from the process of becoming Human on Earth seemed to be headed for an ending that you all had created as you ran your "train of reality" over the same track year after year. But now . . . here you sit days away from the marker [the year 2000], and all has changed!

All humanity, all Spirit, all family (what you call God), knew about the marker—the beginning of the end of time. Indeed, it is almost the end of the test on this planet, and you can look at your indigenous calendars and see it everywhere! Your greatest prophets told you about it, too. You want to know when the end was supposed to be—when the test was supposed to be over? It would have started about 1998, come to a head right about now, and wrapped itself up by 2012. Starting now, and for the next 12 years, would have been the completion of all that ever was for Humanity.

Sounds pretty grandiose, doesn't it? Yet you didn't hear it from this stage, dear ones. It has been written clearly in most scripture. It has been channelled to you through many languages. It came through the ancients, through the indigenous, and through the avatars and shamans. They have all told you through so many different doctrines that this is it! Yet here you sit tonight in a peaceful existence. Instead of a world that is coming *apart* at the seams, it is a world that is about ready to put itself *together* at the seams. And you wonder why we come to you and sit at your feet? The marker is only hours away!

The Grand Setup

The potential for humanity is awesome right now, but for reference, it is time for you to back up and look at some overview points regarding how you created your test. We are going to give you some potentials about this marker you are about to cross. This information to follow is almost an extension of what we spoke of a few weeks ago with lightworkers and family much like this [New Hampshire].

There are some things that you may have never thought of in the grand scheme of things. Some have said, *"Kryon, you have told us that we are divine—part of God—and that this Earthly life is all a part of a test."* Yes, that is correct. *"Then where is the proof of that?"*

It is all around you, yet you have never stopped to look at it! There are facts and realities that you have simply absorbed, or taken for granted. You live in a cradle of a setup that is odd, indeed, but you don't see it as odd. Instead, you see it as normal. When you back up and consider it, however, you can't help but wonder why such a thing would be.

Past Intervention of Human Biology

For the first time, we broach one issue that we have never mentioned before. Dear Human Beings at the top of the evolutionary chain, why is it that there is only one kind of Human? You may ask, *"Kryon, what do you mean? There are many differences in Humans."* Listen: We wish you to look at ALL other biology on your planet. Look at all the orders, species, and types. You are the top of the chain, yet there are many kinds of mammals, many kinds of whales, many kinds of primates. Every single type has many kinds, until it gets to the Human. Then, an anthropological anomaly happened: Only one kind of Human got placed at the top!

Oh, there are many cultures, but only one type of Human. And that, dear ones, was on purpose. You have only one *kind* of Human. Indeed, you have differences of colors and some varying shapes of faces, but only one *kind*. Look at the apes and monkeys. These primates have dozens of kinds, none of which live together, or normally mate with each other—yet they are all monkeys or apes. What happened in evolution to give you only one *kind* of Human? The more your scientists discover about how evolution took place, the more mystified they will become as to why all of the other "starts" they will discover about Humans of different types and kinds, ceased. Go ahead and look, and you will eventually find the basic development of other kinds of Humans buried in the dirt. Some had tails, some had hair that was different, some were very small, and some were very large. You should be existing right now with many types of Humans all around you, yet you only have one kind—the one you take for granted as normal.

Do you think that you had help with this singularity of evolution? Yes, you did. Weeks ago, we told a group much like this that when the Human genome is finally mapped, the scientists will stand back and will have the final blueprint in front of them. And after a time, they will see an overview that will puzzle them. The attributes of this biological map will show the telltale signs of design, instead of the ones of evolution they expected. They will understand that this Human print was not a natural step from the immediate evolutionary steps below it. What they will be seeing is a divine blueprint, made for Humans on Earth who are in a test. This divine blueprint was cast by you and for you, so you could live in Human bodies of one kind that are all uniform.

This commonality was critical to your test, for you all had to deal with each other eventually as a planet. If humanity had been allowed to evolve normally, there would have been many wars between the various "types" of Human, and no effort to ever become of one mind. Species that are different always see themselves as apart from the other, and there would never have been the opportunity for you to call yourselves "one Human family." Most of you never considered this, and it's going to be your scientists who eventually bring up this subject as they discover very early Human development that is *not* like you. Watch for it. It's proof that intervention was accomplished to make you the same. (See page 369.)

We mentioned before [in the last channelling] that you are at the top of the evolutionary chain. Why is it, then, when you lose a limb, you cannot grow it back? The vertebrae creatures that crawl out of the oceans that you evolved from, can! How is that for "survival of the fittest"? Why do you suppose this is? Karmic lesson is the answer. When something happens of this nature for the Human, it is permanent. Karmic lesson wins over evolution. You go from lifetime to lifetime, but when you lose a limb in one, it's permanent until you die. This is a setup of the highest order, and provides for a life lesson. It's an anomaly of evolution that should have had you all very curious, yet most simply take it for granted.

There are many anomalies like this throughout the biological system of the Human. Here is a big one we spoke of before: Certain kinds of nerve injuries in your biology will create something very odd indeed. Instead of healing and rejuvenation, an unusual chemistry will race to the spot of the injury to *inhibit* and *block* the nerve healing. Did you know that? Is that how the top of the evolutionary ladder is supposed to work? You wouldn't think so, yet you have become used to it and never question how unusual this is. You know why the nerve damage is blocked? So that when the spine is damaged, it creates a Human in a wheelchair for *life!* That's a karmic setup and was carefully designed by you. Are you beginning to get the picture? Let the proof of your spiritual setup be in the unusual way the Human has evolved—weaker than it should have ever been, and in a singularity that creates a race that is all of the same kind.

Are you ready to have some of these anomalies change? Are you ready to have the knowledge of why these things take place? All knowledge is already here, and the potentials are grand. It is time to celebrate a marker. Lightworkers who have felt great anxiety in these last years, we promise you—release. It is time to get on with why you came here. There are those in this room and reading this who have felt stymied, stopped, stifled, and feel that they're just marking time. We tell you that you have been waiting for the marker! For as the energy comes forth in these next 12 years past the marker, many of the things that you have designed for yourselves that you feel intuitively are yours will come about. You have been waiting for something, haven't you? Oh, don't you think we know who is here reading and listening? The last time you came across the veil in death, you could hardly wait to return to the planet!

Oh, dear ones, we look at this humanity and we see the angels and family members that you are. The last time we saw you on my side of the veil, you could hardly wait to get back to Earth! And when you were being born, so many of you were arriving into a world that had the potential of termination right about now. Yet you came back and could hardly wait to participate because many of you have been here since the beginning. There is no way you would have missed it! It's the end of the test, and you wanted to be here. So what has happened? Instead of a prophecy of doom, you now have a promise of peace. Instead of horror, you have potential joy. And if you haven't felt your feet being washed yet, give it some time. [Laughter]

World Religious Tolerance

There is so much celebration here! Let me tell you about one of the potentials that is so exciting that we mentioned it before at the last channelling. This is exciting because it has to do with Human perception and cooperation with God. There are many cultures, many doctrines, and many belief systems all trying to exist together on this planet. *"Is it ever going to happen? Kryon, will there ever be a world religion?"* No. We have said this before. It is not appropriate and does not serve the cultures of this planet to have a world religion. We have spoken about the honoring of Humans in the search for God. A singularity of doctrine isn't the issue at all. There is no reward for everyone thinking the same thing.

The bigger picture is at hand. What is going to happen? I'll tell you. It's going to be the beginning of a tolerance between existing belief systems. What you will have is potential coopera- tion and honor—a realization that the other Human Being has the right to a personal relationship with God—and so do you. You can have tolerance, one with the other. And even as you sit here this afternoon, or sit reading this, there are those who meet on the other side of the planet who are beginning this very idea [speaking of the Parliament of World Religions meeting in Africa, only for the third time in 106 years— see page 216]. Look at the overview. There is a cosmic joke here. Where was the end of your civilization supposed to take place right now? The answer is, in the Middle East. Check all of the scriptures and the multitude of prophecies. Israel is the "hot spot," is it not? That is where it all boils over, and that is the place where the energy would bring about the termination of the planet. Indeed, the Middle East is the focal point, as many of you have known and seen.

Now, go over there for a moment. There is no great war. Granted, you have confusion, frustration, and even hatred. But the main emphasis is on how to make peace! From the many sides of the problem, you have the energy of how to make peace! Does this sound like your prophecy? The cosmic joke is this: They are going to create a miracle there eventually, where three major opposing doctrinal religions of this planet can share the same holy places at the same time, peacefully. And how? It's through tolerance and understanding. It begins there, and it won't be easy—but it is happening right now as you pass the marker. Watch for this: Whatever happens at the stroke of midnight throughout the world is a forerunner of the energy of the new millennium. Will there be confusion, riots, and terror- ism? Or will there be joy, celebration, and a feeling of a new beginning? I think you know already.

The 12:12 New Meaning

Past the marker, a potential exists for new gentleness and new wisdom. The greatest admonition of all time will potentially begin to show itself: You are going to begin to "love one another." What a concept! *"Kryon, you mean to tell me that after all these eons of time, energy between religions in going to change?"* Yes. That is indeed the potential. I will say something else, dear ones. Do you wish to know what the facilitation of this is, and where it is going to begin to happen? I'll give you a phrase: *Wait until you see what the children are going to do!* A 10-year-old right now will be 22 in the year 2012, when the last measurement is taken. These children of today called the Indigos will be young adults at the next marker. They will already be changing the consciousness of the planet. Some of you have asked about the meaning of the 12:12. It means more than what you have been given so far.

From 1987's Harmonic Convergence to 1999 is a series of 12 years. From now to 2012 is another series of 12 years. Look at the 12:12. Although it represented a taking of power by humanity in the 1990s, it is also a metaphor for the time frame in the two 12-year blocks given for humanity's change. You have just completed the first 12 of the two, and what you have already done has far outstripped even the potentials given to you in 1987! In 1989, when these writings began and when my partner began this [Lee, channelling Kryon], we had no predetermined potentials of what the energy would be like now. What has happened, and the speed at which it has happened, is awesome! That is one of the reasons we sit here, family, celebrating an event that has a profundity that you cannot even imagine. None of you saw the energy of what it could have been.

World Politics

In past channellings, we've spoken about the politics of the earth. We've talked about financial matters. We said just a few weeks ago, at the last channelling, that the earth is going to have to decide what "things are worth." Now, this has begun, and look at the energy around it [speaking of the Seattle riots regarding world trade]. Look at the old and the new pushing against one another. Look at the third world and the first world meeting together politically, trying to decide what things are worth—what labor is worth, what trade is worth. Take a look. It is part of Earth's new paradigm, and it hurts while it's happening, but it follows along with everything I have told you for the last two years. It is the beginning of growing pains as Earth's societies begin to actually work together. It is the beginning of something we are going to call "the New Jerusalem."

Through a new gentleness, country after country will discover that trade is the answer to war. Let it begin now. Oh, there is much work to do, but you don't go to war with the tribes that you trade with! Remember this: Here is a potential, an admonition, an instruction set for this continent, American. Lightworker, it is time to focus your energy on the third world. There is much there for you. Take your eyes and put them on what is happening in those dark areas that you have not looked at before. There are family members there—lightworkers there—and they need your energy like never before. That is the potential. Remember that we spoke of this, for the balance of Earth depends upon it.

Science

We have spoken about science many times. We have talked about physics and chemistry and DNA. These represent more of the "boxes" of thought that will begin to fall over [have barriers removed from old thought]. Wait until you see what the children are going to do! Let me speak of the oldest science on the planet: the study of the magnetic fields of your solar system and the reaction to them within your cellular chemistry at birth—the setup between the magnetic grid and the crystalline grid as determined by the solar system at your birth. These magnetic instruction sets end up surrounding the crystalline sheath of the DNA. You have them right now. It is the oldest science on the planet, and it's called *astrology*.

Magnetics, cellular chemistry, life prints, and karmic attributes are all the study of magnetics and gravitational attributes of your solar system. Human personality types evolve and revolve around a system that was created so that you, one type of Human, would have great differences between you to deal with! Yet, this oldest science on the planet is an eye-roller to the scientists on this continent [North America]. There will come a time, dear ones, when astrology will begin to receive credibility from your mainstream scientists. Why would such a thing begin to happen? It will be due to the full understanding of the Human genome, and the patterns and anomalies hidden therein. Again, when the scientists see the puzzle, they will study the cause.

Look at your scientists today compared to the energy they had before the Harmonic Convergence in 1987. Look at the astronomers! What was the main objective of their work ten years ago, and what is it now? What is the subject of many astronomy experiments right now, in 1999? It is the discovery of life in the Universe! There is a race going on to discover planets [something that was not an issue ten years ago—22 discovered so far as of the date of this transcription]. Why? To see if any of them are in the "comfort zone" that Earth is, and to study them for life! This search has become mainstream science! The probes to the red planet have life-detection kits! Even a moon of Jupiter is suspected of harboring life in its ocean, and astronomers can hardly wait to get there. If you had suggested this emphasis ten years ago, you would have been laughed at. If you had discussed additional life in your own solar system back then, you would have been dismissed from the room! This is how far you have come. The reason for this attitude change? Accelerated discovery and consciousness changes at the core level of Human thinking. Remember what we said in 1993? We said, "Today's weirdness has the potential to become tomorrow's science." Well . . . welcome to tomorrow!

Think about what the next 12 years could bring. Science is going to discover the divinity of the maker, and will have the opportunity to call it what it is. Some will acknowledge it, and some will not. More than that, they are going to discover something else they did not expect, when they finally reveal that there is energy in Human intent and consciousness. When they discover the science behind the energy of consciousness, they may be surprised, but it is going to make many things fall into place logically about how the body works—how matter works, how God works. There was a time when you believed that God and science were very far apart. There will come a time, dear ones, when that idea is actually laughable.

Let me tell you, there is so much celebration here! I wish to stop now for a moment. Why did you come here tonight? Why are you reading this? Did you have a purpose or hope for your life when you came here or picked up this transcription? Why don't you give intent for it right now? You should know that the things you have requested regarding a higher vibration, healing, peace, and a better Higher Self knowledge can be granted right now. And in the path of these things, dear ones, will follow the synchronicity that you desire in your life. Oh, things might not fall in place exactly as you would have imagined them, but we tell you again, do not sit in front of Spirit and ask for a tree when we have a forest to give you! Don't define how God is going to help you, for you limit the result! Instead, let it be. Sit in front of Spirit and recognize family, and say, *"Dear Spirit, what is it you want me to know?"* Say these things so that we can transmit to you information that is divine for your life!

Dear ones, are you in the middle of trauma, trial, and hardship? Then celebrate it! Can you do it? My partner is correct in saying that when you celebrate difficulties with pure intent, an inner beacon turns on, and you become a catalyst for solution in your life. It brings in synchronicity, answers, and solutions— and a new Human Being evolves out of it. Let me tell you about the passions that are changing on this planet. Human Being, there are some of you who came in with a blueprint that has been totally and completely changed through the intent that you have given. Much of what you formerly desired, loved, appreciated, and thought were important are now gone. Instead, there has been a complete turnabout, and now you are interested in people. You are starting to be interested in family . . . making connections and associations—a web of family. When you find your passion changing, it's a sure sign of a higher vibrating Human.

The New Children—the Indigos

Blessed are the Human Beings in this room and reading this who recognize the new children. Wait until you see what the children are going to do! Blessed are the Human Beings who are ready to take these children by the hand, look them in the eye, and say, *"I recognize you. You have been expected."* These are the children who are going to facilitate the very potentials we have been talking about this day. Parents, be careful. Do not try to pass your biases on to these children, for they will not accept or believe it. There will be no quicker way to have a split of a child and adult, for they will see the bias that you try to pass to them, and will not honor your wisdom.

Indigo Children come to Earth with a set of cellular instructions, and I will tell you what that prime directive is. It is not jealousy, hate, or even survival or protection. When these children are grown, I want you to watch what their words and intentions are going to say to humanity. Their entire purpose will ask this: "How can we find solutions to Earth's problems, and how can we be one family together in tolerance? How can we bring the tribes together who have always fought?" These children can become the leaders who will make facilitation for these changes... something that has eluded most of humankind for eons. Now you have minds that will insist on it.

Wait until you see what the children are going to do!

The Story of Herman—A Christmas Story

Let me tell you about Herman. Herman was a warrior, a real man. Herman is no longer with us. He, and many other men, witnessed something that was unique almost 100 year ago. Just about now, in the year of the Earth 1914, Herman was part of a great battle that was the beginning of what you would call the first war that involved the world.

There was a fierce battle going on that Herman was a part of. In those days, warfare was more crude: Warriors looked their opponents in the eye before they killed them. And Herman and the enemy were in the trenches in the beginning of this Great War—one country fighting another. Herman saw death daily. He lost friends daily. He saw the crudeness, cruelty, and hate daily, and he participated in it with others for his country.

Herman was in a trench that was on the front line. Not too far away was the trench of his hated opponent, and they were battling fiercely night and day. Men were embattled for weeks—exhausted, sore, and filthy. He hated it. Then something happened. He heard from his commanders that there was an agreement between countries that on Christmas day, everyone would stop fighting. For you see, both sides shared a common religion. In fact, they shared a doctrine that spoke of the love of God.

Herman will never forget what happened back then. He survived the war, and he always remembered what happened that Christmas day. For on that day, indeed, all of the fighting ceased for 12 hours, but that wasn't all. Seemingly that night, the silence was deafening to Herman—no more explosions or screams. When night fell, he saw light from fires in the enemy's trenches—something they had never done before. In this moment of agreed peace, they dared light fires to warm themselves. Henry's side did the same, and it became more obvious just how very close in proximity they really were to each other. Henry could see the outlines of some of their helmets, and then he heard them singing!

They sang songs in another language, but the melodies were some of the same he had heard and sung as a child! The songs were about peace on Earth and the love of God. He heard them rejoice, and he smelled their food. It changed Herman. Nobody died that day. It was the most astonishing thing that had ever happened to Herman. He told his children and his grand-children that he experienced a miracle: The men had laid down their arms when it was recognized that they had something in common that was beautiful, and which surpassed their war or their hatred. The thing they had in common was the love of God.

He said to his children, "Would it not be great to find the secret of this miracle? What if you could take that secret that stopped the fighting for a day, and stop it for a week, a month or entirely? What if Humans could look beyond their hate and reach an agreement about the shared love of God?" He told them again before he died, "I saw it! I saw the miracle of what the love of God can do! I know it can happen again. I saw it in an old energy, although only for one day." And he threw the gauntlet to his children when he said, "I know it's possible. Please find a way."

* * *

You wonder why we celebrate with you? This entourage of ours sees the potential of the new Human child, which you have created by choice on this planet. This entourage that floods in here to love you sees the potential for humanity to have an agreement respecting the divinity of one another on the planet. Oh, there may be dissension regarding how it takes shape and form, or how it's eventually facilitated, but humanity can eventually agree about something that can supersede the energy of war. It can agree that before war ever begins, there is a greater divine purpose in finding peace. Do you doubt that something like that can happen? Do you think this is all make-believe, and that Human nature will never provide for such a thing?

Wait until you see what the children are going to do!

Dear ones, you approach a time that is a holiday of love—the time of year when in 1914, they ceased fighting—a miracle that affected the lives of all the soldiers who saw it. You will see the sayings around you now that you have seen all your lives: "Peace on earth," etc. Only now, you and the children hold in your hands the potential to facilitate those words! Will it happen? In the history of humankind, there is no greater potential for it than right now.

How will this be accomplished? It must begin right inside you. How would you like to cease the fighting? How about an agreement between the "duality-self" and the "Higher-Self" that ceases the fighting? Let the duality go its own way and bring in the knowledge that, with an agreement about the love of God, you can cease the fighting.

Oh, but there is more, and I have said this to other lightworkers, but you need to hear it again. Dear Humans, hearing and reading this, who is it that you will not speak to? Who is it that you will not forgive ... dead or alive? Is it not time for that energy to end and for you to begin to see the big picture—the setup that would cause such a thing? What about the love of God? Is that not more important than your drama? Peace on Earth must start here, right where you sit!

There is a divine love spark inside you that is part of every single entity that sits here or reads this. It's time to agree and intend with the angel inside to release all bitterness and hate. And in these subjects regarding Human-to-Human relations, we say this to you: Wait until you see what the children are going to do!

Again, we say, do you want to know what our message is this day? It's *thank you!* Thank you for raising the vibration of this planet and starting something that has profound and interstellar implications that will be felt in the farthest reaches of your Universe. Every family member knows about Earth—every one. There will come a time when we will see you again, and it will not be in this room, or where you sit reading. There will come a time when the Kryon sees you in all of your splendor, glory, and colors. When that happens, we will talk about this Earth day, this last meeting before the marker. We will speak about the celebration we had in December of 1999, of washing your feet, of hugging you, and of the eventual celebration of your return. To me, it's happening now.

But until then, dear ones, until that happens in your reality, we say this to you: Stay here and hold the light! Make this marker count! What will happen regarding this world? Dear ones, when you pass the marker, we will say this: Let the teaching begin! For then, the anxiety will begin to dissipate. Wisdom will wrap itself around you because the marker that you felt and thought would be your end will have passed! The fear surrounding this event will have been defeated, and now only hope will stand in its place—hope of the most powerful force in the Universe . . . the hope of the love of God!

The hardest thing we do is depart from you. My partner wells up, and the words of parting are difficult. He feels what Kryon feels [weeping]. These moments that we have shared in intermingling energies with you are precious, so precious. And now we retreat, leaving with celebration in the same way we came in—with thanks in the message we give. Remember what the Masters have all said and continue to say: "Love one another!" And when you do, the most pressing world problems will fall away as though they never existed. The catalyst to peace is love—say it over and over and over again.

Now, at the marker, you can facilitate it completely.

Thank you, dear ones. Thank you.

And so it is.

Kryon

Live Channelling

"Crossing the Bridge of Swords"

Channelled in
Orlando, Florida
January 2000

Chapter Eight

"Crossing the Bridge of Swords"
Live Channelling
Orlando, Florida

*This live channelling has been edited with additional
words and thoughts to allow clarification and better
understanding of the written word.*

Greetings, dear ones. I AM Kryon of Magnetic Service. This is a precious moment as we come into this entourage feeling so light—not having to set the energy—letting the entourage pour forth as we begin to touch your hearts. For there are many of us who come this day to see you. Indeed, we will fill the aisles around where you sit and fill the places behind and in front of you. Even if you feel there is no room and no space, there will be many of us here.

From the interdimensionality that belongs to all, we proclaim that we are the same as you! The I AM presence is not Kryon. We invite you to feel the I AM presence of the angels in the room. The first angel in the room who wishes you to feel the I AM presence is the one with the archangel energy. As you become accustomed to the peace that may flow into you now, the overlay in this room—this evening—is of Archangel Michael. *She* is pleased to be here! So is your sister/brother Kryon. Do you understand that there is no gender with Spirit?

The second angel in this room that wishes to greet you is the one you carry inside you that is the REAL family. The Higher Self of every individual in this room is standing to greet us all, as well as the doubt within you that this could be happening. It is the other half of the I AM.

Every angel that has ever been reported to have spoken to a Human, and every reported vision with attributes of angelic visitation, are the same in one way. An angel or entity comes into your life, whether in a flock or one at a time [laughter], and the first thing they will do is to sit in front of the Human and say, "Fear not." They are really saying, "Don't fear me, for I am your family." The second attribute of every angelic visit is, in a word, that of *assistance*. These angelic beings are pieces of God visiting you in all their splendor. Oh, if you could see what they look like! They are everything you could imagine! How does it make you feel to know that every single one of them comes to give YOU assistance? Take a look at history and the documented visits of angels such as this.

Does that sound like the God you may have learned about early on in life—the One that tells you that you are not worthy? Does it sound like a God who sits far away, beyond Human understanding? No. It's time for you to understand, if you have not already, what my partner had mentioned earlier this day: You have no idea right now during this channelling who has come to see whom! Let the energy spill forth in this room and give you proof of what is happening in this reality. Understand the relationship between us! Understand that WE are here to see YOU!

For this is the reason, as we have said before, that there is a reunion here. It is an awakening with family. We invite you to feel those of us in the room with you, and this also applies to the reader. It's going to feel warm and moving, with energy pressing upon you, pushing upon the thickness of Spirit—the feeling of home. And you can call that a hug if you like. There is nothing like it, dear ones—nothing like it. With a room full of those who love you so dearly, sit in this place of peace for a moment, and celebrate with me.

[Pause]

My partner wells up with the knowledge that so many of you are now giving spiritual energy that you have brought with you—the intent to let us in—the intent to let us hug you. For just a few moments, let your family on the other side of the veil intermingle energies with you. From hereon in, just for a few moments, let it be your reality along with ours. Feel the family as it comes and proves itself next to you by touching you. Although it is not always the way of things, right now there are some precious entities here who were recently departed Humans—visiting in this room and around the readers. This is not always the case, dear ones, but today there are those hearing and reading this who need to feel this specific energy now. Perhaps it was your intent all along. See what your power does? Here they are! Reader, do you understand the NOW better? This transcription is being heard and seen all at once! Feel the love of those here! The energy right now around you is about *completion*, and it's about a *spiritual beginning*. But then, that's why you are reading this, isn't it? In the teaching today, there are many things that we have to tell you, so we better begin now. Within the process of the teaching today, don't be surprised if the hugs get stronger.

The Crossing

What is the energy about right now? It's about the fact that you made it! We are going to call this teaching today, *Crossing the Bridge of Swords*. A few weeks ago, you all moved into an area of time—linear-time, that even Spirit could not tell you about. If you didn't feel it, we are here to tell you about it. Not only is the *time* different today than it was in the '90s, but lightworkers are different today as well. Indeed, you are all different from how you were just a few weeks ago.

There is a chasm between old and new energy, and you have
just crossed it. Understand that I speak to you as sister/brother
Kryon—in the NOW—and please understand this: Gone is all
the prophecy about war, Human extinction, mass suffering,
planetary destruction, and global technical meltdown. In crossing the marker [the year 2000 time frame], you just created a new
reality. As we told you last month, no entity in the Universe
could do this for you, and no entity could absolutely predict what
would happen. Instead, we gave you the grand potentials [speak-
ing of the channelling in New Hampshire in December '99].

First, we invite you to look at the marker itself in real Human
time. It set the stage for what is to come. Always watch for the
energy around a profound date. It often foretells potentials of
the next portion of your journey. The marker we had discussed
before [last month] has you moving into the year 2000. You were
very aware of the coming chasm, and many Humans knew that
it could represent many things to them. You had a cellular
awareness of the importance of this marker. Most, however, had
no idea of the changes it might create in their lives. It would be
a final separation of eons of potential—a separation of the old
energy from the new—a separation from the whole Earth purpose in the past, into a move to a new Earth purpose for your
future.

None of us could tell you what might happen on this marker,
but in previous channellings, we gave you some potentials. Only
you, as the Humans that you are—in charge of your reality—
could cross the Bridge of Swords. The marker arrived, and it was
awesome! If you want to hold the energy of what took place for
this planet at the marker, take a look at the energy around the
transition of humanity into the year 2000.

My partner spoke earlier about this [Lee mentioned the
celebrations on New Year's Eve]. As the marker was realized
across your world, within the individual time frames, there was

celebration, and then there was celebration, and then there was celebration! [Laughter] It is no accident that there was peace as you passed into 2000, and that's exactly what you gave intent for, lightworker. Do any of you truly understand that YOU created it? This is the power of Human consciousness.

Look at Israel! We told you in the past that all futures would begin there. No matter what happened on the planet, it had to begin there energetically. Remember the prophecy? Wars of horror for the entire planet would begin there. Yet it didn't happen at all when it was prophesied. Instead of war or terror, there was something else to mark this grand event at the time of the transition. What happened on this marker? Celebration! And if you go there today, the emphasis in this energetic, profound land is how to create peace, not how to wage war! Although the energy is changing slowly, and it finds much resistance, the overwhelming feeling in this prophetic land is to create peace. Now I ask you, what prophecy told you about that? The answer? None did. YOU created it yourselves! Of all things, this should be the proof of what we are saying—and your media allowed the entire world to share in the celebration. No wonder these important areas of the world are having trouble adjusting to the energy! Many are still trying to FORCE the old prophecies, and are finding tremendous resistance. Watch for a seeming "pull backward" this year, as the old energy force tries its best to keep the old conflicts alive. This energy is new to the planet, and potentially will bring great trial to those who try to remain in the old paradigm.

If you notice, we never give predictions. We never tell you what IS GOING to happen. Past the marker, we had no idea what you would create. Based on the energy you had developed, however, we gave you potentials. This is because no entity in the Universe could tell you what was on the other side of the Bridge of Swords. That's the kind of spiritual choice that

Humans have. Now you stand there! It's grand! We're never going to underestimate what you've done.

The Bridge

The Bridge of Swords is a metaphor, is it not? The bridge is across the canyon between the old and new energies. The swords are crossed above your head as in so many celebrations that take place for warriors. Some have envisioned the swords as actually being the bridge, but the bridge is pure intent. The swords are the canopy. "Warriors of Light" is what you called yourselves—you named it—the war between old and new energies. Don't be shocked and surprised if that war is not over. In fact, in some cases, the battle has just begun! Call it the final battle if you wish, for again it represents the flailing of the old paradigm of power and control—an old imprint of what could have happened—against a new, unexpected energy of integrity, wisdom, and peaceful purpose. What the chasm represented was a complete change in Human consciousness potential—a change that would rewrite the end of Human history into a new beginning.

The chasm between the old and the new has indeed been spanned by the Bridge of Swords. Look at what the sword represents: Truth! The sword IS truth. The sword sings with the vibration of the heart chakra, which is the F note in music. Crossing the Bridge of Swords also crosses into a new millennium date, and a new energy that's supposed to be about TRUTH.

In past channellings, we gave you information about the kinds of energies that are going to be delivered to you soon. We spoke about how energies are delivered to the planet, and one of the best methods is through your solar system. We spoke of the energies around eclipses and also of comets. Now, even this year, within the planetary alignment to come [speaking of the planetary alignment in May 2000], the energy to be delivered to you can be understood in one word: MOTHER.

Some of you have said it is feminine energy. This is not the whole story. It's MOTHER energy. This is not gender specific. This is an energy that all humans will understand since it's of nurturing, of gentleness, and of peace and caring. That's the energy of the beginning of the balance of the planet, and it's long overdue. It's an energy that will complement what is also taking place with Human consciousness evolution.

Not All Will Cross

Not all of humanity will cross the Bridge of Swords, but then you knew that, didn't you? There are those who will never accept any of the new energy. There are those who will never cross the Bridge of Swords. They will stay in the old and will wallow in it. They don't want to change, and still cling to the old cellular imprint that tells them that we are all doomed. Some might say, *"Kryon, they crossed over into the new millennium, didn't they?"* Yes, they did. *"Then didn't they cross the Bridge of Swords?"* No, they didn't.

Passing the marker is what ALL humanity did. Crossing the Bridge of Swords is a description of what only some of YOU did. The Bridge of Swords is, therefore, also a metaphor for the realized and manifested intent of lightworkers all over the planet. Many have passed the marker but did not change their own personal energy. Dear ones, realize that there is no judgment around this, only celebration that they are here as family just like you. As this new time frame moves forward, you are going to see many who decide that it will be far more efficient at the cellular level to leave this planet and to come back as a new child (with the Indigo vibration). I am telling you that there is the potential for much unexplained death. This is not something to fear, but rather a potential fact to look for. Some of this may touch you, and some may not. But if it does, understand and celebrate what it's about.

Overview of the Time Frame (revisited)

The time frame we wish to tell you about has been shared with two other groups, but it is an overview that you should see again. It gives a new meaning to the 12:12, for the 12:12 has been a metaphor all along. Some years ago in your linear time (1994), it was about the enablement of humanity. We called this the "passing of the torch." It was a time when the control of energy was completely passed to you from other entities who held parts of it for you in the old energy. So that there is no misunderstanding, you always had control, but there was a wonderful group that had to be next to you to hold certain kinds of energy in order for you to operate within your divinity. They are the ones who left. They left because your divinity increased. The earth's "energy bucket" became full, and they had to leave—letting you have 100 percent.

Now, we are looking at another meaning for 12:12, and it is indeed another main event. Again, it will be about Human enablement—one that threw away the old predictions and created a new timetable. The distance between 1987 (the Harmonic Convergence) and your 2000 marker was 12 years. And that 12 years was spent in an old energy with lightworkers beginning to awaken, anticipating the Bridge of Swords, which was your passing in the double '00s.

The next 12 years will take you to the date 20:12. If you asked some of the ancients about the meaning of 2012, they will tell you that it's THE END OF TIME! Guess what? It is! It's the last measurement of an old Earth paradigm, and the end of time for a very old plan. When it takes place, the potential is for another celebration, bringing in a planet at peace. Indeed, it is another marker! The last 12 years of struggle, combined with the next of revelation gives you another 12:12 to look at. There are no accidents within the numbers, and the 12 is the basis of all physics. Physics is the model for choice, and choice is what Humans have manifested to create a new reality on the planet. Sometime later, you will understand what this means as this pattern shows itself all over the Universe.

The potential of the new energy is now limitless, but you had to pass the marker by yourselves to create these potentials. A new kind of Human will populate the planet (the Indigos)—new attitudes will prevail in the least expected places—tolerance will be experienced where there was none before—extended life will be granted through science and spiritual intervention. There are so many things here that we have spoken of regarding the potential of this new age, which we are beginning to call "the Now Age." In so many channellings, we asked you to sit and feel the energies of a celebration—one around yourselves—one around your children, and your children's children. We asked you to celebrate the ones who are waiting to be born—those who can hardly wait to get here—those who have selected YOU to be parents, and some of you—grandparents. And when they arrive, we challenge you to look into their eyes within the first hour—the first minutes of their birth—and *see* the old soul! And if you're there in person for the birth, we challenge you to say this to them in that room of joy, and watch their reaction: "Welcome back!"

What Next?

You have spent the last 12 years getting ready for the dance, and here you are! Now you are going to move into the *action* of this new time. Lightworkers, have you spent the last years feeling stalled, anxious, stymied, under renovation, and nervous? Some of you have been waking up at all hours of the evening and wondering why—not able to sleep. Healers, are you paying attention? Things are going to change! Many of your contracts have been waiting for this new energy. If you have felt held back in the past, it's because you were! Perhaps you felt frustrated that things were not going the way you had intended? The marker was not ready. You were not ready. Your intent has outstripped the energy you were in, but now you sit in the very energy that you created—finally! What you have asked for is now here. The marker has been passed, and it is the beginning of a new paradigm for your life and planet Earth.

The chariot of the new energy is here to carry you into a new land. As the chariot starts to come alive, it's becoming powered up. You call yourselves lightworkers? Well, it's time for you to go to work. And you thought you were all ready, didn't you? You're going to start seeing results, and that is the difference between the way it used to be and the way it can be. How soon? This will not be an instantaneous energy shift. Just as any other shift on the planet, it will take time, and must be enhanced by the will, work, and consciousness of the Humans on it. It also has to do with the overall energy being delivered to the earth—the *mother* energy—the gentleness—the synchronicity. This new energy may now finally be delivered personally to you in a cheerful and wise way, instead of one that comes and kicks you from behind, as in the past.

You asked for a new way of working with Spirit; now look for the evidence of it and celebrate! Don't tell us how to do it. Don't tell your guides how to solve a problem in your life! Instead, be a partner in the process. Visualize it as already having been done. Visualize yourself as peaceful, sitting in a place where all is well. Let your partner [God] supply the means, while you supply the intent. Let us present to you some wonderful solutions through synchronicity—solutions that you never imagined, but ones with your NAME printed on them (since you created them before you got here—just like the challenges). Indeed! This is the picture of a Human Being who understands the NOW.

Many of you are going to go from a state of disappointment and anxiousness about *nothing* happening, to anxiousness about *everything* happening! Many doors may now open—many options may present themselves. Energy for change may very well start to flood into you because the new energy has created it—an energy you were always looking to for help—but now may give you too many things to choose from! You all are very different, and each case in this energy will be slightly different. But all of your names are known to us, and I speak now of the spiritual names that you have. Even those that have come to this meeting seemingly by accident will have changes presented to them through synchronicity. You want to know what synchronicity is? It's being here and hearing or reading these words! It's things that you can look at and see in your reality.

Blessed is the one that is listening or reading in total disbelief, for this one is often one of the most likely to change the earth! Look at Human history. Often the one who is the most opposed to new energy is the one who grasps it the best later on. This shouts SPIRITUAL CONTRACT! Often the ones who are the most skeptical are the best workers later. Sometimes spiritual contracts demand this kind of inward examination before they can manifest. It is no accident, therefore, that there is doubting family here (and reading this). They are as loved as you are!

The Integrity of Holding Your Light

Dear ones, I want to present to you a concept regarding the love of God. We bring up two issues of integrity. Lightworkers, integrity must figure into all you do here, for if you haven't known this already, there must be spiritual integrity in all things. We speak to all of you who are holding a vibration that is higher than you were born with—one that indicates your choice and intent to move closer to your divinity. That's the definition of *lightworker*.

There are two integrity issues surrounding the new energy, healers, and lightworkers in general, that has been asked about.

(1) Some have said, *"Kryon, I am a facilitator. What is our responsibility to those we facilitate? In general, what is the responsibility of lightworkers to those around them? We have much energy to give, but when we do, how much should we get involved? Does any of it interfere with the free choice of the individual?"*

We will give you the metaphor of the lighthouse. The lighthouse is anchored on the rock, no matter where it is built. Sometimes the lighthouse is rebuilt in other areas as the weather and conditions change—same lighthouse—same lighthouse keeper—always anchored in the rock. The lighthouse is there to do one thing, and that is to shine the light. The purpose of the light is often varied. Sometimes it's a warning, sometimes it's there to attract attention, and sometimes it's there to guide. Whatever the purpose, it's always anchored in the rock. Those who built and operate the lighthouse know something that the others do not: They know where the rocks are—where the trouble is—and they are there to guide others around these things.

When the light is able to help steer ships into the harbor safely, the lighthouse rejoices! When this happens, however, the lighthouse keeper does not go over and have a party with the captain of the ship. Instead, the keeper silently rejoices and continues to shine the light. Most captains who reach port safely due to the light of the lighthouse never know the lighthouse keeper. The lighthouse keeper doesn't publish a statement telling others that he saved a ship! He is silent and continues, often alone, anchored in the rock.

For those ships that did not look up to see the lighthouse, and who wound up on the rocks in disaster, the lighthouse may be saddened. But the lighthouse keeper does not go over to rescue the ship. The lighthouse keeper does not take responsibility for those who end up on the rocks! The lighthouse keeper does not go into depression about the event and dismantle the lighthouse due to the ship that didn't look to see the light. NO. Instead, the lighthouse has one purpose, and that is to shine the light, shine the light, and shine the light.

What we are saying to you, especially to the healers among you, is this: In the new energy, you will have gifts given to you as the lighthouse keeper. Perhaps you have heard this before, but we say again that you must not take responsibility for those who do not wish to share in the new energy. Do not take responsibility for those who do not heal. Don't take responsibility for those who DO. Celebrate those who heal, cry over the ones that don't, but don't take responsibility for anything but the integrity of the energy you put out. Shine the light and stay in place. Continue to anchor yourself in the rock of wisdom, and do constant maintenance on the purity of the light you display.

Your lighthouse can go anywhere you want on Earth, but make sure that wherever you decide to stop, you again anchor on the rock and shine the light well. It's important you hear this now, because in the new energy, there will be many brought to you who would have never darkened your door before. Many will be attracted to your light. As the humanitarian that you are, as one who understands and wants the best for everyone, you might feel that you MUST be successful with everyone—you feel that all ships MUST be safe. Remember what we have said before: Healers don't heal—healers balance. It is the choice of the individual who sits before you, ready to be healed, who carries the power. You are the catalyst. Anchor yourself and shine your light. That is where the integrity is.

(2) *"Kryon, what if I shine my light and it affects another person? Doesn't that interfere with free choice? Kryon, you said that this is not evangelical work. Have I not interrupted their lives? Tell me how this works."*

Dear ones, the lighthouse is not proactive. It is not evangelistic. It simply shines. Let's say you walk into a dark room where it's difficult to see. Others in the room are simply walking in a darkened room, doing their best. As the lighthouse you are, you shine the light in their direction, and suddenly it illuminates where they are going. They now have a *choice* to see the path or not—to head in another direction or the one that is now illuminated. I ask you, have you interrupted their choice? NO. You have instead given them some silent options.

Some might say you have affected their lives, and they would be correct, but you have not interfered. You have not coerced or prodded. All you have done is to be silent, anchored, and you shined the light. Some might not even know you were there! That's how it works. There is integrity in the silence. There is integrity in the humanity that honors the free choice and will of each Human family you meet. There is integrity, therefore, in being a lighthouse! Lightworker, you have crossed the Bridge of Swords. I sit in front of hundreds of lighthouses right now!

Science in the New Energy

It wouldn't be a Kryon channelling without speaking of your science now, would it? Something is happened that we never discussed before. Your scientists are now beginning to talk about the atom in a way that WE have been talking about it for years. And believe it or not, this is related to crossing the Bridge of Swords. A full understanding of atomic structure will be an interdimensional understanding. Your scientists are coming to the conclusion that there are pieces and parts of the atom that are not in your time frame. Finally! It's information we gave to you years ago! Some of them are saying that what they formerly understood to be small particles that whirled around each other are now somehow connected! They are somehow put together in an interdimensional way. Your scientists are starting to see the evidence of this, and it is starting to be clear to them that there is special interactivity between the parts beyond the physics they understood.

In addition, it appears as if the particles have choice! And shockingly, they can go where they *want*, instead of following some understood rules of physics. (Don't tell Euclid.) Well, they are right! Let me tell you what they're missing, or about to find. Let me tell you what some of the future discoveries may show. It's time for base-12 math again! You need another kind of math to fully understand the relationships going on inside the atom. (This is an old message we continue to give to the scientists who are reading this particular transcription. We know you're there!)

Let me tell you what's inside the atom that has not been seen, but which has been hinted at. Are the parts somehow connected with unseen strands? Perhaps there is a new force here? Are they influenced by interdimensional strings? What is happening? And we say to this to you! There is energy between the parts, the smallest parts you can imagine. And there is indeed interdimensional energy that connects or pulls on them in an unusual pattern. Do the parts have *choice?* Yes they do. And what is odd and unusual when you stand back and watch the energy strands between these pieces and parts inside of the atom is that you are going to see an actual geometric pattern emerge that you will recognize as the Human Merkabah! You will see the sacred geometry presented interdimensionally and will discover the Flower of Life within the heart of atomic structure. Scientists, think out of the box! The choice of matter in its flow is not any kind of chaos. It is the propensity of balance! This seeming choice is caused by a new rule of physics—a rule of the Universe that says, "All matter seeks divine balance." You will begin to see this at the largest and the smallest level of all matter.

Some of this may seem odd to you, but there will come a time when you will hear it within main science, and then you may remember that you heard it here first. We say this to give validity to this spiritual experience. Some of you are going to need that to believe this message is real. Remember what we said to you ten years ago? We told you that when science is able to fully understand the atom, they will find at the heart of it—the love of God!

I want to talk to the lighthouses and lighthouse keepers now who are hearing and reading this. I also want to talk to the potential lighthouses, as the energy where you sit starts to move and you feel the hugs all around within this family. Within the teaching of today, we have presented some of the concepts for this new energy you step into. To use the metaphor of the train, this energy has no track at all for you to roll upon as in the past. Instead, you co-create as you go—a reality that never existed before. You need a light to see by as you do your new co-creative work, and you and the family lighthouses are the ones who will shine that light. Lighthouse, get on board this new train! Cross that Bridge of Swords and move into an energy you have never experienced before—one that cooperates with you and is far easier to work within. Plant yourselves there and hold your light. Watch and see, for some of the ones that are on the other side of the bridge who would have never crossed it may now cross because of you . . . because of your light.

Do you understand this metaphor? Lives will be attracted to you due to the way you live and act. Some who are alive now, and some who are not even born yet, will have a raised consciousness because of your light and what you do now. They won't have to become new age, metaphysical, believe in Kryon, go to spiritual meetings, or anything you might label as religious. Instead, they will become enlightened as to the wisdom of the love of God. The whole idea is to present an energy that lets the Human

Being decide if there is more to life than what they thought. Is there a God? Is there perhaps a plan? Is there hope? Can a Human live in joy? It starts the personal SEARCH, and that's what holding your light is about!

Lighthouses on the rock, feel the new energy! We are talking to YOU. You wonder why you've been guided to the place in life where you are? Stand on the rock. Rotate the light. Feel peace in that heart-path where there is divinity! Be in pure purpose, even though it might be a tough place in your vocation, or a tough place in your relationships. Understand the light-house concept. Lemurians, this is not the first time you've done this. Shaman, this is not the first time you've done this. I told you we knew who was hearing and reading this, didn't I? That's why this is so personal.

I mentioned those who are on the other side of the veil who are in the room with you now, figuratively and metaphorically. Some of them are kneeling in front of you. Some of them have tears of joy because you have come across this bridge. We have spoken of those who have lived before on this planet and have returned to this spiritual space right now and who sit next to you. I want to tell you what this is all about. For many here, it's about completion—closure. I would like to tell you what is on the minds of each of those who come in with that attribute in this room, who sit in front of you now. They're here to celebrate you! Have you gotten the point yet that you're never alone? They're here to celebrate you! This entourage and this precious energy will go across to the other side of the veil when done here, yet you'll still have an entourage of your own. It's the one that you came in with—the one that sits by the angel called Human.

Some of you don't know what to ask for. Some of you are confused. If you don't know what to ask for, here's a surefire way to help yourself and to get going with better communication. Sit alone. Open a dialogue, simply, to your angels and guides. Don't try to analyze how many there are. The duality even keeps you from seeing your own energy within them! You don't have to know their names. Just simply tell them you love them! Tell them you love them and then stand back. You'll feel them! It's the beginning of recognition, and a two-way love communication. Did you ever think it was only one-way? The old energy was truly deceiving, if you did. Tell them you love them, then be still. Don't be surprised if you hear a flutter of wings! Looking for a sign from God, are you? Sit alone and watch what happens. Be still, and know that YOU are God. The FAMILY is always there.

This is the time when we want to touch hearts. Your entourage is here; they're in place. Everything is ready. The intent is pure, so we say, let the healing begin! Let it pour through you as you read this, and through this family crowd. The messages that will come tomorrow from various facilitators may touch you in the ways that you have asked for [speaking of the second day of the two-day Kryon seminar]. Let the puzzles be put together in your lives. May you feel the energizing of Spirit now. Indeed, let the healing begin!

Let the uncertainty of your lives and your future begin to clear before you in a way that is fresh and precious. Find yourself saying, "Now I know what's going to happen! I may not know the details, but from the depth of my divinity I know that it will be from the love of God, and that means I'm a partner in it." That is why you came, isn't it? To hear this truth? That's why you read this, isn't it? Don't you think we know who's here? That is why you came. Feel alive as the family says to you in these last moments of this message, "I love you."

This family before us is so honored, as we feel it starting to give our love back. Do you know how important that is for us? The family who floods in here from my side of the veil sits absorbing the emotion and the love you are sending! We don't wish to leave.

And so it is that we celebrate those in this room and reading this right now who are being healed in many ways. That is why you came, and that is what led you to these words. We celebrate the angels in this room and around the chairs of those who read this—the angels who protect the family angel pretending to be Human. You've heard this before; the hardest thing we do is to leave. I thank you for inviting us in. We gather our bowls with the tears of joy in them—the ones we have been using to wash your feet—and we begin to exit.

May our parting words to you be the greeting ones as well, for all is in a circle.

Greetings, dear ones! We love you!

And so it is.

Kryon

Live Channelling

"The Third Language, and New Awareness"

Channelled in
Reno, Nevada
February 2000

Chapter Nine

"The Third Language"
Live Channelling
Reno, Nevada

This live channelling has been edited with additional words and thoughts to allow clarification and better understanding of the written word.

G reetings, dear ones. I AM Kryon of Magnetic Service. We wish you to rest in the peace and purity of the moment—all of which is God. I have said the words "I AM Kryon," and again, for those of you who need to hear this translation, I have said the words "I AM." And the "I AM" is the family. It is not a greeting. Instead, it is an identification. The "I AM" is the greeting and the declaration of purity of family, which surrounds me now.

There will be some of you who might say, *"Perhaps what we are hearing and reading is not of Spirit—we're just experiencing the Human Being, Lee."* If so, then you would not feel the energy being transmitted now. Indeed, this would be a good time to address the energy issue of what is before you. Let the spirit and the love of the family pour into this place. We (Spirit) are in the NOW. There has never been a more poignant NOW than this, and I speak to the family who is gathered before me—sisters and brothers of Kryon, as well as to the reader, who is in the NOW. Listener, can you relate to the NOW of the reader? Can you understand that your future is their NOW, and their past is your NOW? Yet, here you are together! Perhaps you

understand a bit more about the NOW experience? Listener and reader are in the same energy!

Reader, we see the potential of who it is that casts his eyes upon this message. We look into your hearts and see family, as well as what we see in the listener. Odd as it may be to some of you seated in this room, this message of love drips with a potential of understanding and awakening for literally hundreds whose eyes will gaze upon this page today, tomorrow, and long into the new millennium. And so I ask the family who sits in this room to welcome the reader, even though they are unseen and seemingly unknown. Can you see these readers as family, also? If you can, you have just gone through the veil partially into our NOW where everything is together. Reader, stop for a moment and feel the love from hundreds who are now greeting you from what you call your past. In actuality, you are indeed all here together!

Understanding NOW time is one of the first steps to truly understanding the divine time that you are in. The family pours into this room with that same kind of understanding. To us, you are the same as you were the last time we saw you! In these few moments, let the proof of the energy that is developing here be the proof that this is real. These are not just words from a Human. The family comes and sits between you—listener and reader. Even though it may appear that there is no space for them, there is, for it is the space in your heart that you have left open for such an event. The family sits upon some of your laps at this moment. We greet the divine energy of the angels at this moment. We welcome and greet the family of the Archangel Michael at this moment. We greet the divine energy of Metatron at this moment. We see the physics and the divine coming together, and we call that *family!*

There has never been any way of being, other than this—the circular NOW—but it is the veil of duality that has kept you from seeing the truth of what I speak. Sitting before me and reading these words are indeed Humans who are pieces and parts of God. Human Being, you are family to me today, just as you were in your yesterday. But for me, this has never changed. I look upon you—those of you hearing and reading—and what I hear, see, and taste is your "name." You are no stranger to me. If you think you came here by accident, that is not so! If you think you picked up this page and are reading it by accident, it is not so! For now we address personal messages to those who have come to be family with me.

We brought you a message 30 days ago about passing the marker. For in identifying this energy to those who sit here and to those reading, we say: This is only the second month past the marker. Yet, dear ones, the energy is very advanced in comparison to what it was! This entourage has come today not to feed you, even though you may feel the pressure upon your bodies from their presence. No. This entourage has not come to do that. Instead, what we have come to do is honor the Human Beings— the ones who have passed the marker—the ones who have crossed the "Bridge of Swords." Human Beings, there are so many of you who came into this planet fresh and new, taking your first breath—and we were there, as children, each one, growing up. We are your spiritual family!

The spirituality of your contract said that you could hardly wait to come back into this planetary energy to finish the test that so many of you, as Lemurians, started long ago! It is so that many of you here, and reading this, will help to balance the very fiber of the earth to the end of the test of the planet. You are here in this new energy to "get the ball rolling," as you say. We spoke earlier to you about those family members who are back again. Some of you could hardly wait to get back here, even though you knew that the potential of the planet was to have you in turmoil—to even have some of you gone by now through death. But none of that happened! Instead, we celebrate a group who is hearing and reading, who changed the reality of old Earth and is going to be part of this creating a new planet!

You crossed through the marker, and you saw the energy of the celebration that took place on that day. We told you before to look at the "snapshot" of the energy of celebration around what happened at that moment of the new millennium, for that energy is a foretelling of the potential that can exist from here on. And the potential, as you saw, was one of celebration—a celebration that has you in peace, not necessarily between all nations, but with yourself.

This is what we wish to talk about, lightworkers, for we have come this day to speak personally about what is taking place in your lives. You may say to yourself; *"Oh, I don't consider myself a lightworker; I'm just here with someone else."* Some of you may have come with ones you honor and love, and you are not really interested in spiritual things. But this may also be an opening of the door of awakening through choice. For what we are saying is this: There is more to life than what you may think. Your presence here is honored fully whether or not you believe this is real. We recognize you regardless of your attitude or demeanor. We honor your life to the same degree as the one next to you. A lightworker? Perhaps you don't think so, but there may come a day when all of this makes far more sense to you than it does right now as you pretend not to be interested! Your potential is as grand as anyone's in this room, and it is only as your linear Earth time passes that this will be shown to you.

You are eternal in both directions—pieces of God. You always were, and always will be—that's who family is! What do you think it is like for this entity and the entourage with me who pours in here? What do you think it is like for this entity called Kryon to come and sit before family? We feel it emotionally, as we touch you. We know you intimately! We know of the lives of the Human family who are here. We know of your names on the other side of the veil, the ones you sing to us in light. We have known you for eons. This play you are in—this test you have agreed to—is a test of love. The duality that has been pressing upon you for eons represents one kind of energy that is now beginning to change!

Let me tell you what passing the marker is truly about. Right before you passed it, there was not one entity on this planet or in the Universe who could tell you what was going to happen. Passing the marker is indeed one of the most energetic things that has ever taken place on the planet. It is true that all humanity passed through the marker, but it is also true that only a handful have crossed the Bridge of Swords. That is the message we gave you the last time we were together. The chasm is great. You have given intent to move across the chasm from old to new energy. Truly, that is what passing the marker is! But perhaps you did not understand what that actually meant in this new energy. Lightworker and warrior of the light, in a moment we are going to give you a new gift and also five "awarenesses," but we wish to enhance again your understanding of what passing the marker has done. Intent is the king of Earthly energy change, for the intent of the Human Being and the piece of God that you are sends a message to the very fiber of the earth as to what you wish to have happen. This is reality shifting.

The earth, your partner, responds with intentlike energy as well. It changes as you do, as we have discussed before. This is why you have Earth changes right now that are so profound. What humanity has given intent to do, dear ones, is to change the energy of the planet in such a fashion as to actually alter the duality. As a review, I wish again to tell you, dear ones, that so many of you who have felt stuck and stymied for so long in these past years are going to finally realize what you have been asking for. Family, as facilitators, humanitarians, healers, and pray-ers, you are about to meet YOUR energy—the energy you have created through this change!

You are about to meet an energy that has your name on it! You are laying the track, dear ones, for the new train of humanity as its engine is picking up speed. Don't be shocked and surprised if the energy that comes forward during this new time feels somehow familiar. It's yours! That is how profound it is. If the NOW is in a circle, why would you be shocked to find yourself in a familiar place? This is the promise, should you choose to create it! The promise is that your reality will change to suit the greatest intent of humanity. It will rise to meet what you create.

We have to say this to you: You came to sit in the energy, to read in the energy, but there is more—much more. Dear ones—my family whom I love—sister, brother—you are in the new energy! That means that the healing that you wanted can now take place. That means that some of the facilitation that you tried and failed to accomplish will work now. Let us say, as we have so many times before, why not let the healing begin right now? We talk about Human consciousness, we talk about the love in your life, we talk about the issues that you came for, and we say: Listener, reader, don't you think we know who you are? We sit in front of royalty, and we know it. This Kryon entourage has known of your decision to be here. Some of you may say, *"Kryon, I only decided to come two days ago,"* or *"I just picked this book up a moment ago."* There was a space in this room with your name on it! And there IS a space in divinity for you to read this right now! That is because the potential for you to hear or read this was REAL to us. It is our NOW.

You are here for these few moments while the entourage touches you, loves you, and sits upon your lap. Just let us love you for a moment. In the process, don't be shocked or surprised if you can feel the presence with us. Don't be shocked or surprised if it feels like home, because that is what it's all about. Before the teaching begins, listener, reader, put down the book—we will pause—just feel us with you, and feel family surrounding you!

The Third Language

Let me tell you about a gift that is coming—one that we have wanted to tell you about for a long time. Those of you who have crossed the Bridge of Swords, you are in the new energy now, but we must tell you that in the old energy, we were very aware of your past complaints. [Laughter] You may think God and your guides didn't hear a word. *"Why didn't this or that happen? Why was I anxious? (Perhaps still are?) Why are things not going well?"* We heard you—we really did! Now, in this new energy, dear ones, you are going to have a completely different set of complaints, and they are going to go like this: *"Oh, too much! Too many choices. Better slow down! Which way should I go? Kryon, guides, I've asked for this and that, and now I have too many choices, and a bit too much energy!"* One Earth year from now, some of you will be trying to cope with new eating and sleeping habits—new ways of dealing with increased energy—and a new clock (one that has sped up)!

It is about time, isn't it? Each of you is different. We cannot tell you exactly what is going to happen in each of your lives because you are creating your changes as you go—laying a new track for your engine as your move forward. But we are telling you that there is an energy with your name on it that is commensurate with your intent. Ah, but there is more. Before we tell you about some of the awarenesses that you are going to have in this new energy, we wish to tell you of a new gift. It is time you understood the window that is coming. To use a metaphoric term, we will call it "The Third Language." The Third Language has nothing to do with three languages. It is a metaphor that describes communication in the language of Spirit. The "third" refers to the honor and the catalyst of the "three." Look at the threes and what they represent spiritually. Here, then, is *The Third Language*. It is the language of the three between the father, the Son, and the Spirit. You have had these metaphors identified to you in past channellings, and you have been told what they meant.

All three of these create "who" you are spiritually. The Third Language cooperates with the grid move and is an enhancement of the spiritual language between the Human Being in duality on Earth, and that which you call God. Let me give you another definition of The Third Language: It is a beautiful, loving, 100 percent, 24-hour meditation working language. Some of you who have felt disconnected are about to connect for life! Some of you are going to wonder what it was like not to have this new connection. My partner wells up now because, you see, this is a two-way gift. You give intent, and we are able to come in and walk with you daily—100 percent of the time—not just when you sit down to meditate, but all the time!

Don't cease meditation! It's beautiful, an honoring of our relationship, but understand that you can leave this place and develop a communication using The Third Language—a walking meditation—always in touch, always with the discernment of God, always with the peace of understanding, always with the purity that is you. Remember what the shamans were like? Remember the wisdom of the holy man? Now it can be yours. This will change lives around you, since YOU change. Your scheduled meditations, therefore, become ceremony instead of just communication. It brings a whole new meaning to the event.

The Third Language is arriving in windows of opportunity that each Human Being will create as he goes—as he lays the new track. Look for The Third Language, for it will fill you in a way that only certain meditations and energies have done—that only certain events have done. Do you feel the energy of Spirit here? Do you feel the family here? Do you feel the pressure upon your bodies now? Do you feel the love that is pouring into you now? I want to tell you that long after this event is over, you can walk from this place and have this energy anytime you wish! The

Third Language is what it is called, the connection of the three. It is the beginning of the connection to HOME.

This Third Language happens slowly and naturally for those who have crossed the Bridge of Swords (passing with intent into the new energy of the millennium, with understanding and a spiritual awakening). Like many other changes, however, there is a learning curve that comes with wisdom. There are five "awarenesses" that come with The Third Language, which can create misunderstanding, anxiety, and even pitfalls to continuing a spiritual life. We will examine them, and in the process, you may recognize some of them as happening already, and in the process, we want you to also recognize US—for this is why we are here—to give you loving information and to hold your hand during the transition.

Sudden Awareness of NOW

Are you tired of Kryon speaking about the NOW? We will continue to do so until you live it as you breathe. It is a different time-frame awareness for you, and to some it is like a slap in the face! You have been in linear time for eons. Your duality supports only the concept of linear time. Suddenly, however, many of you are going to be aware of so much around you that is potential, or that is "past." With new "eyes," the new NOW awareness can press upon you as though it were all taking place as you sit here (or read this)! This is due to the acceptance of The Third Language.

Understanding the NOW, dear ones, is the divine way, but for some it may be confusing because Human time perception wraps up and presents itself in one energy package. It also represents the beginning of your spiritual understanding. The Human Being who understands and is comfortable with the meld of linear time and the NOW time is one that does not consider the future as a problem. For in the NOW, the future is here. All the things that ever will be or ever were, are wrapped up in the potential of the divinity of this moment. This is difficult to explain for those who do not FEEL it. Everything that has ever transpired, and the potential of all the things that ever *may* transpire is present in an energy of knowing. All of the problems and the solutions of *forever* are in front of you. All of the joys and all the sorrows are being lived NOW.

All of the potentials of the challenges you have had and will ever have are all wrapped up into one spot. And do you know what that spot is [and this is important]? It is your "divine spot," which is being fed by The Third Language. It is the trinity of YOU. That should give peace to some of you, but to others, it's just not understandable.

For some who do not have this message, it may present an awareness that makes you uncomfortable. We say to you, dear ones, that you have one foot on the other side of the veil. Welcome to the NOW! The feeling of home is the NOW time. The feeling of knowing that things are well, since they all "belong" to you and are within your co-creation power, creates a peaceful Human. But this is much different from the old perception, so "living it" must be learned and understood. When the NOW visits you in a way that you have not known before, it may cause unrest within the confusion of its percep-tion. If this occurs, celebrate the confusion! Then ask your Higher Self for guidance to understand and be peaceful with the transition. Some of you may feel that this message is cryptic information—written for someone else. Just wait.

Awareness of "What Was"

Wrapped up in the awareness of the NOW are four other awarenesses that you should know about—all caused by The Third Language. When you have an awareness of the NOW, you have a profound awareness of the old "you"—all of the things you were before the marker. Looking back in wisdom, some of you will be distraught by what you see! You might ask, *"How could I have ever done that? Who was I really, back then? Was that really me doing that stupid thing? Why didn't I do this or that when I should have? What about the fact that I made some wrong decisions? I was stuck so long! Now I realize that all I had to do is this or that. .. but I didn't!"*

Hindsight is perfect in the NOW. Some of you will blame yourselves. Some of you are going to lay guilt upon yourselves for what took place before you passed the marker, for you are now filled with wisdom of the NOW. You are now filled with information that is going to make the past look different to you. It is going to make you look different to yourselves. I have a message for you, if you are one of those who might tend to look back and bemoan the past, or are sorry for what you might have missed. In the old energy, things were different. You are sitting now in a bright light, and it is easy to look back into the dark and see formerly hidden things. I want to tell you who was with you back there—helping you with those "errors" you see now. We were! Family stood next to you in all of your "wrong" turns. If you want to know why you didn't press on that door of opportunity, or didn't do the thing you were "supposed" to do—didn't turn left when you should have turned right—here is an answer. The loving hands of your God and family kept you right where you were! In other words, you had HELP from Spirit to remain stuck!

Do you want to know why you were stuck? Because there was a giant angel sitting on your lap, and you couldn't get up! You can't begin to understand the things you could not accomplish before this energy came in. You were not ready, and the love of God kept you where you were. Think of it. You received answers from God during the time you were complaining that there were no answers. This is common with Humans, in that a "no" from Spirit is often seen as "no answer." That angel sat on your lap, and you could not do anything! Timing was every- thing, and you were honored with a "no." You have to know how perception and awareness works. Those of you who look around and say, "*I am a fool*," let me tell you that you will have to agree, then, that your spiritual family became fools with you, for you were kept from doing certain things until this new energy passed the marker.

Perhaps you felt that you were walking in circles, or mark- ing time? Now you say, "*I wasted it!*" No, you didn't. Celebrate the event, and celebrate your lives then and now. Celebrate what is to come, and understand that all is appropriate. You had help then, and you have help now. You missed nothing!

Awareness of "Missed" Synchronicity

The third one is synchronicity—awareness of synchro- nicity, "missed." There is no such thing, dear ones. You live in a circle, as we have told you before. If what came around when the timing was not appropriate was missed, it will come around again. That is an honor in the NOW, is it not? When you are in the NOW, you understand the circular way life works. You will also understand that it is Spirit Who brings what you think you missed. Lightworker, this has many meanings and is a meta- phor you cannot even imagine.

What you have asked for has many faces. Many things in your life will be presenting themselves to you with a new face. But when you look at the core energy around it, it will be something you asked for a long time ago. Lightworker, there are new paradigms of awareness here, and there are also new energies working for you. Let me speak of a new item you never thought of. Why are so many of you heavy in body? Facilitators, healers, workers in the light: Why are so many of you doing fine work, but heavy? There is an old paradigm of "protection" at hand here. We also call it "fortressing." It is wrapping many layers of energy around your persona to help you protect yourself from other energies in order to do what you do.

You might have done this to yourself as the only thing you could do to mesh with the energy. And it seemed to be the only thing you could do at the time to let yourself exist. You have been aware of it, and many who are heavy have given up trying to make it any better. Some may have said to the Universe, *"I cannot be anything but what I am—looking the way I am. It's me, and this is what I am, and all I'll ever be."* Well, guess what? Watch the new energy change that! How many of you would like to change that attribute, finally? You know who I'm talking to!

It's time to try some of the things you did before to help with the weight. Whereas before not much happened around certain tries, watch what happens now. For now, the energy is cooperating with you and your cellular structure. Do you want to gain some health and shed some of that weight? Try it now. Didn't you think Spirit heard your call for this? Now is the new synchronicity! The family is here, sitting with you, saying, "It is time now to try again. Do it, and you will have the results and the cooperation of an energy you never had before." Believe it. It's true.

Oh, there is so much here! We want to stop and celebrate the healing that is taking place right now. It took a little while for you to know that we are really here, did it not [speaking to the anonymous one receiving some kind of healing in the audience]? We are pouring energy into you that you have asked for— for a long time. That is why some of you came, is it not? That is what family does—it loves you so much that it changes who you think you are!

Awareness of Responsibility and Human Relationships

Number four is responsibility, and also relationships. We have told you about this before in certain ways, but you have to understand that in looking backwards, you may again flog yourselves for what you think didn't happen. And again we tell you that in hindsight you might have a sudden profound awareness of being part of the Human family, and might say, *"I am a humanitarian, and I should have helped this person or done that thing."* This is nonsense. You missed nothing, and the family was around you in those times where you feel you might have failed. An older, lower energy inconsistent with your divineness kept you from making certain decisions that you easily can make now.

In this divine hindsight, you are beginning to see what some of the past old-energy relationships were all about. We speak of Earth family relationships. Some of you are finally beginning to see, in this energy, what death was about—and it is affecting your heart as you see the big picture. Again, some of you will blame yourselves that you did not see it earlier, and you will think about wasted time—or worse, you might think of things said or unsaid that you now are sorry about. Remember: This is a study in NOW awareness. There is no linear time, only the NOW. There is nothing that existed in the past that cannot be corrected NOW. Perhaps this did not occur to you?

If what follows seems redundant, it is redundant on purpose. Dear ones, we say this to you now because this is the catalyst for your enlightenment. Do you want to know how to advance to what you call the ascension status—how to vibrate at a higher level? I will give you the answer again, as we did in the last channelling. You are starting to "see" or to become aware of Human-to-Human setups. The setups in the past require closure in this new energy for you to proceed. Some things need to be closed—really closed.

Remember when the character Wo packed his bags for the new millennium? Remember his hidden compartment? It was Human drama. Again, in love, we say, dear ones—dear Human family, who is it you won't talk to? Who is it you will not forgive, dead or alive? It is time for closure! Perhaps that's why you came here—to hear this! Perhaps this is why you decided to read this! Pull the divine love out of the bag of the new energy, and face yourselves in a forgiving way. Forgive the child inside you. Forgive the one who harmed you. Take the word *victim* off of your person—out of your vocabulary, and place the word *family* there in its place. Appropriateness is in all things. It must start sometime, and perhaps that should be now. You know who we're talking to. Let it be now. It is inappropriate for any lightworker who thinks he is in ascension status to have a situation where he refuses to have a relationship with any other family, dead or alive. Let that sink in now.

We remind you that the past is NOW. Perhaps there are those Humans in the NOW who are waiting for closure? Perhaps you are ready as well? You decide.

Removal of Vows to God

We bring you the fifth awareness. We have saved the most potent one for last. The Third Language is at work now—at its best. Lightworkers, shamans, listeners, readers, I am talking to most of you now. I am going to give you some information here. There is something you need—something that can be dismissed, removed, and peeled off of you so that you will never have it part of you again.

Listen: Shaman, this is not the first time you have awakened to spirituality in some lifetime. In recent past lives, almost every one of them, you had an awakening to your spirituality as well. Some of you even know who you were, it was so profound! You were the monks, sisters of the church, shamans, medicine men and women. You were the ones whom the tribes depended upon for the potions and the energy healings—the hands-on work. Let me tell you what came with that—an old energy that required a focus on God. If you were going to make the potions, send the energy, and heal those who came for it, you had to truly focus. In order to focus in that old energy, you gave something away in return. Some of you took vows to remove Earthly humanistic characteristics of normal life in order to focus. You made promises to God, and the promises were in the form of sacrifice.

How many of you remember being the shaman and the medicine man? Remember what the attributes of the medicine man were? So many times the medicine man lived on the outskirts of the village. The medicine man lived alone. Remember? Listen to what I am saying. This is important. Did you take a vow that in order to be spiritual, you were never going to enjoy the intimate company of another Human Being? Did you? Did you take the vow of celibacy? I have new information for you. A vow to God given in pure intent in ANY lifetime is taken into the next lifetime, and carries through the veil over and over. You could not easily drop the vow, because your inner soul is committed to God. If you were going to spiritually awaken and be the shaman in those past lifetimes, you had to sacrifice many things back then.

Lightworker, are you having trouble with keeping and holding relationships? Abundance? Having a normal life? This could be why! Let me tell you now that for those of you who have crossed the Bridge of Swords, this new energy gives you permission to drop all vows! Perhaps some of you thought you would be alone forever? You do not have to forsake relationships anymore. Let us hold a ceremony right now.

Visualize the old vows you took in those old days, releasing themselves. See them floating away into the air. Celebrate the release in this new energy! Kryon has never said anything about this, ever! I could not even begin to broach this subject in the old energy. This was not possible before. This is a new gift for you and is just the beginning of the tools of ascension—an ascension you can share with a mate if you choose. You can have a light body, if you choose. You can have abundance, if you choose. Let the old vows be released from you right now. Let's create a new vow together: *"I vow to use The Third Language to become as close to my Higher Self as a Human can get! And in the process, I claim that I can be abundant, peaceful, and never lonely. I claim my Higher Self as my best friend. I claim the divinity that I AM."*

Understand that you have permission to focus on God using The Third Language without sacrificing anything. You can be the shaman and enjoy your humanity, have relationships, and abundance. Monk, it's about time, is it not? Sister of the cloth, it's about time, is it not? Oh, family, don't you know that we know you intimately? We have said this at every single meeting to you. Don't you know that when the family comes in that this is not some kind of generic visit? It is heart-to-heart, dear family. If it seems that we are talking to YOU, it's because we are.

The hardest thing we do, listener, reader, is to leave you. You can re-create this energy anytime you wish. You do not have to attend a meeting like this to create this. You do not have to sit with other lightworkers, although it is pleasant and you can feel the love here. You don't have to buy a book or a magazine or anything else. We have told you so many times that you can go home and create this yourself with your own divinity. Now we tell you that The Third Language is the key! We celebrate you! We celebrate the energy of the family member.

There have been questions this day from lightworkers about your guides and how they work. I'll tell you what it feels like when your guides work with you: an *expansion* of you. Enjoy the many "you's" that are here! Enjoy the family that surrounds you. Enjoy the pieces of God that are all you. Enjoy the angelic presence of the gold color that we show you now. This is you!

The entourage retreats from this place in perfect love and purity. It basks in the revelations that have been given—the gifts that have been shown to you, which each of you can take. There has never been a closer time with family than this, dear ones. You are now able to draw very near to those on the other side of the veil . . . that's US!

Dear ones, take care of yourselves, and shine your light. Indeed, others around you will change as you use The Third Language, and your light is "seen." This has been our message from the beginning, and it is our message now as this entourage says good-bye. There will come a time when I will see you again, and it may not be on this planet. At that time, dear ones, you can climb that grand staircase, and you will see all the ones in your play and will recognize each of us.

Happily, we will break into applause and say, "Welcome home!"

And so it is.

Kryon

Cooperation Between Religions?

> *"There are many cultures, many doctrines, and many*
> *belief systems, all trying to exist together on this planet . . . We*
> *have spoken about the honoring of Humans in the search for*
> *God. . . . [There is] going to be the beginning of a tolerance*
> *between existing belief systems. What you will have is potential*
> *cooperation and honor—a realization that the other Human*
> *Being has the right to a personal relationship to God . . ."*

Kryon, December 1999 . . . regarding world potentials, this
book, page 165

(1) In Capetown, South Africa, on December 1, 1999, religious
leaders and thinkers from around the world met. It was only
the third meeting in 106 years of the Parliament of World
Religions. An opening prayer by chief Rabbi Cyril Harris
said, *"By joining this parliament we do not have to give up the*
beliefs and practices of our faiths, but we do have to give to the
Human family of which we are all a part." [1]

The meeting was opened by Nelson Mandela, and closed
by the Dalai Lama. Did you see this on CNN? Probably not.
It wasn't mentioned in most U.S. cities.

(2) The United Nations, June 26, 2000. The birth of URI-UN
(United Religions Initiative at the United Nations): *"With*
the signing of the charter on this day, the URI is born. It has been
developed in consultation with people of many faiths around the
world. It is a growing community dedicated to promoting endur-
ing, daily interfaith cooperation, ending religiously motivated
violence and creating cultures of peace, justice and healing for the
Earth and all living beings." [2]

[1] *Reuters News Service*—December 1, 1999
[2] Quoted from the UN invitation to the charter-signing celebration,
June 26, 2000. The actual signing was done in Philadelphia.

Live Channelling

"No More Fence-Sitting!"

Channelled in Kansas City, Missouri March 2000

Chapter Ten

"No More Fence-Sitting"
Live Channelling
Kansas City, Missouri

*This live channelling has been edited with additional
words and thoughts to allow clarification and better
understanding of the written word.*

Greetings, dear ones. I AM Kryon of Magnetic Service. There is an energy here, which *you* have invited into this place. It is an energy that has come from Home, and it has your name on it. It has your energy on it. It has many of the attributes of you, and it flows into this place freely, for it was designed by you. It ought to feel familiar to you, for it is the love of God—what you have also called the love of Spirit—and is no more than a spiritual essence that is you.

Dear ones, there are those here, who in the next few moments will become used to the fact that what you are hearing is not necessarily the voice of a Human Being. Oh, we use my partner for the words, but the energy is from Home. The energy is from Spirit. We will say something that we have said so often before: Let the proof that this is real be contained in the fact that the energy will be delivered to you and felt! For, flowing into this place, there are those whom you have asked to be here. We have said to so many hearts before: You gather in this place, and you give of your energy to come here and sit in front of  this chair of mine. Perhaps you've wanted to feel the energy of this family as it flows onto the floor and around you? It encompasses the room and creates a bubble of thickness here. Perhaps that's why you came? In this new energy, this family that pours though the veil has stood in line to be here today! Perhaps this may give a whole new meaning regarding who came to see whom!

It is no accident that you came and sat in the chair where you are sitting now. We knew of the potential, dear one, dear lightworker, that you would be here for this reunion. The grand potential that exists in the "now" is what we speak of. We knew you'd be here. The potentials were great that you would come into this very place and hear these words today. I speak now even to those who might feel that they were dragged here. This is for you as well! Finally, I speak to the reader, who is right now in front of this entourage as well.

The entire energy around this episode in the play called "Earth" has one name to it—and that is love. We are here to love one another, and if you did nothing more today than that, then when you stand and go from this place when we are finished, you will remember that this day you sat here to be loved. And as you feel the arms of Spirit around you, I want you to feel the messages as well—messages given in The Third Language— not the one I'm speaking in, but the language of the new energy—the one that is delivered to you energetically, and emotionally [as defined in the last Kryon channelling as a "walking meditation" energy]. This Third Language says this to you: "We know who you are. We know what you are going through. We know what is being presented to you. We are celebrating with you. We are dancing around you. We love you!"

The solutions to the challenges you bring here, listener and reader—the reason why you came—are at hand. The synchronicities that you asked for, some of them a long time ago, are before you now. Much of what you have asked is before you on the plate to behold, and it's a plate that you created. All we do is hold it out and wait for you to put the solution upon it that you already own.

We have much to teach you today about the energy of this new millennium. We are calling these messages to you from Kryon, "The Marker Channellings." They all deal with the same subject, which is the energy that you have created, dear ones, as you moved into a newly created reality on this planet. Sometimes there will be short reviews of what we have said earlier (in past channellings) to enable you to understand this current message. So again we say that we sit in front of a family, many of whom have decided to cross what we have called the "Bridge of Swords." Passing the marker of the new millennium puts you into an energy—a potential of which is being developed daily.

Permission was given on January 1 to move into "the beginning of days." The old energy from the other side of the chasm, which we will call the "other side of the marker," is no longer the major force of the earth. The reason for Earth to exist, within the test, is wrapping up and completing itself. You have a 12-year time cycle in which you can develop much of the new energy for what we call the "new beginning of the planet." Grandiose as it may sound, we ask you to look around and see it. My partner says that you can see the consciousness of the Earth changing.

There is far more happening here, dear ones, than you know. We see your sun changing. We see the center of the earth changing. We see it vibrating higher. The humanity upon the planet is the catalyst for Earth change. We remind you of this: As you see the earth change around you, and obviously you are in the center of major change, we would like you to remember who is responsible. The earth does not "do anything" to you that you did not sanction. It responds. It responds to the consciousness that you put forth. The geology is speeding up to represent a higher vibrating planet.

I sit in front of family this evening—a family whom I know so well! As I deliver these concepts to you, I will say that there is a Higher Angel in each of you who knows these things, also. We ask you to resound with the truth as it comes your way. We have been here long enough now in this communication [speaking of the time since the channelling started] for you to begin to feel the truth energy we carry—these messages from Home. In fact, some of you are now in that place where we can deal with The Third Language. And so we can say these words: "Let the healing begin." It's why you came, isn't it? We know it's why you came.

There are changes that can be made in Humans today. I'm speaking about the biology as well as Human consciousness. I'm talking about dealing with the subject you came for. Family, we know who you are, and we continue to say that in the most loving way that we can. What has brought you to this place and taken you to where you sit now, hearing and reading, is the knowledge that family is before you. The sister/brother Kryon is before you—not in a grand way, but as one who kneels before you in honor and says, "I celebrate your light. I celebrate all of it. Eternal, you are. I celebrate you. I know who you are. The last time I saw you on the other side of the veil, I recognized you. You sang your name in light to me, and I saw it. I sang my name back, and you saw it. We intermingled energies. We are family! You know me!"

The love of Spirit is strong here. For those of you who came for a specific solution, this would be a wonderful time to open your hearts and receive what you came for. Reader, are you with us? You think this channelling is something that happened a long time ago? Think again. Even as we teach, we say to you that there is healing going on in this place. That includes the place where the reader sits as well. That's why we came. That's why you came. We are intermingling our energies now. Blessed is the Human Being who comes to the planet and is purposefully ignorant about the other side—the side that is Home. We are going to reveal a secret that you already know intuitively, and we will do it before we close this message. To some it will be well known and understood . . . and to some, a revelation. For humanity in general, it is a revelation.

The Widening of the Chasm

First, let us again discuss crossing the "Bridge of Swords." Here you come, lightworker, across the chasm between the old and the new! Here is where it starts to get interesting. You are learning the new Third Language that we have spoken about, and, in review, this is the language of Spirit. This new energy on this side of the marker, where you now sit and stand, is different and will be growing stronger all the time. Part of the strength of the attribute of this energy is a separation from the old. If you would like a visualization, I will give you this: The Bridge of Swords that you crossed was spanning a giant chasm. I want you to see the following in your mind: Since you have crossed the Bridge of Swords, there is no more reason for a bridge at all, and soon it will tumble. As it does, the chasm will begin to grow—representing history—the distance between what was, what is, and what will be. It is the opening of a gap, wider and wider and wider between the old ways and consciousness of the old earth and the developing energy of the new Earth.

We have told you that you will have various delivery systems of energy to your planet, and one of them is coming in May 2000. We have told you what these systems may bring you. In particular, we have said that the one in May will have the energy of "mother." The alignment of the planets will bring you the energy of *mother*. For those reading this, it was your past. For those hearing, it is the future. To Kryon, it is all NOW.

Look at the date, for the date shouts that it is a catalyst for change. The alignment will bring (and has brought) nurturing.

The alignment will pour into this planet an attribute that you have been asking for and asking for. But the only time we could have granted this request was past the collective fear—past the old energy and the old setup—past the marker when you gave permission for it to be. Not one entity knew this would take place until the marker had been passed. Now, here WE sit—the beginning of the *New Jerusalem*. Dear ones, you sit in a grand potential change, ready to begin to write Human history again.

The chasm will widen, and as it does, we would like to tell you what may happen. It is as though your reality train that was given to you as a metaphor [earlier in the seminar] had several cars. One of them was detached—the old energy car. Slowly as you accelerate, it drifts away from you. It belongs to a different time, and even though you are on the same track, the old energy drifts away as though it were from another time. This truly is a metaphor for your interdimensional shift!

Here is the attribute that the opening of the chasm will cause. Watch for this, for it will be all around you shortly. It is literally, dear ones, the *end of the fence-sitting*. The "fence-sitters" that we speak of are those who have one foot in the old energy and one in the new. In the old energy, this was very, very doable. In fact, it was a common way of life. These people never had to make a choice—a little bit of the old, a little bit of the new—it served them, and they never had to make a choice. As the chasm widens, there is going to be an energy released from it. Although this is metaphoric, let me tell you that the energy released from the widening chasm is going to make the fence-sitter extremely uncomfortable. Those who were formerly without a reason to move are going to *have to* make a decision, for their biology will scream at them if they don't . . . such is the way of the new Earth.

Never has the Human on this planet received so much new energy—divine energy—different energy of change and of balance. You want to know why the nurturing has to come in?

You want to know why the *mother* energy is here? It's going to feed the children—feed the energy and consciousness of the new children! You are seeing much imbalance in the children at the moment. You are seeing those who do not understand them, and you are seeing the children react—even the children killing the children! This action is the epitome of a lack of balance within their ranks. An energy is needed on this planet—an energy to be delivered in May of *mother*. Those who will react to it first will be the children. That's what they are going to need in order to balance themselves better. This is what they need to create the "children of the children," which you will eventually call "the peacemakers." We have spoken of this before. It is an energy that must be delivered to you this year.

The fence-sitter is going to become very uncomfortable. The chasm will open, and it will simply tear them off the fence. And in their uncomfortable state of being prodded and pulled from the position that they carried before, one which was so very comfortable for them, there is another thing that you can watch for. We will call it *"**spiritual rage**."* Some complacent fence-sitters may ask, *"Why do I have to change? What is it, Kryon, that is prodding me? I was happy before, and suddenly I'm not. You say I'm going to have to make up my mind one way or the other, but I don't want to."* The answer is in your cellular structure. You cannot sit in one energy and practice another without being anxious. In addition, the very purpose of your being here is now far different from before. Your cells know it, and so the message comes from inside you at the core level of your being. If suddenly in your life, everyone started speaking another language, do you think you would react? Yes! You would have to, in order to exist. Some will get off the fence and learn the new language, and some will retreat with others and demand that the old language be the *only* one. You will see.

Spiritual Belief Systems

Belief systems all over the planet will tear apart with change. Oh, they will remain, but there can be no more fence-sitting in regard to the old ways that no longer work. Those who talk about the love of God but do not practice it are sitting on a fence, are they not? Those who are trying desperately to follow the laws of God, but instead are following the laws of men and women, are on a fence, are they not? In addition, the world is beginning to hold them accountable for what they teach. As the entire population of Earth is able to observe [due to communications revelations such as the Internet], some systems will be shown to be unbalanced, and those who were never spiritual will become the first critics of doctrines that profess one thing and do another. The result will be that there will be fewer and fewer young people in their ranks, and many of the organizations will wither from lack of respect.

What has to happen next is a search for the divinity within core doctrinal belief—a return to the principles of love. You will see it first in the belief systems of the planet, and if you are astute in world events, you are seeing it now. (See page 238.) The greatest spiritual leaders you have who search for the divine on your planet are coming to a reckoning even as you sit here. Some of this has been discussed with you [in the seminar]. This is an end to the fence-sitting. This is a return to a quest for integrity—the morality of the search for the love of God and the core issue of family.

In this new energy, you are going to have a tough time professing one thing and doing another. If you do, you are on the fence. Those who say, *"I'm just going to stay put here. I know what Kryon said, but I'm going to stay put,"* are going to be very uncomfortable. You will see this "spiritual rage" more and more—those who are so angry—perhaps they are angry with God, perhaps they are angry with themselves—they don't know. They just know that they're being pulled off that very comfortable place where they used to be. No more fence sitting.

The spiritual belief systems of your planet are about to have a house-cleaning. Most will survive, and in the process will become closer to the intent of those who created them—to celebrate the love of God in a way that honors humanity, and does not tear it down.

Pulling the Energy Backwards?

There are other areas where this is going to manifest itself, but let me tell you another thing to watch for—another kind of rage. It has already begun. We will call this area "those that cannot believe the prophecy did not happen." Dear ones, in these next years, you are going to see some reversals. You may look at these reversals and say, *"You know, our Earth seemed to be doing pretty well until we got to this place. Now it seems that there are some reversals of the good things that were happening."* How many promising peace agreements on this planet are suddenly now stalled? How many issues politically and tribally have simply reached a stalemate? Have you seen any agreements simply fall apart lately? What's happening here? Isn't this the new energy?

Also, there will be action one way or the other within some issues that have simply been stalled for a very long time. Things that have seemed stuck will unstick themselves, and some will appear to move backwards into chaos! Let me tell you about that. There are those on the planet who love the old energy—are uncomfortable with the new, and are in a rage about the new language being here at all. What they will do until their last gasp as a Human Being is to try to make the old prophecies take place . . . and they will be with you for a while.

They are convinced that the prophecies should have happened but somehow did not. They will wonder if perhaps they didn't do their part in the divine plan, and they will try to pull you backward across the chasm that indeed is widening, in order to provide their own redemption. The only thing that will happen is that they will fall in! In the process, we want you to observe and remember that they are loved as much as you are. They are family as much as you are. It is their choice, and their decision on this free-will planet. So what I am saying, dear ones, is that there is family who will try to pull back what has been accomplished—the last gasp of an old energy Earth. You will see some apparent reversals until they give up. Some will never change, and some will have a revelation as far as the promise they now have in their lives. It's up to each individual to accept or deny the reality of one's "new train."

Tolerance

Do you know one of the big issues that this Earth will not tolerate? Intolerance! [Laughter] You will not tolerate it. You are beginning to see this. Some of those belief systems that have felt pressed upon—picked upon—is due to their spiritual box becoming intolerable to those around them. They may think that it's their box being picked on [reference to the boxes of different religious beliefs]. However, it is not. It is their *intolerance, not their doctrine,* that is being watched and seen. Intolerance will absolutely show itself. So many will say, *"I recognize this seeming two-faced action, and I do not accept it."* It's odd, isn't it, that so many who didn't care about anything moral before, will now become the watchers of spirituality? The un-spiritual becoming the accusers? What is happening here? It's called "getting off the fence." It isn't about religion. It's about the morality and integrity of the Human spirit. It's really about divinity *not* in a box [spirituality without the accompanying doctrine or organizations to go with it]! We will call it the *new personal spirituality*.

Personal Change at Home

There will be some who are in a neutral position, personally. This refers not to nations and not to religions or the many boxes, but personally... again, the personal spirituality. Dear ones, you are going to have to get off the fence! Some have interpreted this as, *"Oh, Kryon, does that mean that I'm going to lose those at home who are on the fence? Are they going to disappear in that train car called old energy as it pulls away?"* Not at all. Remember, they're just as apt to come your way as not! Getting off the fence doesn't always mean falling down the crack. It means introspection and self-awareness. There will be change—the end of neutrality, for you can't sit in the new energy and pretend nothing has happened. If you do, you are in denial, and that creates imbalance and anger ... spiritual rage. It simply means that there will be many who are going to start asking questions about who they are.

Personal Change at Work

Lightworkers, you have had a unique thing happen in these last years. Many have awakened at three or four in the morning. You've been uncomfortable. You have been pushing at doors that did not open [a metaphor for things that didn't seem to work]. You have had all manner of uncomfortable events present themselves to you as we raced toward the marker [the millennium shift]. The middle of change is never pleasant. Now, the energy is starting to be developed that you have asked for—that you have created. Now it's your turn! But look at what this really means and what it doesn't mean.

Some have said, *"I can hardly wait to get into the new energy, because that person at work—finally, I'll be done with them. God will get rid of them for me."* That's not so. Let me tell you, they may go into a rage. It may get worse. They may wish to pull you backward in their anger. Here's the difference: Finally, your "buttons" they push within your interaction with them will become disconnected. You are in the new energy. No matter what they do, all you will do is love them. This will not be hard, and you will find the love energy far easier to access now. Standing in the "now" will not be the problem it was before. Disengaging from their drama won't be nearly as difficult, but the energy now supports you in this.

Whereas they were "the sand in your oyster," there's no more oyster! It was in the old energy car left behind. Dear ones, you go to work now with a clean slate. When someone irritates you and tries to "push those buttons" of your personality, now you can understand the wisdom of their path and who they are and why they came here. What you are becoming is peaceful! Wisdom and love transmute the irritation. That will make it very interesting. What will they do when you no longer react? What will they do when you no longer fear? No more fence-sitting! Watch for this. Some will give up and become your best friends. Some will begin to ask questions. Some will even begin to carry a light—something you thought they would never do. They have gotten off the fence and have decided to join you!

The Expanding Human!

I have good news. I would like to tell you about an attribute you are being given—and we celebrate with you! It's an attribute that we can now reveal, that some facilitators in this room are starting to experience. The *Human energy field* in the posturing of the old energy was approximately three feet, or about one meter. Facilitators who work with energy will tell you that this is the distance in which they can often sense energy as they approach a Human Being for healing. They can sense the field that is the personal spiritual energy of a Human. It belongs to each Human. Those who can feel energy will tell you that this is more than an aura. It has your "energy stamp" on it—your name on it—who you are. Often, medical intuitives and energy workers can feel all manner of things within this space. Some energy workers can put their hands within the field and discuss what is indeed happening at the cellular level of your body— imbalance, as well as enlightenment and even sorrow or joy! This is the way it has been.

Now, that distance is going to change, dramatically. We're here to tell you this, dear ones: You now have permission to expand this personal field, slowly through these new years, foot by foot—taking your power to its full potential of 27 feet! This is the size of the full Human Merkabah. When I see you here . . . I always see you in your fully divine size. It is indeed the outer perimeter of the Merkabah that I experience when I come into this place to communicate with you, but this perception has been limited to approximately one meter per Human Being for eons.

When the Human energy matches the Merkabah energy, you will indeed be an interdimensional being, standing there in your 4-D, but radiating love, light, and understanding that is filled with multidimensional aspects. Shaman, this is what you asked for! Lightworkers, this is what you always wanted! Start visualizing it and working on it right now. You have permission to change and expand.

Fortressing—Revisited

Speaking of expanding, we will now review something very important to many of you. Some of you may remember this from the last channelling. It is very real! Because you only had a three-foot expansion limit for eons, many of you felt a spiritual inconsistency at the cellular level. Healers and lightworkers *knew* they were bigger than that! They sensed it. To provide both protection from the old energy, and to try to expand into an energy they intuitively knew they actually were, they did what is called "fortressing." Fortressing is the name given to the Human Being who puts layer upon layer of protection on their body to make up for the expansion of the I AM, which seems to be missing.

Now, what I am telling you is this: Lightworker, for the second time, I will say that this is why so many of you carry around the extra weight. Whereas it was something appropriate for you and what you came here for, it can change. When you look at yourself in the mirror, which *you* is it? The one in the old energy train car trying to survive, or the one in the new car? The ways that you tried before to lose the weight may work now. Also, look for new processes that are more intuitive, many having to do with water, to take the weight off. You don't need the layers anymore. The fortressing is over. Through these next years, you have permission, finally, to reduce yourself to whatever weight you choose as the Human who stands in total health. This is new, and is part of the cooperative nature of the lightworker and the new energy.

There are some who sit in disbelief about what is being said. *"I have tried everything. Nothing works. I'm stuck with my bigness."* This is not so. Some will not change, for they like who they are as the size they are. Indeed, that is all right, too. For those who wish to change, however, we tell you the process is at hand. Fortressing no longer is needed in your life. It doesn't help the spiritual, and may limit your life span. The invitation to expand in another way—a spiritual way, is open. This information has now been given two times due to the importance of your understanding of it.

The Big Secret

Let's talk about the big issue: Shamans, you are here hearing and reading this. I keep calling you that because I know who you are, and who you were. Who do you think awakens now? Who are the first to awaken on the planet in this new millennium to this divine energy? I will tell you. The ones who awaken now to their spirituality are the priests and the nuns—the monks and the shamans—the medicine women and men of the indigenous peoples—YOU! If I could give you a flashback of who you are, those who sit in this room and read these words—that's who you are. This is not the first time you have awakened to ask about your cellular spirituality. This is a review, and we said it last time we were here. We reminded you of the vows that you took that passed through the veil, lifetime after lifetime. We asked you to drop these vows. We told you that you could drop the vow of celibacy and being alone. We told you that in order to focus on God, many of you decided to be poor, and we told you that this vow could be dropped as well. We told you that all of those vows could be dropped. This is information that has been transmitted and transcribed. Perhaps you've even read or heard it already?

But there's another big issue. It is the one we have talked about since the day that you began your search for the divine. There is a secret of humanity that hides. Humanity has been looking for the divine since it arrived on the planet. Look around you. Look at the religions and the structure of how things work. Look at the thousands of doctrines, and the global, historic search for God. Look at those who have brought you into their lives and into their own religious groups, because they are searchers and wanted to help you. Look at the search for all things holy. What about the fountain of youth? Look at the search for the fountain of youth. You've heard about it all your lives. Could it be real? The search for this is ageless! Humanity has searched for these things forever. The basis behind governments coming and going on Earth is about the search for the divine. Most of the earth's religions and all the ceremony is about the search for God. History shouts about this search over and over, and kingdoms have been won and lost due to it. Look at the resources put forward by humanity to find God!

I would like to tell you this: We hid it. You hid it. We all hid it very well. We hid it in the least likely place for any Human Being to ever search for it! The Human Being that crawls up the steps one at a time to be honored by God would never suspect where it was hiding. The Human Being who prostrates himself daily on the prayer rug would never suspect where the real divinity was hiding. The Human Being who counts the beads over and over so that transgressions would be forgiven would never suspect where it was hiding. The millions who give homage to a greater power, and who walk through hardship to gain God's favor, would never suspect where it was hiding.

So, lightworkers in this room and reading this, you already know, but still there is doubt. The biggest secret on this planet—the biggest one—is where the divinity really is. Let me give you a hint. Why is there so much energy around the words "I AM"? The least likely place to find the fountain of youth [eternal life]—the least likely place to find a divinity that can heal the Human Being and make him whole—the least likely place, the one where no Human would ever think to look, ever, is where we all decided to best hide it. You know what I'm talking about, don't you? The place where it is hidden is inside every Human Being alive. That's where the power is. That's where the fountain of youth is. That's where eternal life is. That's where you will find the Holy of Holies. That's where the love of God is.

The biggest issue of the lightworker, the fence-sitting in the lightworker's life, is this: You cannot accept where the divinity really is . . . even when you know the answer. The piece of God inside you—the Higher Self inside you—is so well hidden that the duality will shout to you for the rest of your life that it is *not* so. That's the way you designed it—so that it wouldn't ever be obvious.

One of the biggest issues that we would like to give you permission to clear this afternoon, together as a group, is this: You can't believe you've made a difference. *"Kryon, who am I, really? Who am I, and what difference do I make? Am I really a piece of God?"* I'm going to give you some numbers. Look backwards at what just happened a couple of months ago. You gave permission to change the planet, and within these past years, you now have evidence within your reality that it *did* change. You changed the track on the train of humanity from an old reality to a new one. And who might you say did that? God from above? No.

It is those awakening on this continent, and on the other continents of the planet, who did that. I'm going to give you a fact now. Less than 15 percent of all Humans are aware of what you are aware of right now. They don't know what the secret is. Yet that 15 percent has changed the planet forever! We have talked about the critical mass of those who are aware and what happens when they "hold the light." We have talked about what happens when you shine a light in a dark place. We have given you the parables of the light and the dark. We have discussed the attributes of spiritual light—the active attribute of light and the passiveness of the dark. Listen, lightworker: If you consider yourself a lightworker on this planet, you're part of the minority of the earth's population and the majority of the energy that changed the planet! You 15 percent are responsible for what you see. Does this give you a hint of what Humans can do when they give permission to vibrate higher? Like the power of the angel inside, this also hides from you.

And you don't think you did anything? Oh, I want to sing your name! You are so valuable! In that closet where you pretend to be alone and you cry, we dance around you. You are never alone. The entourage is always there that you call God. It's always there. It's always there! Go ahead and pretend to ignore us. Leave this place and go home. Put down this book and carry on. We are wherever you go. We're even there in your car! Each lightworker who has given intent to vibrate higher takes on an entourage! That's where the power is! It is what has given you the ability to change the planet. As the energy on the planet changes, more of it will awaken. And those who awaken are not all going to be lightworkers. They're not all going to speak The Third Language. They're not all going to come to a Kryon seminar! In their own way and within their own boxes, many will begin to get off the fence and slowly change their minds about how big God is. They will start to have wisdom and new integrity. Many will expect more of themselves and start searching. So this will not change what they are doing in life, but it will simply expand it. And with the expansion will come tolerance and love of one another—the core issue. Many will discover the secret. The search will reveal the hiding place inside.

Lightworkers, shamans, you dropped the vows. Now it is time to bring out the angel! It is time to take your power. Many of you know what I'm talking about, but few have really implemented the reality shift of bringing out the angel! There is no more fence-sitting. Some of you will have the passions that struck you early in life—the ones you put in your back pocket will reemerge in your lives. In the past, some of you put things on the shelf and said, *"That's not for me; I don't think I'll ever be able to do that."* You are now going to go to that shelf and revisit it. It's all part of getting off the fence. This is the energy that you have asked for, and in this process, don't expect to sit down much. Get ready for the work.

In the process, dear ones, here is the promise. This entourage around you ... the ones that are going to leave in a moment ... the ones that you call family, belong on my side of the veil. There is also an entourage that you own, on your side of the veil, which is also family and is always with you. Both kinds have a language now to communicate with you. The Third Language is the language of God. That's claiming the new vow! You are going to *own* that angel inside as you speak this language. Some have even called this the final communion with God. You are going to know we're around you as you speak it. It is time to accept this. Drop the past, where you were searching for the divine. Bring out the angel!

I AM, that I AM—the circle of the words that describes the Human Being as God, is the truth. It is the ultimate secret. The very names of the I AM in spiritual history refer to the Human Being. The most divine scripture ever written came from Human Beings. Think about it! The most profound thoughts ever thought on the planet were not delivered to you on a few tablets. They came out of the core of the Human Being. That is where the divine has been hiding all along.

Now it is time to find the fountain of youth. It's in there, you know [Lee touches his heart]. Oh, we told you, it's in there. Don't be surprised if you find the new water cures having something to do with it. Perhaps that's why it was called a fountain? It is coming. You will see what I mean. You've asked for it, dear ones.

All we can do is celebrate as this entourage withdraws from this room. We have spent more time celebrating than anything else this day. For the Human family has allowed this now—allowing us to come and share this time with you. It is time to see those around you. They are showing themselves now. We want you to be aware of whom we all are in this room and reading this. We want you to be aware that this is not an exercise. We wanted you to know, so you could leave this place and say, *"Today, I felt the touch of God."* Yes, but you also felt the sister/brother Kryon—family—not some divine being that came in and did something to you. No. Instead it was a brother or a sister who walked between the aisles and between the chairs, even next to the chair where you read. A family member who touched you and said in The Third Language, "I want you to know I am here, that I love you, and what is being said now is accurate and real."

The family that visits, now leaves. In the process it says, "Welcome to the new Earth." There is no predestination. It is continuing to be in your hands. You can do anything you want with it. That is the choice. That is an example of the divinity in you. The Kryon grid-moving entourage arrived in 1989. The move of the grid will be done in 2002. The entourage, which was responsible for moving the grid, will be on their way. They will not return again, because they will never have to. You now have all the power to do anything here spiritually that needs to be done. Your sister/brother Kryon has been here since the beginning and will continue to be through all of Earth's history, past and future.

Listen: This is important for you to know. You are empowered! There is not one of you here who has to come back to this room to experience this. No person ever has to read the words again if they choose not to. No Human has to join anything or profess any system of belief to find the divine inside. The Third Language is your guide! We are all available—all in that closet, if you will. You are all God!

And so it is that the new energy of the planet fills this space and gives you the wisdom of God. And so it is that you have asked for and have received instructions this day about the potentials of the planet and who you really are. And so it is that the secret has been revealed about the last place you might expect divinity to be—inside the Human. And so it is that we have given you permission this day to drop your lack of self-worth, and to come off the fence and let your angel shine. And so it is that there is sorrow as we back out of this space—sorrow that this time was not longer—sorrow that we don't have you Home yet, but also celebration that the I AM is starting to be recognized, and celebration that your light is so large!

And so it is.

Kryon

About the channelling you just read:

Kryon was referring to two current events as this seminar was given:

(1) The Pope's sudden decision to try to obtain forgiveness for past Church actions this year (2000) is an attribute that brings people across the chasm, and unites them in love. He is the first Pope to visit Israel and to celebrate their right to worship God. .. even participating in Jewish ritual. I believe he also recognizes the new spiritual energy and is preparing the way for his replacement to continue this radical change within a very old established religion on Earth. This was predicted in July 1999, and you can find it in this book on page 78. Seldom have we had such fast validations of what Kryon told us we had the potentials for!

(2) The suicides in Uganda in March 2000 were a direct result of the anxiety of fence-sitting. Those who committed the murders within the cult were in "spiritual rage" that the *end of days* did not come with the change in the millennium. God did not "take" them as they had expected. They believed that it was better to kill the membership, and then take their own lives, rather than live on a planet that they were certain was now in the hands of Satan—such is the way of the widening chasm of the old and new perceptions.

By the way . . . Kryon mentioned that the leaders of that suicide are still alive.

—Lee Carroll

Live Channelling

"The Journey Home, Revisited"

Channelled in
San Francisco, California
April 2000

Chapter Eleven

"*The Journey Home,* Revisited"
Live Channelling
San Francisco, California

This live channelling has been edited with additional words and thoughts to allow clarification and better understanding of the written word.

Greetings, dear ones. I AM Kryon of Magnetic Service. Dear family, this is indeed a precious moment. There was a time when the entourage would pour into a place like this and Human duality would have kept us from *feeling* the family's love back. Now I can report, dear ones, that we have something that we *feel* and have asked for but that only you could grant. It's a new energy that allows us to immediately feel your hugs to us, and this is new.

The last few times that we have entered with the entourage, which we call family, instead of simply taking our places at your feet and around you, we had to pause for a moment to absorb the wave of love that came our way. This is proof that there are new abilities within those here and those reading this. It's a divinity, a handshake, that says, "Yes, we recognize you, brother/ sister Kryon, and the entourage that you call family." There is no other name for that feeling, other than *precious*.

And so it is that we feel you profoundly as we pour into this place. Here is something that we have said to you many times: We come here to celebrate you! Oh, it is true that there will be teaching this afternoon, but for a moment let us celebrate *you.* Dear ones, we say this to you often, but perhaps you are not aware of the energy in this place. Even around the chair where you read this transcription there is a change, if you allow it. Perhaps you do not understand or realize that we knew of the intent for you to sit where you are now . . . reader and listener. Perhaps you did not fully comprehend or grasp the fact that we saw you on your way to this place and knew of your intent when you gave it. We knew that some of you made your decisions at the last moment, and some gave their intent weeks ago.

Yet, it is in our *now* that we see this group of family before us—listening and reading. And we say to you that we knew of your arrival before you came! We knew of the potential for your eyes to meet these words! In this assemblage, we knew of the names that sit in the chair—not names you would recognize as Humans. Kryon and this entourage assembled here more than three days ago to match the energy of who was coming. Perhaps you did not also know that the entourage is different every single time the Kryon comes in. It is made of entities of family members who know you. It is sometimes constructed and gathered from those who were once on the planet but have passed on. Sometimes this is the case, and other times it is not. It is different each time, due to the Human who agrees to come here . . . or to read the pages before them.

The entourage floods in here and takes its place around, behind, and in between you. It knows you well. Three days ago, there was a celebration for the potential of who would sit in the chairs and be here. There was joy and an outpouring of love, and there was patience until you arrived this day. And so it may give you pause to think about exactly who came to see whom as you hear these words or read this page. Although it is difficult for you to understand, the incarnations of transcriptions of these words in many languages is a potential that is already here for us. The thousands who will read these words are all lined up in your linear life in what you call the future. To us, however, these are potentials that manifest in our *now*. Therefore, we congratulate the reader, and tell you that all this applies to you, also. Indeed, we saw you there with the book in your hand!

And that is why our emotional heart is so stirred with those whose energies are here as readers and listeners. You may ask yourselves, *"Who am I to be called divinity? What have I got to do with anything?"* The question that you ask is due to the duality working at its best, dear ones. For here you sit in an energy you have created that is far different from anything any creature in this Universe could have predicted. You have collectively decided, even without meetings, to change the track of your planet's reality.

Even to those who do not call themselves lightworkers, there is a divineness and understanding—the beginning of passion for the planet. You will begin to see it in your religious leaders—your politicians—and in the world itself. You will begin to see the potential for changes that you have been wondering about for years. Some have asked, *"Why did they not manifest before?"* The old energy was not suitable for much of what you anticipated. But many of you are beginning to see these things now, however, because the new energy allows for it.

Some of you stand in front of the mirror and say, *"I am insignificant. Who am I to be called an angel or lightworker?"* I want you to know that we collectively celebrate you! Without what you accomplished, it would have been far different as you sit there. "The Great I AM" sits in front of me today. You call yourselves Human, yet you are pieces of God. Dear ones, when you're not here and on my side of the veil, you will know what I speak of, for your grandness is celebrated there! It is difficult for us to teach you, when all we want to do is hug. Your duality completely hides who resides in that frail Human body!

For many years, our messages have said, "You can do it! You can move past the marker without any of the prophecies coming to pass." I have spoken of "holding on" and being patient. We often gave you the words, *God is slow* . . . and you didn't want to hear it. But now you sit in the energy that you've created. Look at it! It is not the *end* of days. It is the *beginning* of days! The creation of a new Earth is at your fingertips. The track that your train is on has nothing in front of it at all. It is virgin, creative territory and has never been touched. It is territory you have never seen before, and it will create itself as it goes out of your consciousness. Some of you are aware that you're even building the new track, and it's the first time you've been on it.

It is true that you continue to have free choice, and anything can happen. But the critical mass has been reached, and you are starting to see it within the way the earth behaves. Certain kinds of problems that have presented themselves before, regarding moral issues, are now being dealt with. Whereas the planet didn't seem to care about these things in the past, now they are paramount in your news. This is the beginning of spiritual evolution, as defined by your vibrational level.

We are here to give you a revelation this afternoon. We are going to walk you through seven new meanings. Finally, we are going to reveal for transcription what was meant by the channelling that you have called *The Journey Home*. [This refers to Kryon Book Five, a novel.] Those of you who have read or heard of that channelling story will know of the things to come in this teaching. Those of you who *do not* will still be given the message in its completeness.

The channelling called *The Journey Home* is an allegory. To some it is a metaphor, and to others a simple story. To many, it was created in your past time and transcribed years ago. But to us, it was in the *now*. As you sit in the *now* that *we* have always sat in, the potential of this afternoon was there . . . and the information to follow was at hand. Even as this book was channelled, we saw the potential of your being in the chair where you sit... such is the power of the *now* time frame.

The Journey Home message was really given for those in the new millennium. It is the story of the potential of *ascension*, a word never mentioned within the story of Michael Thomas and his journey home. Within the story, spiritual metaphors were presented for you to examine and see, but never have we revealed what we reveal today. It will now combine information from the last two messages of this new millennium [channellings from the last two months].

The Journey Home, revisited

The story was about a gentleman on Earth. Michael Thomas was his name—the name derived from the energy of Archangel Michael, combined with the energy of *the doubting Thomas*. This is the energy of a Human in duality, for that is exactly what you have before you—a duality that is part angelic and part doubter. The Human hides an angel inside, but the duality hides this, so it doubts and fears. The Human Being is filled with wonderful potential, for you have the choice to find the divinity and discover the angel. You, therefore, have the choice to find one of the greatest secrets of humanity. But this also hides from your thoughts.

This gentleman was taken into seven houses of training on his way to a journey that he thought was his sacred home, and he longed to return to it. He was on his way in training to what he felt was Heaven. And in those seven houses, there were energies that we will reveal to you now—energies that combine only with things we have given you subsequent to January 1, 2000.

Oh, dear ones, some of you came today for something other than this information, did you not? Some of you are reading and longing for something other than this.

We wish to stop now and say, "We honor you for the healing you've come for, for the healing of the heart. You know whom I'm speaking to! We honor you for the biology and the healing that you have asked for. We honor the secrets that you carry. Don't you think we know who's here? Don't you think we see you reading there? We know of some of the quandaries in your lives!"

[Pause . . .]

Now would be a good time for you to heal, would it not? Now is a good time for you to see the colors as they pour from this stage and fill the hearts of those in front of us. Now is the time for many of you to celebrate the healing that has just taken place! You didn't expect it at this moment, did you? The teaching has hardly begun, yet your intent and purity is allowing the energy to speak to your crystalline sheath [speaking of the DNA information presented the last time Kryon was in the San Francisco area].

Let the energy right now be the proof that this is simply not just another meeting—or words in a book. There is nothing more precious in the world—on this Earth—than the Human who begins to discover that he/she has power from inside! For it is not necessary for you to ever come back to a meeting like this. It's not necessary to ever pick up a book about channelling if you do not choose to. You can walk into the smallest closet and perform your own healing, because the entourage is there, the healing is there, and the power is there! It's the Human who has the power. It's the Human who is the Higher Self—the divinity inside, but who walks the earth disguised as a frail biological entity. And you wonder why we celebrate you? Let the healing begin!

The First House—Maps

The first house that Michael Thomas entered was the blue one, the House of Maps. We have talked about this many times.

We have trained many times and given explanations of the metaphors. But the full explanation has never been given in this new energy. We spoke of The Third Language in past channellings. This is a new language that is yours for the asking. It is very new, and it could not exist like this before the marker. This is the language formerly only available to the shaman, for it took training, discipline, and understanding. Now that the fear has been reduced on Earth, The Third Language can permeate itself into lightworkers and all those who wish to have it. It is the epitome of the new age. The Third Language is the language of Spirit. It is a constant, 100 percent, "in-touch" language between the Human Being and God. It's a walking meditation, while being aware and awake—going about your lives normally.

Michael Thomas received a magic map that only seemed to work at the last moment when he needed it. In addition, the map never gave him information about what was coming, but rather gave him solutions to situations only after he stood in the middle of the energy of the challenge. Here is the metaphor for the map in this new age, past the marker.

In the old energy, dear ones, you might visit the shaman for advice . . . for wise information. You would listen to the wisdom from Spirit coming through the shaman, much like some of you are doing now. The shaman would give you information about potential things to come, and what to do when you got there. You might ask him what's going to happen when you meet certain situations, and the shaman would help by giving guidance for those items.

Later, you would leave that wise shaman and go forward in your life, hoping that you had the information you needed and could remember it all. When you encountered obstacles and forks in the road, you would try to call up what the shaman had said, and apply his knowledge to the current task, hoping that you got it right! That, dear ones, is the old energy. It represents the giving of information through Spirit to the Human, but requires that the Human remember what was given.

Here's what the new map is about in the blue House of Maps, the first house. The House of Maps represents The Third Language as a "shaman on your shoulder." Instead of going out and trying to remember what was said by others of an enlightened state, how would you like to have the information live with you? Then, as you approach every fork in the road, the divinity of the shaman says, *"Turn right or left. Feel it—turn this way or that—feel it."*

Instead of trying to remember what was given to you during a lesson, now you have instant communication with the divine. Each situation that arises gives you wisdom about what to do, and there are no surprises. A communication like this gives you peace over any situation in your life, does it not? You have the shaman on your shoulder! That's what the map is. It is The Third Language visiting you all the time so that there's never a question about which way to turn. The House of Maps describes the energy on Earth past the marker. It's also very much within the *now*, a shaman who is silent until you need him within the energy of the challenge.

Using the map, or The Third Language, is to understand that the energy of challenge must marry to the energy of solution. This sacred language is available anytime, and you can look at your map anytime. However, only the times when the energy of the challenge is paramount will the map work. Celebrate this attribute! It is the circular *now* of how spiritual things work. It is how you can walk into uncertainty with a peacefulness that you never had before. But you must understand the timing of it all to fully comprehend the beauty of this gift!

The Second House—Gifts and Tools

The next house in the journey is the orange house—the House of Gifts and Tools. We have already given you information about some of the new tools of the energy of this millennium. The last time we met in channelling and the time before that, we made reference to dropping the old vows. We made reference to those who sit before us, family who have been through many lifetimes in spiritual quest. We reminded you that the vows you took before God, even lifetimes ago, carry through the veil over and over. Now, you come into this incarnation... seemingly fresh and new, but carrying pieces and parts of past vows to God.

We told you about your new gifts. This is the House of Gifts and Tools, and the vows can now be dropped. This is reviewed information, but necessary for some of you to hear again (or for the first time). We told you that you could drop the vow to be poor! In the old days, you gave this vow in order to focus on God. Now you have The Third Language instead. We told you that it would be appropriate to drop the vow that said you had to be alone for the same reason! Some of you actually married God and followed a pattern of sacrifice in order to focus on spiritual things. Now you have a gift that replaces the vows, so you may drop them.

Let us revisit one that was actually shown in the parable, however. Michael Thomas was given a sword. At the time, it seemed like a sword of battle, and it was. It is also part of the Bridge of Swords that we spoke of in past channellings, representing the crossing into the new energy. The sword represents a battle against the old energy. It isn't a battle between Human and Human. It's a battle between the old and new energy. It's a battle against duality, and therefore no energy but your own.

This particular sword was also a weapon that sang when you used it! It sang the F note, which represents the heart chakra.

Do you understand now why you need that note in this new energy? The alignment of planets in May of 2000 brought *mother energy*—nurturing energy—to the heart energy of this planet. The children will feel it, and many of you will, also, as the gifts and tools you are given in this house of training match it and also sing the F note. We give you these things because it is time to cut the ties, to release the binds, to take off the shackles of the old energy and the old contracts.

The sword was the sword of truth . . . one that signifies a part of the Bridge of Swords that broaches the chasm over the old energy, and helps you to prepare for the new. Indeed, it is powerful, but it now marries perfectly with the nurturing and love energy that it was meant for. Now the actual dirt of the earth resounds in cooperation with this wonderful gift. If a battle is to be fought between energies, this is the tool to have.

The Third House—Biology

Michael Thomas walked into the house that was green— the House of Biology. In the original story, much was given to him and he trained in this house. We have spoken many times about cellular rejuvenation. We have given you health admonitions. We have given you advice and told you many things about your DNA, but not like this! Dear ones, in that green place called the House of Biology, Michael Thomas was shown something that was never transcribed. We can tell you now in this new *now* energy, that there will be more profound live essences coming forward in these next 12 years than in the past 100! We are going to tell you what many of them are going to look like, and you are going to be in quandary, for they will not sound to you like live essences.

Now we can tell you what we really mean by live essences. Much discussion has been manifest regarding what is a "live essence." Oh, it is true that a live-essence substance is indeed derived from those things that have been alive on the planet, used in herbology and in essences and in aromas. But there is one that you never thought of. And when we tell you, you will say, *"But Kryon, that is not alive!"*

We are going to tell you what it is. It's water! Water! And it's alive, interdimensionally. Water will now start to show you something you never saw before . . . energies of healing. Watch for a plethora of water cures on this planet! Water is the life of this planet. It is alive with the essence of healing. It is the vehicle for live essence, and this is what has been meant all along—a live-essence curative energy in water!

The very cells of the body sit in a water bath. Life sits in a water bath. The earth is mostly water. Some water cures that are needed by some of you specifically can now be provided. Some cures will be selective to match the energy of what you specifically need, while others may not do anything for you, but none will harm you. There will be an explosion of water cures, and some of them may surprise you. There will be a whole number of them that you will think of as being "energetic water." Some water will contain energy only available in certain parts of the earth, now holding the energy alive in containers for one of the first times ever. Water from one energy to another will travel well for the first time. Look for waters that you can drink, and which cooperate with your body where you can feel it within moments after you drink it.

This is new information revealed now on this day. It is something that could not have been revealed before the marker, for you were not prepared to accept this at all. It is only past the marker that these things can be brought to you in the manner that they can now, as you hold the sword that sings the F note high above you head. The battle between you and the old energy and the old self includes a rejuvenation at the cellular level. It includes permission for life extension, and it's going to start with the water! And that's what the green house was about. We will have more about the water in future channellings.

The Fourth House—Responsibility

Michael Thomas went into the violet house, which was the House of Responsibility. Here he learned about contracts and how he had helped plan all that had happened to him on the earth. This may sound like old metaphysical information, but with a twist in this new millennium. He learned about his contracts and predispositions to potentially do certain things if he decided to. He learned the difference between predestination and predisposition. He learned what it was like to come to this planet with a propensity to do something, then follow that feeling, in part because he didn't feel he could change it. That's a contract.

Some of you have yet to understand what the word *contract* means. We wish you to examine the word now. The word *contract*, as defined in your language, means "an agreement between two entities." If you have a contract on the planet, who is that second entity? Now we reveal this: The largest contract you have—the life contract—the one that says how long you are going to live on this planet, the one that specifies that you may become sick, all of those energy concepts embedded upon you—is between the "Earth you" and the "angel you," the Higher Self. This is a binding agreement between the Human in duality and the Human in divinity. Perhaps you thought it was an agreement between you and Spirit? Actually, it is, but it's Spirit inside you.

Before you can move ahead, this agreement, this contract you came in with from an old energy, can now be dissolved. We have spoken of this before, regarding erasing the recipe you have at the cellular level for an old contract that "wants to be cooked." Many of you have the residual feelings of the recipe! It has that kind of an energy, for the contract still exists, waiting to be acted out or altered.

It's time for ceremony. When in doubt, have ceremony! [Laughter] Dear ones, we say that lightly, but it is so revered by Spirit. For the Human Being to prepare something of significance regarding ceremony, whether it be an altar or a quiet time, it is very honored. If you should do this in the new energy, here is what to say:

Agree to drop the vows of celibacy, to drop the vows of poverty, to dismiss a contract you had with your Higher Self, developed in an old energy. Agree to erase the ingredients of the contract recipe and rewrite it, to renew the vows of the love of Spirit, to renew the vows of the love of the earth. Validate that you DO NOT have to be poor; you CAN have a loving partner; you DO NOT have to carry out some of the challenges that you signed up for. This is a new Earth and one that did not exist when you came in. That is what the House of Responsibility is for. It not only represents the responsibility to the family via the contracts that *were* yours, but now it represents the responsibility to the earth and you, to change them!

The Fifth House—Relationships

Michael Thomas moved into the red House of Relationships. There he was taught about karmic interaction between Human beings on the planet. Here is where he learned about the death of his parents and the meaning of it. We have spoken of this many times, but in the last sessions, we have said these words to you: *"Who is it you will not forgive, or not speak to?"* The red House of Relationships is about forgiving family!

Do you want the tool to forgive the family? Who are *you*, really? What do you carry around from the past? We are telling you this, dear ones, whether it is in the House of Relationships or the House of Responsibility: *You* have the sword to cut the binds of these old chains. That's what the sword is for! It's the heart chakra, and it wields the power that only compassion can give . . . and what a power that is!

Who is it that you will not forgive? That's what we asked. This question has come right out of the House of Relationships, for all that was presented to you in life was a setup for this moment! Perhaps it's time right now for another kind of healing in this room, another kind of healing in the chair you sit reading in? Maybe it's time for some of you to move off that old peg of comfortable drama? What is it that you can't seem to get through in your life? Who is it that you have to forgive? Who is it that you won't speak to? That is what this house actually presented. That's the training that Michael Thomas received: the ability to see all in the scheme of life as family with a purpose.

You must realize something: For the map to work, for The Third Language to be effective, for the dropping of vows to be meaningful, for the biology to begin to change, for you to become responsible to the earth, there must be a purity of spirit present that you absolutely cannot fake. Forgiveness of the unforgivable shows a compassion for life that only divinity can muster up. Compassion of this kind creates a divine spirit, and that is the catalyst to all the other areas. The battle is won when you have the ability to forgive and mean it. And what if you don't? Then it's time for ceremony! Tell Spirit that this is what you wish to have, and watch your attitude change. Compassion is a result of the willingness to see the big picture—the willing-ness and intent to learn to forgive. Soon the learning will become manifest, and you realize that you have indeed accomplished much.

"Dear God, show me how to be compassionate. Show me the divinity in all things. Show me the love in all things. Let me shine with understanding, and give me the ability to forgive those I have trouble with. Let me have the peace of perfect understanding. Let it begin with me. Let peace on Earth begin in my heart."

The Sixth House—Love

All of the other houses made sense when Michael Thomas got to the house of white—the House of Love. Here he learned the four attributes of love. He watched the Human Being, Mary, in an unfolding vision where she forgave her abusive father, covered him during his death, and blessed him. She told the Universe that she was proud to have the abusive man as her father, and she showed the kind of purity and compassion that only comes from a Human who is practicing The Third Language. And Michael Thomas stood in amazement.

Dear family member, where is your *block?* Perhaps that is why you are here today . . . or reading this . . . to ask yourself in this silent time about that very thing. When you get through that truth, dear ones, it's going to be a tremendous release! These things must be cleared one by one, and understood one by one, in the training of the seven houses. Ascension is the raising of the vibratory level of yourself, then of the earth. You cannot have an ascended, graduate Earth without the Humans on it doing it first.

Now, here is something new. We have mentioned The Third Language all the way through this message, and it was also presented two messages ago [two months ago], and here it is again. It is now possible, dear angels, to have The Third Language not just between Human and Spirit, but also between Human beings. This will affect your attitude toward those who have indeed been the sand in your oyster. [Laughter] In other words, you can speak The Third Language to others!

Some of you who may have regular heated arguments with another will actually find yourselves *listening* to the other person during this interchange. [Laughter] Some of you may find yourselves actually weighing the merits of what the other person is saying! What's happening? The Third Language is not just between you and Spirit. It is between the other angels as well [other Humans]. What we are saying here is that there is going to be the potential of attitude change within situations that have seemed untenable before. This will only be allowable because there is another energy present at the same time you are speaking and talking—a new energy of The Third Language! It will change the way you do everything with another Human Being . . . even the way you argue. Anger will be slower to develop, and patience will be much easier to find. Humor may temper it all and be the catalyst for agreement rather than separation.

With intent, many of you might experience this soon and know what we are talking about. You may find yourself talking to a person for business reasons, and at the same time find yourself loving them at a level you never thought possible. At first, this might be disconcerting! After all, there are some attributes of humanism that seem unchangeable. This will be different. Some of these will be people you would never, ever have thought this about in the past.

The Third Language is a strong one, since it's what we call the "core language." It's going to be here for those lightworkers who want to grab it. Some of you will call it "new intuition." You might even call it "moving into a new dimension," and you would be correct. Remember the dimensions are hidden until you tune in to them. This, therefore, will be one that some of you will tune in to. It makes you see Human Beings differently. It lets you forgive those from the past who may have done things that created much hate and strife for you. Now, you will see them as family and love them anyway. Regardless of their own attitudes toward you, you will love them anyway. In this, you are drawing closer to who you really are—a 27-foot-wide entity that spins—each of you. (But you knew that, didn't you?) That's what I see as I look around here. I see magnificence in you, sitting there in that chair pretending to be Human.

The Seventh House—Gold—Self-Worth

Michael Thomas went into the House of Self-Worth and had many surprises—including what happened when he opened the magic door to "Home." Read the transcription if you wish to know more. We told you in the last channelling that self-worth is the key to all spiritual growth and all spiritual ascension. What this gold house is about is humanity's search for divinity. This house was to reveal a secret, and it did.

In the last channelling, we also told you that humanity's biggest secret was that the fountain of youth and the Holy Grail were all inside the Human Being, hidden well. This is not just a metaphor. What the gold house is really about is the ability of the Human Being to provide personal changes and Earth changes that can change the very reality of what you think is possible on the planet!

As you move into the new millennium, there are some very scary possibilities as humanity grows in numbers. You have overpopulation problems and diseases that are yet to be seen, which may very well be unstoppable with your technology. You have a warming of the earth, and areas of ice that may melt and break off. You have atmospheric concerns and weather that is seemingly getting worse and worse. It doesn't sound like a joyful scenario, does it?

When you understand what you have already done, you then can also understand that through Human consciousness, and claiming the I AM energy, there is still something else hiding. We speak of your ability as a Human race to change all the physical items I just mentioned. *"Kryon, can we do that? Can we change the weather, diseases yet to be released, and ice flows? Can we change the temperature of the planet?"* The answer is YES! All that and more. That is exactly the message of Kryon for the new millennium!

In this new energy, how many of you are going to stand in front of the mirror and look yourself in the eyes, and say, "I AM THAT I AM"? How many of you can do that and mean it? It's tough! But when you understand where the power comes from, and that it's also where extended life is going to come from, perhaps you can begin to change your mind about who you are and what you can become. Then you can also understand what a collection of the I AM can do with the planet!

When you can claim the I AM in pure understanding, you will begin to understand how to hold the sword. When you do that, you will know how to use the tools and release the vows. When you do that, you will know how to rewrite the contract recipe. When you do that, you will know all about compassion and forgiveness. Isn't it odd that this is the last chapter in *The Journey Home*, yet it is the first one to complement the others? And the reason is that these house-lessons were meant to be presented in a circle! Yet, in linear time that is impossible. So we ask you to see these houses in a circle—six houses around a center. The center is the gold house, the one of self-worth, the activator. For once it is accomplished, indeed, all of the others will be added unto it.

This is the promise of Earth! This is the secret of the ages … that humanity has the power to not only change itself, but also the very dirt you stand on. Your partner (the earth), waits for you to make the changes.

We sit in front of those who are shamans, those who are known to us, and we have to say good-bye. We sit in front of family, and we have to say good-bye. It's the hardest thing we do, leaving. For it's just about this time when we start feeling your love for us. We've told you only three times now. We are starting to feel you! We come into a session of this nature, and so often in these past years, it has been a "one-way push." There has been an energy of fear and duality that never would have allowed for you to hug us back. Now when we come in, we are beginning to feel love returned!

My partner wells up with what he knows, and what this entity, Kryon, feels. There are those in the room who set the magnetic grid at the beginning of Earth with me, and in the *now*—in the blink of an eye—we sit here together again in your year 2000. Is it the end of days as your prophets told you? No. It's the *beginning* of days.

Blessed is the Human Being who understands these seven houses and their meanings. Blessed is the Human Being who knows the secret of where the divinity lies, for much will be added unto their lives using their own creation, using their own power, using The Third Language, which is theirs for the first time in Human history.

And you thought you weren't worth anything!

We celebrate the preciousness of this moment, and we say, until we see you again . . .

And so it is.

Kryon

Live Channelling

"The Interdimensional Human"

Channelled in
Clearwater, Florida
June 2000

Chapter Twelve

"The Interdimensional Human"
Coloring Outside the Lines
Live Channelling
Clearwater, Florida

*This live channelling has been edited with additional
words and thoughts to allow for clarification and
better understanding of the written word.*

Greetings dear ones. I AM Kryon of Magnetic Service. This is the moment that you have given permission for, which would allow an entourage of those whom you know so well to come pouring into this place.

Quite often you will feel it from the back of the room, moving toward the front, as we encompass all of this room and the surrounding areas with a bubble of love. Dear ones, we invite you to feel something unique. We invite you to feel the interdimensional spiritual family as we come forward to walk between the seats, some to kneel in front of you and wash your feet.

I speak to lightworkers—not only those who have been doing spiritual work for many years, but also to those who are just now becoming aware. The spark inside is starting to vibrate, and to some, the vibration is turning into the note of F, which is the heart chakra. That's where it all starts, you know. Understand, dear ones, that awakening to the divinity within does not begin in some strange way that feels odd, unusual, or fearful. Every recorded angelic communication experience known to humanity started with the words "fear not." This communication, as before, is about love. Therefore, the awareness of it begins at the heart chakra. This is where it emanates from, and where it is felt first. Then it evolves into the head, moving into wisdom, then into absolute knowledge.

So what we are saying, dear family, is that the invitation is open for you to first feel it here [Lee places his hand on his heart]. That is why we also say that those who feel Spirit in the fullness of love in this hour will find themselves feeling it first in the heart. This is also where discernment starts, and this is where you often feel a validation of energy. There is much to say about the energy of compassion regarding the ability for Humans to change themselves.

There is nothing that can get to you faster than the love of God and family. That is what is here today. Other family members are here, also, to honor you and sit next to you. Some of you will feel them manifesting themselves here in this very room. Some of you will see colors on the stage before you leave this room. The "see-ers" are invited to watch the colors as they develop and change on this very platform, indicating the 4D reality of what is happening here.

The love of Spirit manifests now in this fashion because you have asked for this. I've said this before, but perhaps it will be more understood now: The experience of the channelling of Kryon, as you are hearing and feeling it now, cannot happen unless there are Humans in the room! That may give you a hint as to what is to come. It is a two-way event! You are not simply listening to, or reading, the words of a Human Being as he gives you messages from the other side of the veil. Indeed, what you have here, as you hear and read, is an experience in what we have called The Third Language. There is energy moving between us—an energy of love at the heart level. There is an energy of knowingness at the angelic level. There is a divine language that spreads through this room and creates a remembrance in those who wish to remember.

This is going to be an unusual, interdimensional teaching event here today, and I'll tell you why. I am designating this, my partner, as the last channelling to be transcribed in the new publication [speaking of the book you are holding]. It concludes with this message, although this one is the actual beginning of a new series of interdimensional training. In addition, today's interdimensional information may seem strange indeed—perhaps as strange as any information brought forth yet. We are asking that this particular message be transcribed and published, and therefore, we are indeed speaking directly to those sitting in the chairs, as well as to those who are reading this material.

Whereas, listener, you may say that this energy is specifically for you (and it is), you might not realize that the energy of this moment is for everyone who is reading, also. Therefore, what is taking place involves many more than you can actually see in this room. In our reality (on our side of the veil), we see those reading this right now. We see the thousands who will be touched by the energy, along with you who are listening.

So, listener, we invite you to practice your interdimensionality right now: Envision with me, will you not, that the room goes far beyond the wall in the back. There are those reading these words with one pair of eyes, feeling the energy that you are feeling as well. And so we ask you, as you sit here listening, to welcome the family that is now also reading this! It's a good exercise, is it not? It's a suspension of the "time rules," as you know them. And this is only the beginning of the exercise—suspension of time.

Can you, dear linear one, suspend the linearity of your time clock and feel the energy of what is to come? Can you participate in the potentials of those who will read these words and also have a chance to feel what you feel? Moreover, reader, can you feel the energy of the room in what you now call your past? I want you to understand that to those in this room, I am speaking to the future. To those reading this, I am speaking to the past. But the middle is the true reality, where the NOW exists. Can you be in both? Can you join with us all in such a way that you actually meet and greet the thousands in this "now room"? I think you can.

Let the thickness of the love of Spirit lay upon this group and those reading right now, to facilitate understanding in what we have to say. For we are going to give you information that is interdimensional. Some of it will be understood, and some of it will not be until a second reading, perhaps even a third. Then you will begin to know what we are telling you.

Here is a good exercise in interdimensionality. My partner has told you this in the past, and you can even read it in this book that you hold: We expected you here! Reader, we expected your eyes on the page. Listener, we expected you to sit in the seat where you sit, and do you know why? I must tell you that there is something a lot bigger going on here than just words on a page or sound in the air. There's a mutual communication going on. There's an angelic group who knows who you are, sitting around you. There's a system for you to be here, and to be reading these words. It's a system of care and unconditional love—of protection and intent. It's a system you designed, where your intent is so powerful that it's transmitted regarding your potentials, even before you arrived—even before you obtained the book you're looking at! It's a system that validates all that you suspected about the interdimensionality of your spiritual family . . . a very caring and aware group of interdimensional angels.

We know who you are! There's more than one of you here for healing . . . there are hundreds! Aren't you tired of frequent trips to the doctor? Why don't you transform the reality you *think* you're in, to the one you *can* be in? We're going to talk about that in a moment—and perhaps that's why you came to hear and read. Dear family, we know who you are—by name! You are one who sits here and reads or listens, and you are seen right now by all of us.

I speak to others now who are doubting that this could be real. We know of the challenges in your lives, too. Maybe that's why you came, to hear a few snatches of words here and there—maybe to feel some energy, perhaps not. We're going to tell you something anyway, now that we have your attention. There are no problems in your life that are not solvable in a win-win situation. You can create a reality that you thought impossible—and you can get out of a situation that you think is impossibly black and bleak. There are solutions that are truly interdimensional that you cannot conceive of, but that your spiritual being knows of. It's up to you whether you will receive them or whether you wish to follow the old setup—the old contract that didn't allow for your new interdimensional aspects to be used. Which is it for you? You are truly in charge of what happens.

We are going to speak of the true interdimensional Human Being. We are going to give you an example and a visualization to start this teaching off. Let's say that somebody gives you a piece of paper. On that paper is drawn the outline of a Human form—and they give it to you along with some coloring sticks and say to you, *"Go ahead, color yourself in."* What are you going to do with that drawing? Visualize yourself coloring it in. What's your color? Where do you start? Now we're going to tell you that this has nothing to do with color. [Laughter] It was a trick. We give you this visualization, for we wanted to test your consciousness. Did you stay within the lines, or not? [Laughter]

For those who colored outside the lines, you're getting the idea. Perhaps you filled the page with color! If you did, you're still only half right about what you "look like." The page isn't big enough to contain who you are! The old energy paradigm has you coloring the illustration very carefully and neatly— within the lines. You instinctively feel that the Human Being is defined as the entity in your skin. Well, it is not and never was. Those who "see" the colors will tell you that. For they do not see you "within the lines," but rather they see the colors surrounding you. Many energy workers are apt to "feel" you from a distance. What's going on?

We have told you before that the higher you vibrate, the farther out your energy field extends. We have told you that some of you can actually claim the higher length of your Merkabah, up 27 feet. Did you know that? How's that for coloring outside the lines? Dear Human Being, it is time to see yourself in this fashion—every day. You are far larger in your energy field than you think you are.

I'll give you one of the tests. Do you know who can sense this, if not actually see it? The Indigo Child! The Indigo Child can sense imbalance. Certain kinds of Indigos are better at it than others, but there are interdimensional Indigos who sense it profoundly. They are actually "intergalactic" Indigos, but you have called them interdimensional. These Indigos have their "antennae" out, and they see you coming! Test it! Go into a room where there is a small child—perhaps a public place. Say nothing and make no noise. Intuitively "call" to the child with your mind. Smile and look his way. Unless distracted, quite often the child will turn to see the origin of the energy! He wants to find out where the "light" is coming from.

Lightworker, I challenge you to try this with an Indigo and feel the proof of what we speak. The child knows at some level who has entered the room, and at some level there's an awareness that is far beyond what you've called the five senses. And when it happens, you have to ask, *Why would the child turn and look at you?* This is real! It's because the lightworker is far larger than you might think, in interdimensional energy.

We have spoken of this only briefly before—coloring out-side the lines. Now it's time for you to understand what you can do that relates to this interdimensionality. In previous channel-lings, we have given you information that says, "You shine when you enter a room." We have explained the integrity of that so that you would be comfortable with the fact that you are not forcing your energy onto anyone else, for that would not be appropriate. Instead, you enter quietly, with the four aspects of love in place. You are quiet, with no agenda; you are not puffed up with pride. You are there just to be there, drawn to a certain place, just to shine your light for a moment or two. In the process, you allow those around you to see their paths more clearly. This is not evangelistic energy work. This is enabling energy work. Those in the room may not even be aware of who is among them, but they will be aware of your light at some level.

Decisions may be made, and paths changed, because your light showed them a clearer sight. Do you have any idea what we're saying? Maybe this explains why you're "stuck" in that job! What about the people around you? Do you think about that? Maybe you're not stuck at all. What if you were an ambassador of light? Maybe that's part of the puzzle you *didn't think about*. Maybe you were drawn to that "awful" place because that's where you belong—to hold light in a place that needs it. Maybe it's time for you to look around, ambassador, and start seeing where your light is being anchored. Is it in a place you feel has no good energy at all? Have you ever contemplated your magnificence? Angel, disguised as a Human Being, you are magnificent! How many times do we have to tell you that the angels are here to honor your path? How often do we have to sit next to you, unseen, and love you so strongly that you "feel something weird in the room"? How often do we have to give you the 11:11 "high sign" before you understand that we are around you?

I want to give you information about three attributes—three gifts that you haven't really thought of, that are inter-dimensional. As my partner says, *"Here come the eye-rollers!"* We are at it again, are we not? For every few years we open a box that sounds odd and unusual until science proves it. Then we do it again. So it continues here in this room for your listening, and for those reading.

The Compression of Time

Each of you has the ability to personally compress time—that variable that you always felt was unchanging. It is now yours to play with! And you can test it tomorrow if you like. Dear ones, some of you are beginning to understand what we call the ascension process—that of moving into higher dimensions. Do you feel as if things are going faster? Are some of you sensing the movement of time quickening, even though your clocks read the same as usual? This is because you're beginning to sense a time attribute where you can manipulate your own lives. We even ask you to try it!

Some of you will be aware of traveling distances in a portion of the time it took before, and you wonder where the time went! Some of you are task oriented, so we give you a challenge. You know how long certain tasks normally take to accomplish. Take a look at the clock when you start a task like this, and look again when you're finished. Sometimes you will find yourselves creating a situation where you've accomplished far more in a short period of time than is humanly possible! What happened? You're practicing "time compression."

Some have been doing this unconsciously for years. Now we're telling you that with practice, you will be able to schedule this kind of event for yourself. For this is a personal attribute and a personal gift . . . this time compression. And when you start to see how this works, it will simply be the beginning of understanding your interdimensionality and what it also means with respect to what you call "reality." Time compression—some of you have experienced it already and some of you will soon. The invitation is out there for you to actively practice it.

Now, why would we be telling you about this? Because many of you are going to find out soon that there's just too much to do! [Laughter] Remember the complaints to Spirit within the past years? Perhaps you didn't think we heard you? Some of you have said, *"I wish to do this and do that; I'm stuck and stopped."* Well, the new complaints will be, *"Dear Spirit, slow down! There's just too much for me to do—too many avenues—so much happening. Which road do I take?"* Some of you will need time compression.

Within this interdimensional gift, there is also the promise of time compression while sleeping. Here is what this means: Dear ones, it is a four-hour sleep period that gives you eight hours in rest. Do you understand what I'm saying? It's sleeping less, yet being far more fulfilled than ever before in energy for the next day. We invite you to practice this, for it is yours for the taking. The old paradigm is gone. If you find yourself saying, *"I need this much hourly sleep to exist,"* you are then placing a clamp upon a specific reality and holding it in place, not allowing it to change. Instead, say this, *"I will take as much sleep as my body needs."* Before you retire at night, say, *"It doesn't matter how many hours I sleep; when I awake I will have the same rest as though (in the old paradigm) I had slept eight hours."*

Now, watch what happens—you'll experience productivity and rest like you've never had before! This gift is well within your grasp. Everyone is different and on a variety of levels of training and wisdom, even of the acceptance of the hugs that are here today. Some of you don't wish to be touched with our energy yet, and we know that. Some of you are just beginning to understand that there are angels and guides around you, and we know that. We honor all your processes. For the rest of you—

those who are seeing the colors change [on the stage] and feeling the energy in the room, it's because we're hugging you, if you haven't noticed. Some of you have felt your feet washed and you can't seem to move your legs. That's a reality of what's going on here, if you didn't know it before.

Shifting Reality

Interdimensional Humans have the ability to shift reality and heal themselves. This is information we gave you in the middle of last year [1999]. But now you sit in a new energy where you are able to not only absorb this information, but to work with it. Here's how it works and always has, and we can now explain it in a way that an interdimensional Human can understand. You want to know what miracles are? They're shifting reality! You want to know how they work? The Human shifts the very reality of time, and the cells respond!

Did you come and sit in your chair for healing? We'll examine how it's done. This shifting of reality is going to take practice, but the interdimensional Human Being will know how. A moment ago we asked you to do something—to place yourself into the future where the readers of something yet to be transcribed are in the same energy as you are [speaking to the listening group]. Can you do this, and feel the family who has their eyes on the page? If you can do that, then you can also go in the other direction. We want you to participate in a reality that is as solid as the one you think you're sitting in now. You're actually looking at a multiple reality, like shelves in a cabinet. You carry around the cabinet deciding just which reality you may wish to sit in today. Let me tell you, there are multiple realities in the cabinet. There may be one you wish to sit within that you haven't thought of—the one we are going to display now. Get rid of the idea that the "reality cabinet" only has one shelf!

I ask you to take yourself to a place, or a reality of an energy, that made you sick. Go back to the time before the event happened. We want to take you back to a time that was peaceful and joyful in your life. *"Kryon,"* you might ask, *"you are asking us to remember?"* NO. I am asking you to re-create something that is yours, something that you experienced as a reality in what you call your past. I'm asking you to bring it up to your vibration and *feel* it.

"Kryon, you are asking us to move around in the reality of time." Yes, I am. We have established that time is variable, and that reality is only what you make it. It is not set and not established for life. It is not something that is uncontrollable. Can you bring back that joyful reality of your past? If so, there are now two realities in front of you. One—the one you came here with, where you are troubled and think you're sick. Two—the one you call your past, where you are youthful and healthy, or unburdened with worry.

Take yourself to a time when you were whole and peaceful. Live in that moment totally, and own the reality of it. Now there will be those who say, *"Kryon, you are asking us to pretend."* No, I'm not. I'm asking you to visually go there, encompassing all of the sensations you can muster—the loved ones, sights, sounds, tastes, smells, emotions, and weather. Perhaps only for a moment, but when your cells begin to understand and feel that you've changed the reality of your consciousness, you will begin to understand why spiritual people can live longer.

You have always had this ability. That's a miracle! It's how profound healing works. You don't get healing in your body by hoping it goes away! You don't heal your body by praying and asking something evil to leave. You heal your body by taking it to a time when it was clean and perfect—maybe at the moment of birth! That is a shift of reality, and the cells will willingly go where the divinity asks them to be! Did you know that? But you absolutely have to feel it for this to work.

I'm giving you information here that is years away from fulfillment for many, yet it's very real to some who sit here listening and reading. There will be those who grasp this today and will walk out of the room different from when they came in. There will be those precious ones whose eyes are reading this, who are beginning to understand why they picked up the book. I know this, because I'm seeing the healing and the colors. Remember, Spirit sees potential!

Youthing

The third one is related, and we're going to call it *youthing.* Can you slow down your aging? Yes! You can do it magnetically, chemically, energetically, and interdimensionally. Let's discuss the interdimensional one. Dear Human Being, you can do it while you sit in the chair. I'm going to give you something you haven't thought about, and it may be confusing because it has to do with relative reality. The interdimensional part of YOU is speeding up. The chemical part of YOU that has the clock in it is seemingly staying the same. But when you put the two together [meld Spirit and biology], you have an interesting process: The interdimensional YOU is speeding up, and it makes the chemical part of YOU *appear* to be slowing down.

Think of it this way. Which is the *real* YOU? Many would say that there is no difference, but there is! The interdimensional YOU can live faster, have more energy, and sleep less. This is almost like creating time between the clicks on the watch—time where you live actively, while the biology still chugs along at the old pace. Why is it, do you think, that you can compress time? It's due to this very relative principle.

You have the ability, with the understanding of this dimensional relativity, to slow the aging process almost to a crawl! Angel, you have the ability to change the reality of your life in the very aging of your cells! Again we say that in order to do this, there must be a communication between the spiritual YOU and the physical cellular YOU. They must both become a meld of the spiritual YOU. This creates this relativity of reality, and every cell in your body must be involved.

This is not magic. There is a chemistry in your body that regulates how long you live and how fast you metabolize. You are sending signals to this chemistry to change, and therefore your cells will take on a new, slower inner clock. Also, don't expect to feel the same! Don't do this unless you're ready to feel different than you have most of your life! This is very real and will take your intent, practice, understanding, wisdom, and permission.

Practice this. It may take time for some of you, but also some of you may start to feel it—sleeping less with more energy, feeling more youthful. Some of you will actually start to see it in the mirror! And then, dear ones, when some of you start to see it in real 4D, perhaps you will also grasp the other stranger parts that we've also been giving you.

In review, the body meld works in a wonderful way when the interdimensional Human Being begins to vibrate faster. Time is transcended, and the cells seem to age less. Perhaps now you will understand why some of the documented deaths of the shamans had the cells of the body unaware of the death of the whole! They lived on, and very slowly expired, long after a normal time of decay. This is the exact process we have discussed. Becoming interdimensional tends to change the apparent body clock and cellular awareness of an old 4D paradigm. The proof of this is all around you.

With spiritual knowledge and vibrational increase, comes an overview. With an overview, comes wisdom. With wisdom, comes joy. Blessed is the Human Being who understands that to walk the Earth can be a joyful experience. Blessed are the Human Beings who understand that even while being tested, they can smile and hold hands with the guides and family members around them, and know that they are dearly loved. They can have an element of joy, no matter what the test is. Do you think you're in trouble? We know who's here! We know who's reading! We challenge you to have joy through it. It is the catalyst for healing, and your cells will know it and feel it. Why do you think it is that a deep laugh is felt from the toes to the tip of the head? Joy! The great healer. Joy is also compassionate.

Dear ones, I hope you're grasping all of this. We have given you some of the secrets of longevity and the secrets of healing the most profound diseases that may invade your body. It may turn around some of the biology that has been disturbed and unbalanced for years. How would you like to be rid of it? You *can* be. You can leave this place different from how you came in. You can raise from the reading place differently from when you sat down. You can have the beginning of a cellular understanding of this entire concept of becoming interdimensional. It is appropriate in the angel body that sits in front of me or reads the words on the page. You cells know about this!

Interdimensional Business

Now I'm going to change directions and speak about something very different. Some will ask, *"Where did that come from?"* I want to talk about business! Interdimensional Human Being, do you think that God knows of the culture you sit in? What about money? It has been called evil and the root of sorrow. It is simply energy. Energy worker, do you know how to move energy? Then you'll know how to create abundance. That's all it is, yet you assign value to it where it seems hard to obtain. In addition, you assign to it an attribute that is fearful! You say, *"There's only so much money, so if somebody gets some of it, I lose that portion."* In reality, you set yourself up for failure, due to rules you also made up. Again, your consciousness clamps off what you might otherwise have.

Understand this: Your feeling of abundance in business is the way the contests work on your planet—someone wins and someone loses. It's an old paradigm that has nothing to do with your interdimensional life, and does not represent the way things work interdimensionally. No. Your life is much different from this, and so is business. I want to talk about business and money challenges for some of you. First, you don't think Spirit knows about this, do you? Spirit is a master business partner and knows how it all works! [Laughter] But we know you don't really think so.

Perhaps you are a good businessperson. You might not want to consult Spirit because you think God is about things that are spiritual—and business is not! I have news for you—the best business people in the world are the ones on the other side of the veil, sitting next to you, called your guides! They know more about your business than you ever will. They're experts—every one of them! That's where the source is and where the synchronicity comes from, you know. Why would you separate business from energy? Why would you separate business from spirituality?

You might say, *"Kryon, you and those on the other side of the veil don't understand competition. Humans compete for the same space—even with other lightworkers."* [Laughter] Who is going to win, you might ask? Interdimensional Human Being, you are in a circle where you all win! Let me give you a challenge. In your current reality of business, you are in a very small box. It's one of small thinking, where you think that if you bring in certain customers, then someone else is going to lose, or, heaven forbid, others would get customers and you would lose! Isn't this right?

Here's how interdimensional business works. It's done with visualization in a very special way. It depends on the unseen, and also on the fact that linear time is not the important factor. Oh, and did I mention that it works? And did I mention that it takes compassion?

First, visualize your competitors. You know who they are. Visualize them with more customers than they could ever handle. Think of the one competitor that gives you the hardest time in business, and make them abundant in your visualization. That is the test. Create compassion in your mind that aligns with what they will feel like with all that business!

"Kryon, now we absolutely know that you don't know about business!" Some will shout when they hear this. *"That's crazy talk!"* But dear interdimensional Human Being, if you can do this, I'm going to tell you what will happen to you: Double the abundance. Give away the fear, and fill the pockets of your competitors with your visualization. Then see yourself abundant as well, and feel the same joy as they do. See both of you successful. Then watch what happens in your own life. You think we don't know about the dynamics of business? Try it. You see, we're looking at an interdimensional situation where the games end with a win-win. There's no finite amount of abundance. It comes from so many sources that you never knew were there!

When you have a room filled with Humans who need healing, is there fear that there isn't enough to go around? No! There is never a question about the abundance of Spirit's gifts. Then why is there a problem with business or money? It's from the same source!

We speak now of money. We speak now of health. We speak now of joy. We speak about peace in situations that are impossible to have peace within. Are you listening? I know who you are, and this is for you. Interdimensional Human Being, this is for the taking. You can shift reality. The exercise is easy. Take yourself to a place "before" where you are now. If you were ever in an abundant place, take your reality there and make yourself feel it.

You didn't think we'd ever speak about business, did you? Yet it's as sacred as anything else you do in your culture and in your life. You can honor people by the way you do your business, and you can co-create abundance for you and your family with it. But many of you have isolated it from anything spiritual.

Speaking of this kind of bias, there are businesses on this planet and in your culture where you would never associate integrity and spirituality. You think it's one or the other, and you never see them as partners. I'll give you an example of one you would never associate with Spirit: your law profession! Most of you have never associated it with anything spiritual. Yet this profession is about justice and correct thinking. It's often about morality as well, and it calls for great wisdom.

I want to tell you that this profession is no different from any other business. It's time that those in it, and there are those here [speaking of the Clearwater audience] who hear these words and what I speak of because they are practicing it now. You can have integrity and be in this law business and still have a win-win, but it will take interdimensional thinking and coloring out of the lines. Open up and color outside the lines. Light is seen in all businesses, where there is intent, compassion for the competitor, and interdimensional thinking.

Interdimensional Life on Earth

We are going to give you more information right now about one of the highest curative substances known to Humans. You're going to see more cures arise in these next 12 years than you've ever seen in Human history from "water." We've opened this subject before, but we told you only a small portion of what we wished to.

When we were talking about live-essence medicines in these past years, we can now tell you that we were talking about water. You may say, *"Kryon, water isn't alive, and it never was or will be."* Dear ones, you may say that since you don't know the truth. Water is teeming with interdimensional life. I told you there would be some *eye-rollers today!* The very atmosphere of your planet has interdimensional life in it—life forms that live on the planet in the air and in water, that are interdimensional, and which you cannot see. Science is going to begin to discover anomalies about this very thing. The brave ones will also begin to mention that there could very well be interdimensional life, things they cannot see, but which, by their very definition, must be alive. Water.

Here's what's happening. Certain kinds of treatments of water, both natural and by using magnetism, chemistry, and atomic structure alerting, affect the interdimensional life within it. This, therefore, changes the very attributes of the life within it. When ingested into the interdimensional Human Being, these attributes of life in water then interact with the water in your body. Do you understand what I'm saying? It's time to understand why this is taking place.

You may find that chemistry enhances some water, but let me tell you that there's far more going on here than you can see. The word *holographic* has also been mentioned today [by Dr. Todd Ovokaitys], but it is far beyond that, too. By addressing water magnetically, you are actually changing the life within it. This then changes the reactions within your body to the water. You actually touch into the interdimensionality of a certain kind of life that lives in the water.

Now, don't compartmentalize this. Color outside of the lines, and understand that this interdimensional life is not like your life. It's interdimensional, and do you know why it's there? It's there for *you!* Just like the dirt of the earth, it's there to help balance humanity when the Human gives it recognition! It's so that water will become a healing attribute on the planet. There's water coming out of the ground in three places that you have discovered already on the planet, which has some attributes of interdimensionality within it. Therefore, it has powerful curative effects on the Human body. Yes, there really is a fountain of youth. Perhaps its reputation was exaggerated, but there is water that will slow the aging process! It functions in this way right out of the ground due to the specific magnetics of the ground areas where it traveled from, on its way to bubble to the top.

There is interdimensional life in water, which *shakes hands* with the interdimensional cellular life of your DNA. It will actually change some of the imprints, some of the instructions sets, and some of the ways in which your biology works. I'm talking again about the clock inside you. This is just the beginning of an explanation we are only now beginning to evolve for you—things we could not tell you in 1999 or before, since the vibration of your acceptance wasn't high enough. For there are those in this room who will understand fully what is being said. It exists for you, right in front of your nose, to complement and heal the Human body. That's why it has always been there. Those of you who understand and have felt the interdimensional life in nature, in the rocks, and in the plants, have felt these life forms.

"Kryon, do you mean real life forms?" Yes. *"Do you mean life that reproduces and lives in an interdimensional space in water and air?"* Yes. *"Why haven't we seen it, then?"* Because you haven't been willing to look! Who in your biological sciences could get funding for an interdimensional life study? This is still a very uncharted area of research, and your science doesn't even have a program yet to examine the possibility.

Here's something, however, that you should know. As we told you sometime ago, this life has *shadows* that are visible in the atmosphere. In other words, portions of it can be seen as the result of its existence, but you can't really look at it. The same is true in water, but it will be far harder to see, since water is fairly uniform.

In review, we are speaking about a brand new issue—interdimensional life on Earth both in water and in air. And in water, your magnetic treatment of it changes the characteristics of the life within, thereby carrying an invisible curative energy into the body. Since your body is made mostly of water, the treated water then commingles with the very fluid of life, passing a live-essence healing into the biology at the cellular level.

And you thought there was nothing new!

I'm going to give you another visualization before closing. It's not pretend. This is your ability to visualize another reality. We've told you in other channellings that the catalyst to an increased vibration is forgiveness. We've talked about dropping the vows that you've made in the other lifetimes—the vows that were promises to God. We've invited you to do that in channelling after channelling. It is now old core information, but it's still important, so we remind you again.

So many of you sit here hearing and reading this, who were shamans and monks in past lives. You all made important vows to God. As we've said before, these promises carry over the veil. Perhaps you didn't remember that? Perhaps you are one here, sitting alone, and you feel that your romantic relationships never seem to work out? Did you know that you gave a vow to God so they wouldn't? It's called being alone and pure so that you could be married to God. These are vows of celibacy carried through the veil from lifetime to lifetime, and we've given you this information before. There are also those of you who are reading this who gave vows of poverty. And you wonder why you don't have abundance? It's time to drop all those vows.

Interdimensional Human Being, you're outside of any lines you ever knew before. They are gone, and so are the old ways of thinking. It's time you claimed the new energy as your own. I'll give you a visualization. I want to gather around you every single relative who has ever lived on this planet whom you can remember or sense right now. Take yourself there. Gather even the difficult ones whom you remember, dead or alive. Surround yourself with them. As you do, they're actually here waiting for you to do this at an interdimensional level.

If you want to, create this reality. Make it very real for yourself. Feel it! Now I want you to look them in the eye and to the appropriate ones, say, *"I forgive you."* Surround yourself with the people where you work, and do the same. Look the family in the eye and release that edge that you carry around of things that were said, or a situation where you felt you were wronged. I want you to surround yourself with the entire family and get interdimensional!

Let the thickness of this forgiveness spread all over them. Don't be surprised if it's reciprocal, since this is a catalyst to being loved. This process is needed if you want to go to the next step in your evolutionary trip of spirituality. Call it clearing, if you wish, but this is needed. You can't carry these old feelings into an area that is pure. Use your compassion of inner spiritual knowing to create this forgiveness. Then feel the joy of the release!

The hardest thing we do is leave. We only come for one reason, and that is to enable the Human Being. There's no agenda in this visit. As my partner has said so many times, we are not taking your names so that we can find you later! [Laughter] I'll tell you something that's kind of funny in retrospect. Some of you will leave here with energies that you didn't come in with. Some of you will rise from the chair where you read, and you'll feel different. If you gave interdimensional intent for it, this can be so!

Some of you will leave here with guides-within-guides. This is interdimensional! It's time for you to understand that a guide is not just an angel or an entity that has a name and lives with you. Did you know that part of YOU is within your guides? *"How can that be?"* you might ask. Did you know that part of YOU is not here? It is because you are an interdimensional piece of God! When you can understand God, and the secrets of the Universe, you will understand your guide situation. Don't try to compartmentalize an interdimensional energy and then define it. Instead, celebrate that it exists in any way you can understand it! Celebrate the fact that you are never alone! Celebrate the I AM!

We have come here to sit between the chairs and hug you, blessed ones. For a few moments, we wanted to be intimate with family, and we have felt your hugs returned. For a few moments, we wanted you to know we exist and perhaps touch you on the shoulders or neck to give you a sign that this communication is more than just words. It's real.

Reader, this is for you, as well as those here in these chairs. You think you sit alone reading this page? There is an entourage around you that does nothing more than want you to have joy, claim your divinity, and begin to feel your angelic pieces and parts. We want you to be peaceful because you deserve it!

You haven't come here to suffer. You have come here to find the reality of joy that surrounds the Human Being who discovers the truth about spiritual things. You have come here to find the angel with your name . . . living far outside the lines!

And so it is!

Kryon

The 2001 International Conference on Science and Consciousness

There has been a major surge of interest recently in studying consciousness as more and more people have experiences that cannot be explained by traditional scientific approaches.

At some point in history, a split occurred, and we ended up with Science and Religion. Science limited its study to the material world, and the Church took charge of the metaphysical realms.

Now, with science studying consciousness, we are ready to reintegrate Spirituality and Science.

At this conference, we will explore the scientific and spiritual dimensions of Consciousness. Come explore with us the frontier where Science and Consciousness meet.

"There is a great desire now to find the connections between different parts of our society, our civilization—science and religion being the two large subdivisions that need to be reconnected."

—Vice-President Al Gore

(The above, reprinted from the
"The Message Company" web page)
For more information, contact: (505) 474-0998
[http://www.bizspirit.com/science/index.html]

"The Death Phantom"
and
"The New Kids Have Arrived!"

Jan Tober

Chapter Thirteen

"Expanding on Concepts"

From the writer . . .

A few years ago, Kryon channelled some information that is now "in our faces," in this year 2000. This is what he brought to light:

(1) As odd as it sounded at the time, he spoke of "Shadow Termination." You can find this term described on page 276 of Kryon Book Seven, *Letters from Home*. It talked about how some of us actually felt that it was time to go, with the whole body beginning to shut down, including the emotions. This was due to what Kryon called "the recipe for termination most of us have regarding 1999 and 2000." As you know, we didn't fulfill our own prophecies, and instead, we remain here. This is the subject of this very book.

(2) The Indigo Children. You can find the first information regarding the phenomenon of the Indigo Children in Kryon Book 6, *Partnering with God*, page 255. Then came the book, *The Indigo Children*, released in 1999 by Jan Tober and myself. (See page 389.)

The Indigo Children book has become our bestseller of all time, and it has been on the top of metaphysical distributors' bestselling lists for almost a year (as I write this book). Not only that, but it has broached mainstream publishing, and you can go to the major bookstore chains in almost any English-speaking country and find it in the "Parenting" section! Jan and I laugh about the fact that many readers only know us from the Indigo book, and are shocked to find out that Jan and I have been involved in the Kryon work, traveling extensively for ten years. Portions of the Indigo interview (to follow) show that this was actually the case with the interviewer, who had no idea who Kryon was.

In this next section, we would like to give you further information on both subjects. Jan Tober, my spiritual partner and fellow channell/author, has had direct experience with Shadow Termination, which is being renamed "The Death Phantom"—*phantom* meaning that it isn't real, but it certainly looks like it.

Here is the dictionary's definition of *phantom*: "Something apparently seen, heard, or sensed, but having no physical reality."[1] The first section of this chapter, "The Death Phantom," has been published on the Kryon Website for some months, and letters we received have indicated that it has helped many understand this experience. Just for the record, this is an experience we gave ourselves, not something that Kryon gives us.

Jan has also been concentrating on the Indigo Children issue, presenting seminars and interviews in these last few months on the subject. We felt that it would be a good idea to produce a recent interview from *The Spectrum* newspaper written by Rick Martin in Las Vegas, Nevada (two months before this book was published), to add to the Indigo information already out there. In addition, some of you might not be aware of our book, *The Indigo Children*, so this article may help you better understand what we're talking about. Also, see [www.indigochild.com].

—Lee Carroll

[1] Excerpted from *The American Heritage® Dictionary of the English Language, Third Edition* © 1996 by Houghton Mifflin Company. Electronic version licensed from INSO Corporation; further reproduction and distribution in accordance with the Copyright Law of the United States. All rights reserved.

"The Death Phantom"
by Jan Tober

There is an interesting process afloat that many of us are moving into. Tobias, part of the Kryon group, refers to this clearing as "The Death Phantom." This is a situation we have set up to terminate life as we know it in the physical realm. It is based on old information—information that says that the body-mind-soul does not have the strength (for whatever reason) to move into Ascension and the new energy. We have been programmed with trepidation regarding the next 12 years, and much like Atlantis, we have been deciding whether to teleport, die, or stay; and for many of us, teleporting is unavailable at present.

Tobias, my twin flame and divine complement, very soberly and firmly walked me through my Death Phantom. Tobias is the part of the Kryon entourage that has been in the physical body—this is his specialty, so to speak. As we move into pure intent to activate and integrate our remaining strands of DNA, our intent is to release the death hormone and activate the youthing hormones, "the youth and vitality chromosomes." As this happens, it seems that for many, The Death Phantom also gets "charged." I now know four other people (three are close friends) including myself who have gone through this experience. Because it can be quite challenging, I would like to share pieces of my experience with you.

I realize that I've been dancing around this phantom consciously for two years. This spring I watched one of my closest friends go through three heart attacks in two weeks during her stay in the intensive-care ward of our local hospital. During that time, I phoned two *very large* prayer groups, and my own personal group of around ten powerful prayer group participants/healers. We began the long-distance healing. We did not speak to each other much that first week, but just stayed focused "in love" for my friend. The second week, the news became more grave. Pneumonia set in. We kept up our vigil. However, looking back, we now realize that we were being kept at a distance energetically.

For all practical purposes, we felt as if my friend's soul was really turning over its options. We confided in each other that this felt different from anything we had experienced before—almost as if we were losing her. As we diligently held the intent of "Thy will be done," we felt a sinking feeling. (Was this listening to the soul go through its choices?) We felt helpless—an extremely different feeling for those of us who have had miracle after miracle occur as a result of pure intent and prayer.

Just about the time we had emotionally released my friend and had begun to miss her, she sat up in her hospital bed and said, "That's it. I'm fine now! I'm staying!"

My own phantom experience was not so dramatic to anyone but me. As I went through my own medical scares, I suddenly did not feel the prayer group's "high." This was very different from normal. Usually, I sail through anything. I felt that I had passed the point of "no return." Heavy darkness set in for about two weeks. This was not my normal Pollyanna optimism. At this point, I must say that the support of my friends and energy soul sisters and brothers kept me on my feet. When I was at my lowest ebb, I even manifested 450 people at a seminar in Seattle, Washington, being told that I had "passed on" by a well-respected lecturer and teacher! Now I *knew* that I was in the middle of this event. At this point, I was able to access the origin of my Death Phantom (500 B.C.) Once this piece had been emotionally established and released and my polarity had been restored, the linear brain became activated. I realized that I had been "out of my body" most of the last two years. This was a protective and loving mechanism from my Higher Self as I prepared to move into death and resurrection.

I hope that the following information will help you understand and nurture yourself, should you encounter this challenge.

To summarize:

(1) You may feel very alone, even separated from Spirit. This
     seems to be the process.

(2) If you don't know what is happening, you're probably
     "doing" The Death Phantom. You will think you're
     making the transition called "death."

(3) Find the source and clear it from your past or present lives.
     Seek healers to ease you through.

(4) Be extremely kind and gentle to yourself. This is not the
     time to "push through." Take time off. Take time out.
     This is between you and your soul—no one else.

(5) Know that more can be accomplished in this new energy
     in the *physical body* than being in another dimension "on
     the other side."

(6) Repeat the above often. Create a mantra, such as, "I
     choose life. I love my life." I took long walks every
     morning and chanted in positive, loving mantras.

(7) Be with loving people of similar soul-energy. No one can
     fix you. However, the love and vitality of loved ones can
     ignite your own life force. Hold hands with loved ones and
     spiritually connected beings (physical touch is very im-
     portant).

(8) Lovingly bring your thoughts back to the Light. Hold
     your pure intent for being here in love. "Fake it 'til you
     make it!" Consciously take control of your inner dialogue
     and remember to affirm: "I CHOOSE LIFE!"

(9)   Place your name on lists of prayer groups. I have called Silent Unity for almost 30 years (for Silent Unity Prayer, call 816-969-2000).

(10)   Know that this experience may feel different. We're making it up as we go.

(11)   Do body cleansing—Epsom salt baths, meditation, and gentle exercise (walking, yoga, tai chi, etc.) is very important, as well as body polarity alignment.

(12)   Know you can get through this! We all did, and we're all here to help you.

(13)   When The Death Phantom is complete, when you have walked through it, you will remember walking through the Atlantean/Egyptian Seventh Door Initiation. It will be a grand time to celebrate! Ask your friends to join you. Bring in your inner child (the seat of your emotional body). She/he probably hasn't laughed for a while.

(14)   Most important, you will now manifest through thoughts and words more quickly than you've ever known you could. So be aware of your visions at a clearer level. Stay conscious for all that you manifest. The field is clear.

(15)   Verbalize to yourself daily:

"NOW, in Pure Intent,
 I CHOOSE LIFE!
 I CHOOSE RESURRECTION!"

—Jan Tober

"The New Kids Have Arrived!"
An Interview with Jan Tober
by Rick Martin

THE SPECTRUM newspaper
interview by Rick Martin[1]

The great Master Teacher of 2,000 years ago said: "Blessed are the children." These children will be the guides to return us, as a world, to the path of love.

To a lot of people, it's not really news that there is something very special going on with the children in this world. It's been happening for some time. There are those who say that the "forerunners" to this modern-day phenomenon started being birthed as long as 20 years ago. Futurists, such as Gordon-Michael Scallion, have been speaking of their planetary entrance for some years now, labeled by him as the Blue Children. To Nancy Ann Tappe, gifted with the ability to see the auric field of the human body, they are simply referred to as *Indigos*.

What does the presence of these "super kids" mean? What is their message? What is their purpose for being here, right now? Is this just a fanciful idea, or a reality? What are the Indigos, and what makes them "Indigo"?

Although it took some months to coordinate, I was finally able to speak with Jan Tober, the co-author of the provocative book called *The Indigo Children*, about this fascinating subject.

The book, while merely an "introduction" to the subject, is one that every teacher and school administrator should be required to read. If you have a child who is "a handful," if you have a child who has been diagnosed with Attention Deficit

---

[1] Portions of this article have been edited and revised. Complete interview not shown. Used by permission of Rick Martin and *Spectrum* newspaper. See end of article for *Spectrum* Website and address.

Disorder (ADD) or hyperactivity (ADHD), then by all means read this book! It should be in every library across the land.

It is obvious that, in an hour and a half, we were only able to scratch the surface on this subject. But if you've been feeling that there's no hope for the world, you'll get a definite "boost" from this story!

Let's move now directly into my discussion with Jan Tober on the subject of these wonderful, wild, provocative, and often exasperating "old" children.

Martin: Let's begin with a fundamental definition. Exactly what are the Indigo Children?

Tober: The definition that we are sharing, which rings true for us, is: An Indigo Child is one who displays a new and unusual set of psychological attributes, and shows a pattern of behavior generally undocumented before.

Martin: How did you arrive at the phrase "Indigo Children"?

Tober: The phrase *Indigo Children* comes from the color of the aura around these children. There's a dear friend of mine, whom I've known since the mid-1970s, by the name of Nancy Ann Tappe. Nancy has authored a book called *Understanding Your Life Through Color*.[2] It was printed in 1982. In that book is the first documented information about what she has "coined" the Indigo Children.

How does she see the color? How accurate is it? Nancy has been diagnosed with a situation where two of her neurological systems cross, and it creates a situation where she, literally, can see the human aura. She's like a Kirlian camera, if you will, and she sees electromagnetic fields and the colors and the frequencies. She's a fabulous gal, and a wonderful counselor and metaphysician and teacher.

[2] Nancy Tappe's book, *Understanding Your Life Through Color*, may be obtained by calling the Kryon 800 line—(800) 352-6657

She noticed, very early on, that there was another auric color associated with some newborns, when she was working on her Ph.D. Nancy has said that from 1980 on, about 80 percent of the children born have been Indigos. And, since 1995, we have a much higher percentage, so much so that we need to look at what's happening here.

We're seeing a new generation of Masters coming into the planet, and they have been called "Star Children," "Blue Children," and through Nancy's work, they are called, from our perspective, the "Indigo Children." They are our hope for the future. They are our hope for the present. And that, esoterically speaking, is what's *really* happening.

We try to keep the focus as pragmatic as we can, because we've got a lot of parents out there dealing with very *old* souls, in very tiny bodies, who, in most cases, know more than the parents!

And then, what do the parents do with that? There are metaphysicians/parents who have some ideas about alternatives. However, in the mainstream world, I don't know where they go, except to our book and a few other books that are getting out there.

Martin: I'm sure you've been asked a lot of standard questions, and I'm not sure if my questions will be quite as standard. One question that I'm just curious about—I want to move right into some of the deeper aspects—but have you been surprised or overwhelmed about the response you've gotten since this book has come out?

Tober: Yes and no. One is always a bit overwhelmed when they're in the middle of something that is in its perfect timing.

Martin: Good answer.

Tober: This information about the children came to me, intuitively, in the mid '70s, about the time I met Nancy, without realizing that she would be so connected with this information. To my knowledge, she was not talking much about the Indigo Children because the information was quite new. However, I would have dreams where children would come to me, and they would tell me who they were, why they came, who their parents were, and why they came karmically to be with these parents.

And it was fascinating. I would wake up from these dreams, and I would find myself being drawn to various babies and small children. I'd look in their eyes, and there I would see these little-bodied old souls. Then I would look around me and ask my friends: "Have you noticed a difference in the children?" And my friends would say, "Well, kind of."

I knew this was one of the reasons why I'm here. And I know, from the work that Lee and I do, that it certainly is a part of his mission, too. From that aspect, I was not surprised.

I knew it *had* to be done. It was like two very powerful hands pushing me forward into that area of my life. And then, as we traveled and worked with people, particularly over the last four years, parents, day-care providers, and teachers have told us that they've been frustrated by, and have acknowledged working with, some very unusual old souls.

And the question "What do we do?" is coming from the parents. And how on Earth do they help their children interface with the school system? There was so much frustration, and so much interest, that by the time we actually got the book out, we *knew* that its time had come!

Martin: Are you working on a follow-up?

Tober: Oh, gosh. (*Laughter*) Yes, Hay House has asked us to do a second book. I would also like to explain how your readers can contact us through the Kryon Website. [3]

Martin: And what is Kryon?

Tober: The Kryon Website address. [3]

Martin: This is different from the Indigo Children address? [3]

Tober: Oh! (*Laughter*) This is a whole other interview for you. Have you ever heard of the Kryon writings?

Martin: No.

Tober: Well, Lee and I don't talk much about this in Indigo interviews because the Indigo book is aimed at the mainstream public. We want to assist those parents who need help, and who have their nose right up into a prescription of Ritalin. You know what I mean?

Concerning Kryon: Lee and I travel worldwide speaking about the writings and teachings of Kryon—a Master angelic energy. We have actually spoken at the United Nations for the last three years. Lee channels Kryon, and I also channel the feminine aspects of the Kryon entourage. I do the meditations. We do balancing and group energy shifting. We spoke to 4,000 people this year in France and Belgium alone over a period of two days. It was amazing! The work is basically centered around the idea that "we create our own reality," which is certainly not a new concept, but it is our job to be clear channels for that information to come through repeatedly, to help people take back their power— to *re-member their power.*

Martin: This is just an aside. Have you heard of the book called *China's Super Psychics*, by Paul Dong and Thomas E. Raffill?

---

[3] The Kryon Website is: [http://www.kryon.com].
   The Indigo Website is: [http://www.indigochild.com].

Tober: That's who Drunvalo Melchizedek's speaking about?

Martin: Right.

Tober: People have been e-mailing us about it, and Drunvalo promotes our book in his workshop. He's a wonderful teacher.

Martin: Yes, he is.

Tober: And the information that we receive is that these super-psychics are all Indigos.

Martin: I assumed that. And, I would imagine, the same thing is happening in just about every country, but nobody has written a book about it; they just happened to choose the ones in China.

Tober: Well, China [and Asia, in particular] is very interesting. According to Nancy Tappe, basically all children now coming into Singapore will be Indigos. I realize that Singapore is technically not China, but it is in close proximity. We gave a very important seminar in Singapore in 1998 where Kryon described an opening portal. Nancy gave me her information before I told her about the portal. Lee and I needed to do a lot of clearing and cleansing with the land to hold the energy of the space we were in before we even started the workshop.

Martin: That makes sense.

Tober: She said, "Well, of course. There you are. That's why it's in Singapore." The trip was challenging for us in many ways, but very rewarding due to the fact that we knew we had helped in being a conduit for getting some of this movement focused—to help the Indigo souls come in.

You know, Rick, this is basically what we are dealing with—the Masters are coming in as right-brained individuals, coming into a left-brained world. Actually, they are right/left-brain integrated souls, and with that we're experiencing more right-brained consciousness than ever before—that is, developed intuition, etc.

Martin: It's gotta be tough.

Tober: I suppose you're hearing this as much as we are, but we're talking about the Divine Feminine coming in at this time—and not a moment too soon, may I add! [It's as if the last 3,000 years or so have been God's "out-breath," and now we move into the Goddess "in-breath."]

And the Divine Feminine and the Indigos go hand-in-hand. Who is to say where one starts and the other leaves off, or what came first? My feeling is that the Indigos have made the way for the Divine Feminine to be accessed and anchored here with relative smoothness. We needed a "critical mass."

That's what the Kryon work is about—to get a critical mass going who accept that through their consciousness, their thoughts, and their words and deeds, they create their reality; hence, we could create the reality here on Earth called Heaven.

That critical mass needed to be up and running, as the Indigos were starting to come in, so that there was a frequency that was refined enough so that they could come into the physical vehicle and have a higher frequency environment where they could stay—where they wouldn't have to "crib-death" themselves out of here, or leave even sooner, such as in spontaneous abortion, in some cases.

Martin: Along these lines, I want to talk to you about the misdiagnosis of Attention Deficit Disorder (ADD) and (ADHD), and the use of Ritalin to drug these children. Have you encountered a lot of Indigos who have been drugged, and, in your opinion, misdiagnosed?

Tober: Again, I work as an intuitive counselor. I do not work out in the area where a lot of my clients would put their children on Ritalin. They would go to alternatives, innately. However, in some of our audiences, which have a broader cross-section, we are experiencing instances where, maybe our audience member wouldn't go that route, but they would say: "My sister-in-law's child, my niece, my nephew . . . ," where they (audience members) are not the primary child caretaker. But they certainly know other Indigo parents or primary care-takers and teachers, etc.

I want to quote the percentages we shared in the book about the increase in the production of Ritalin: "Ritalin production has increased sevenfold in the last eight years, and 90 percent of it is consumed in the U.S."

The trend over the past few years has been clear: The percentage of children with an ADHD or ADD diagnosis walking out of a doctor's office with a prescription jumped from 55 percent in 1989, to 75 percent in 1996. And, if the truth be known, it's higher than that.

What's happening? What's happening is, we have a new paradigm of souls, of beings, coming into the Earth. We have them being shoved into a left-brained society, where, to be left-brained is to be honored; to be right-brained—that is, the artist, the musician, dancer, painter, writer, or creative thinker—is not to be honored. The Indigos are integrated and will help us as we move into brain-hemisphere balance.

So, they're coming into a left-brained world. To get their kudos, to get their strokes, to be *really* honored and respected, they have to try to fit into that old system. These souls, as Masters, *know* the truth and know that we are now moving into honoring the right-brain mode, and they are a significant part of that.

So, they're not going to fit in, even if they choose to. They're here on a mission lifetime—and that's a very impor-tant statement. *They're here on a mission lifetime!* They're *not* here to fit in. We are here to understand *them*, to learn from *them*, and to allow *them* to teach us a new way of being.

Back to your question. Because they're new and different, where do doctors go? Where do parents go? Where do teachers go? They've got children who would appear to be hyperactive, who have a low attention span, who can't stand in line—all of the symptoms that fit into something like the chicken or the egg.

I mean, which came first: ADD or the child of ADD? It's fitting into a type of pattern. They don't know what to do with it.

Now, if Ritalin healed the process, it would be different. I don't want to get into an AMA discussion, but there are so many incredible alternatives that take, maybe, a little bit more work, but my goodness, isn't your child worth it?

If the drug, Ritalin, heals, then fine. But it doesn't. It's just a coping mechanism or a Band-Aid. Inevitably, they will need to discontinue the drug and deal with life experiences they were meant to have. [And what about the lost "drugged time"?]

I recommend a book on ADD and ADHD: It's *The A.D.D. and A.D.H.D. Diet!*, written by Rachel Bell and Dr. Howard Peiper. I want to include this quote from the book. Although your audience is very savvy, it's a good idea for us all to stop and take a deep breath and think.

> *"People with ADD/ADHD lack sufficient supplies of neurotransmitters, especially seratonin. Seratonin is manufactured in the brain in the presence of B6 and tryptophan. Tryptophan is an essential amino acid. If tryptophan and B6 are in short supply, the body cannot make seratonin.*

> *"Therefore, people with ADD/ADHD may require supplements of tryptophan and/or B6. Protein supplies amino*

acids to the body. If the body contains sufficient protein and tryptophan-rich foods, the supply of amino acids will not usually be a problem. The calcium/magnesium ratio is a key factor, also. Insufficient magnesium can result in high insulin levels, which reduce seratonin. Therefore, it is necessary to ensure an adequate supply of magnesium, in addition to B6 and amino acids." [4]

It goes on. This is one of several books we recommend. The book is short, sweet, and concise.

First, we've got the Indigo constitution. We've got Indigo Masters coming in on a mission, saying: "We're going to help this planet shift into the Divine Feminine, one way or another. We're going to do it by coming in and being an example of love. You're going to learn how to treat us, and as you learn how to treat us, you're going to learn how to treat each other with love." I mean, that's the bottom line to all of this. When we learn how to love, be with, and parent the Indigo Child, we're learning how to operate at the highest level with each other. That's what they're teaching us.

So, we've got ADD/ADHD, okay. We've got a new paradigm coming in. They carry a lot of what has been labeled Attention Deficit Hyperactivity Disorder. It doesn't mean it is. What we're saying to parents is this: Please look at alternatives. We know it's challenging. That's why the book is out, so you can pick it up and look at the list of traits, and you can see that maybe there's not something wrong with your child; that your child is part of this new paradigm.

Now, how do we work with that? That's what the book is filled with—healthy alternatives, from diet to techniques. There's a technique called sleep-talk, where you work with

---

[4] Dr. Howard Peiper, Rachel Bell; *The A.D.D. and A.D.H.D. Diet!*; Publishers, Safe Goods; ISBN 1-884820-29-8; 1997; Ordering (800) 903-3837; Email <Safe@snet.net>; Website [http://www.animaltails.com]

the child in their sleep state. It's very powerful, and it needs to be taught to parents. I'm bringing some teachers with me, as I put together Indigo workshops around the country, who will shed light on some of these alternative choices.

There are all kinds of choices that parents can look at. Does your child respond to food allergies or environmental poisonings? We all have to get very, very savvy about all of this, and these children are going to force us into doing it—for ourselves, as well.

Martin: Because I'm aware of the time restraints we have here, let me ask you: You have a fantastic list on your Website of Montessori and Waldorf schools. And you talk about those as being excellent places for Indigos. What about those Indigos born into families that are economically disadvantaged? What do you say to people who just can't afford that kind of education?

Tober: There have been some wonderful results we've been hearing about with home schooling. There's a group in Houston—I believe there are about 40 families, maybe more, as of this interview, and they are successfully working with home schooling. That might be an alternative. That, certainly, would be an inexpensive alternative. They're getting wonderful results, and the children are walking right into Ivy League colleges.

I also know, within my heart of hearts, that there will be other forms of schooling coming up that may be not as cost prohibitive to families who don't have a comfortable income. And I know there is such a huge interest in Indigos, and what we can do to help them, that there are a lot of educators now who are also metaphysicians, who are joining forces and working on putting this schooling together.

I just worked with a client last week who asked me what I saw for her, and it was very, very clear that she was going to be working as part of this group. This was part of an intuitive counseling session that I did, and it turns out that she is ready to get her degree, and she does have people who are principals and vice principals who want to interface with her. So, where there's one, there's many.

I know that books are stirring—there's this book, and there will be many more. I'm in the process of about four more at this time; one with Lee, and three or four with other people in various areas of education, health, and Indigo-related subjects. We need to get these books out and get the attention of the people, because we must make enough of an inroad to create a "wedge of light" into the educational system and make space for these children. They are now arriving at such a high percentage that it can't be overlooked anymore.

Martin: Are there any foundations or clearing houses for information, other than your Website, for the Indigos? Is there a central place, or places, that are being established to study and work with these special children?

Tober: My information is that it will just be a matter of time before these are set up. It's too important and it's right in our face; and it's the next step in our evolution. So it will be done. And it is probably being done as we speak.

Martin: You've been around a lot. You've been traveling a lot. What do you think people need to know? What is the most useful information that you can pass on to our readers about this subject?

Tober: There are two words that, if we could say nothing more to you, we would say, in the parenting of the Indigo Child. In relating to the Indigo Child, the two words are: *choices* and *negotiate*. If you can remember nothing else, if you do not read our book, please just give them choices, and negotiate everything. I mean, certainly, they're not to run rampant over you.

But that is the parenting guide. If we can remember that they're here to teach us, that gives more of a balance to those words.

I want to share with your readers what parents can do to make a difference. In addition to giving them choices and negotiating with them, you can make a big difference by guiding them, rather than giving them explicit directions. Treat them and interact with them as your best friend, because in truth, they are. Treat them with respect. Honor their existence in your family. Help them create their own disciplinary solutions. You'll be amazed as a parent what they will come up with. And give them choices about everything. Never belittle them, ever. This is just good parenting advice. If we wanted to be the perfect parent, we would say: "This is the list I will follow." So, they are very simply saying: "Now is the time, and you get to practice being the perfect parent. Now is the time on the planet to do this."

Always explain why you give them the instructions you do. Never say, "Because I said so." Instead, say, "Because this will help me today. I'm a bit tired today. I need some help from you," knowing that honesty will always win out with them because they're intuitive. They know what's going on as you're thinking it.

Make them your partners in raising them. This is *extremely* important. This goes with choices and negotiation. Make them your partner. Let them know they always have a vote. Be *present* with them. And, of course, as a friend, as a grown-up family member, we ask always to be present when we're in a situation with people. I mean, that is "be here now." That's being in the moment. Metaphysicians innately know a lot of this. And explain everything to your children, if you think they don't understand something. Know that they *do* understand at the soul level. And we know we can talk to them before birth. Start early—how about even before conception!

If serious problems develop, and you feel you want to test them for ADD or ADHD, we do not say, "Don't go to doctors." What we say in the book is: "Look at some alternatives. For instance, diet, supplements, nutrition, homeopathy, chiropractic, and reverse polarity." Look at what's out there holistically. We offer a large list, and access to, alternative authors and alternative teachers to whom you can e-mail your questions and concerns.

Provide safety in your support. Avoid negative criticism. Encourage them in their endeavors. This is all stuff we know. An Indigo is not a follower. Let them decide what *they* are interested in, and what they want to do. Talk *to* them, not *at* them. That, basically, is the information we have found from therapists, from very conscientious parents, from Nancy's work, which seems to really help guide the Indigos.

They know who they are. They come in feeling and knowing. It does not serve us to try to mold them into a pattern that we possibly had to learn to break out of, the pattern of how our parents raised us.

There is a new way of being. There's a new way of parenting, and it's about moving into love. The bottom line is love—being present and loving and understanding. In the months and years ahead, we're going to see new school systems where parents and educators work together.

These souls are coming in from the tenth dimension. This dimension is about sound and color, and radiates an opalescence energy. As you think about this, doesn't it set up and paint an interesting love-scape? This says a lot about their amazing energy and going back to honoring the right brain, the arts, the intuitive process, and listening to the children.

Allow their knowledge to flow. Tell them you know who they are so they choose to stay. Create a sacred and harmonious home. This may be achieved by burning sage, burning alcohol and Epsom salts, and certain types of incense. Honor your home as a temple so that your child can come home to a loving parent or parents in clear, loving surroundings.

Even if you're tired, explain this to them. Set aside some special time just for them, when you can be fully present. Always make them feel safe, and let them come home to their best friend—you.

Martin: At the end of the book, you have some information on the message that the Indigos bring. Can you comment more about that?

Tober: Specifically, which part, Rick, were you talking about?

Martin: The fact that they bring the message of love.

Tober: Oh, yes! The message *is* of love; it is of honoring that piece of us. Again, I mention the Divine Feminine, which comes in and honors love, compassion, the intuitive process—all of the pieces that need to come together to make this Heaven on Earth—and they are here to show us, one way or another.

Martin: You talk about them as being "systems busters." What do you mean by that?

Tober: We were told, many years ago, that the first things that would break down would be the old, established institutions and systems. Do you remember that?

Martin: Yes.

Tober: We were told that, as we move into this New Age, this Golden Age—the old systems don't fit into the new mold. So they're right out there as those who will break, for instance, the educational system as it has been for a hundred years or so. They will not put up with something simply because that's the way it has always been.

So, knowing that we've got a large group of entities coming onto the planet, and that they are "system busters," it can really give you a pretty good picture of where we are going.

In my mind and in my heart, it's awesome. It's just so awesome to know that they're here working with us—*finally!*

Years ago I would say to my friends, when I was having the dreams about the babies, "You know, we who are conscious are the 'rainbow bridge' from this civilization, from this group of souls, to the new group of souls coming in. We're the 'rainbow bridge' for them." It fills my heart with great hope and joy.

We're seeing amazing things happen, and we who know who the Indigos are can certainly help the parents who are having difficulty and don't understand. We can share with them our knowledge, as these little ones are getting old enough to speak for themselves.

Martin: Let's talk about using the old tricks of guilt and shame as behavior tools with these kids.

Tober: They won't work! The Indigos know who they are. It will just frustrate and devastate the parents. It will bring in a very agitated energy field around the parents and around the child, which will defeat any discussion, any real help. It just won't happen.

They *know* who they are. They're on a mission. They are aware of that. So, this is a challenge, because we have a whole culture that has been raised on "You just wait until your father gets home!" I'm sure you probably heard that a few times. *I* certainly did, and that won't work now!

I don't have children. I'm around them a lot, but I can appreciate what parents must go through when they go back to the old modus operandi and find out that it doesn't do anything. The children will test them to see how far they can go.

However, these children are not brats. That's not in their consciousness. They will test the parent, in this respect, to see what the ground rules are. How far can I do this? What can I do? What, really, is important to my parents? What isn't important? And they're going to learn to see how they can negotiate with the parents. So, if a parent comes back with a *negotiation* point of view, then they're going to be on the same page.

It's quite amazing to see them in action. It's joyful when you experience them with conscientious parents, who are coming from love, who certainly are from a mind/body/soul integration, through love.

Martin: It's going to be interesting to see, in the years ahead, what kind of new professions open up as a result of these children.

Tober: And inventions, new ways of doing things!

Martin: I mean, it kind of takes the old doctor, lawyer, fireman rut right out of the choice equation. (*Laughter*)

Tober: It does. And it's going to really move us into new ways of thinking and being.

Martin: Have you had contact with many parents who have Indigos who are just totally beside themselves?

Tober: We've had a lot of mail from parents who are so thrilled when they read the book, and they realize that their children might be Indigos, When they started working with the principles we talk about, they started to find success in their parenting.

They're all helping each other. They go on-line, interact, and offer each other solutions, ideas, and alternatives.

I feel that's going to be the way a lot of this is going to work. The parents are going to have to get really proactive and put together support groups where they can help each other, because we're making it up as we go along.

Martin: That makes a lot of sense.

Tober: Yes.

Martin: Do you find much awareness among family therapists?

Tober: If they honor their intuitive process, yes. And, of course, in this area, we do have a lot of people who are counselors and do honor their right-brain, intuitive side.

Martin: Let's talk about Kryon. What is the Kryon message?

Tober: The Kryon message is that we create our own reality. The Kryon message is that love is all. These sound really "unusual"—I bet you've never heard these things before. (*Laughter*)

Martin: Oh, once or twice! (*Laughter*)

Tober: The Kryon message is, basically, Universal Truth. We deal a lot with the Earth changes. A lot of the work was to get us all through Y2K, and to change the consciousness about that, because there was so much fear.

Martin: A lot of fear.

Tober: And we needed to counteract it by honoring our God-given power—for us to acknowledge the power of who we are—and to realize that we can create a critical mass where *love* is in charge.

Enough people heard, enough people prayed and pray, enough people meditate, enough people envisioned the planet circled and surrounded with Love and Light, that the planet can go through these changes with a minimal amount of discomfort.

Much of the work of the Kryon is about realigning the earth's magnetic grids and preparation for what is called ascension. It's about the knowledge that we walk on this planet as co-creators with Spirit. We are great Golden Angels all working on a Grand Master Piece.

Martin: Well, our readers can easily identify with that message! How have you found your reception to be at the United Nations—for example, speaking of Kryon.

Tober: They invited us back three times; it was very surprising to us. We spoke in one of the smaller rooms, for the Society of Enlightenment and Transformation (SEAT). It is one of the charter organizations created for meditating members.

So, it's a smaller group. It's about 75 people or so, and we're always amazed, when we're in the middle of the group, that we're in a room where major treaties between countries and leaders have been signed. And here we are, talking about ETs, bringing in a Council of Elders from the indigenous peoples of the world and talking about what's happening with HAARP [*High-Frequency Active Auroral Research Project*].

Martin: Yes, we're familiar with that.

Tober: We were honored, and we always feel very welcome there.

Martin: Okay, let's shift back to the Indigos. What would you like to leave our readers with to think about, with regard to this infusion of new energy in the form of these children?

Tober: If you had a knock on your door, opened the door, and you saw a great Master in your doorway, you would be joyful and thrilled! And you would invite the Master in. Then, you would probably sit down, thank him or her for coming, and you would say hopefully, "What is it you want me to know? How can I help you, and how can I help the planet? What wisdom do you wish to share with me?"

This is the way to honor the Indigo!

Martin: That's a good place to end. Thank you for a thoughtful and "inspired" interview. Our readers will truly enjoy this, and I'm sure some of them will be contacting you!

THE SPECTRUM newspaper
interview by Rick Martin
Las Vegas, NV 89117
(877) 280-2866

Website: [www.spectrumnews10.com]

Jan Tober is co-facilitator for the once-a-month large Kryon Seminars. She also channels her polarity opposite, Tobias, of the Kryon Entourage and the council of 33.

Jan Tober
The Kryon Writings, Inc.
1155 Camino Del Mar #422
Del Mar, CA 92014

E-mail: kryonemail@aol.com
Website: [http://www.kryon.com/jantober]

What is before you is the most profound and altering spiritual energy of any in all Human history. What is before you is your ability to change the very essence of your existence—to live longer lives, have a more peaceful and joyful fulfillment, and the power to change the very Earth under your feet. In the process, you get to learn, learn, and learn. And also in the process, you get to be loved without measure, and begin to feel the *family*—as it is one step closer to you spiritually than ever before. These are *not* the end times. These are the beginning of times!

Kryon

"The Search for Indigenous Wisdom"

Marc Vallée
Woody Vaspra

Chapter Fourteen

"The Search for Indigenous Wisdom"

From the Writer . . .

If you read the statement on page 315 given at the United Nations (U.N.) by Kryon in 1998, you will understand what this chapter is about. Whereas so many grand humanitarian ideas seem to fall in the cracks, or belong in that place that says, "Good idea, but let someone else do it," the idea of including the indigenous peoples of Earth as helpers in a high-tech world is being actively pursued as you read this.

Marc Vallée and his sister, Martine, are Canadian publishers of the Kryon books in the French language worldwide. They were actually both in the room at the U.N. when the words were spoken by Kryon. These words moved Marc profoundly, and as a result of that experience, Marc has formed the *Convergence Foundation*. This is an organization still in its infancy, dedicated to building a network of people of high consciousness and purpose who will provide better choices for society—providing a critical mass that will have positive and lasting effects on politics, economics, and the ecology of the earth.

And the method? To begin with, the plan is to contact and connect with the wisest people on the planet. Marc's belief (which is similar to mine) is that these wise souls can be found in the elders of the indigenous peoples of Earth.

The mission is to acquire wisdom from those who have never separated themselves from nature. There is a saying that states that as man separates from nature, he also separates from himself. To assist in the next evolutionary step of man, therefore, Marc is seeking an evolution of consciousness, guided by those who are closest to nature.

He isn't alone. At about the same time, but independent of Marc, Woody and Catie Vaspra of Colorado decided to quit their jobs and spend all of their time contacting the elders of this planet. Their goal? To create a nonprofit foundation, the *World Council of Elders* (WCOE), which would assist in the very same mission that Marc was aiming for—a critical mass of elevated consciousness stemming from those who had never lost it.

All three of these individuals have traveled the world in search of the elders, and they're very interested in what their reception might be. Most of my readership is American and Canadian. What do you think the American and Canadian Indians think of us on this land? What do you think the reception will be when we enter their lands and ask for help?

The answer should make your heart skip a beat. If you've come this far, you've read Kryon's statements about forgiveness, about a new energy on the planet, and about the indigenous peoples of Earth having a "knowing" about the timing of it all.

Marc, Woody, and Catie have reported that as they present their ideas to these elders, the elders tell them, "You were expected." No matter if it's in Canada, the United States, Peru, the Ivory Coast of Africa, or the inner circles of the indigenous peoples of the Hawaiian Islands, the answer has been, "You were expected." Within the true elders, gone is much of the hatred relating to what we did *to* them, and what we took *from* them. Their wisdom has to do with how we can work together and reestablish the link with Mother Earth that humanity greatly needs now. Just the energy of sitting with the elders makes you understand why we need them so much!

Along the way, Woody and Catie met Marc. They shared their ideas and experiences, and now they're working together. Can they make a difference? That depends on you.

Dear readers, take a moment to look at the work of these fine people in these next few pages. Perhaps there are some of you who have something to add to Marc, Woody, and Catie's work. Perhaps you've been waiting for this very thing in order to help in some unique way. If not, perhaps you might include them in your visualizations and meditations as you send energy to Mother Earth, and the humanity that lives on this planet. Your energy and visualizations are far more valuable than you think.

These are pioneers in the new energy. They are explorers in the untouched jungles of consciousness. They will forge a bridge that needs to be crossed across a chasm of the new and the old—but *we* are the ones who must do the crossing of that bridge.

I present my friends, Marc Vallée; and Woody and Catie Vaspra.

—Lee Carroll

"There has never been a greater time for you to implement a Council of Wisdom, a nonvoting council of indigenous Human Beings on this planet to reside in this building. And we are telling you that the consciousness of the building will eventually support this. The consciousness of the people will support it. The consciousness of the planet is pushing you toward it. It is the next logical step—and when you present it, present it to the public first. They will do the rest to help you implement it."

Kryon at the United Nations—1998

"Assisting World Awakening"
Through Indigenous Traditional Wisdom
by
Marc Vallée

As a publisher of spiritual books over the past ten years, I've enjoyed reading important teachings relating to the creative potential that individuals have to affect the events of their own lives. Like many others, this has brought me to study the implications at a collective level—the potential to choose consciously the world in which we wish to live.

For the past two years, I have been involved with a group known as the *Convergence Foundation*, which aims to link various groups in order to form an information network on a significant scale. Our goal is to bring about a coordinating action of these groups so that a critical mass of conscious people may have a real influence on the choices made by our societies.

We realize that to hope for any productive results in this endeavor, we have to target our actions, and we have done so, guided by the understanding of man's essential link with nature. We are made from the energy of Mother Earth. Human beings, by attempting to dominate nature, have severed essential ties with the nurturing aspects of Earth, in turn, negatively affecting the connection with their own spiritual selves and to others. We believe that by renewing this essential link, humans will access higher spiritual wisdom, inspiring them to find a better way to resolve the problems they have—whether they are ecological, or issues of world economy and politics. We believe that there is an important key here in man's renewed relationship with nature and the consciousness at work within it.

Now, the dominating Western world seems to have lost the ability to resonate with this understanding and truly harmonize with the life flow prevalent in nature. On the other hand, the indigenous, or *First Nations* people, have preserved that precious talent and wisdom throughout their history. When I first read the 1998 Kryon channelling at the United Nations (U.N.) stating that the time has come for a Council of Elders of indigenous representatives within the U.N., I really felt attuned to this idea. Working to assist in this endeavor has grown from a smaller project within the Convergence Foundation to our main purpose. The idea is to involve indigenous tradition and wisdom in our modern social choices. We need their assistance. Western ways have brought humanity to a very precarious state of living, and we truly believe that many indigenous values are fundamental to our survival. Our foundation would like to study these values specifically.

My own brief experience in Africa and the Amazonian forest of Peru has enabled me to understand some basic values in indigenous ways that could be quite useful to us here in the West. For example:

The welcoming of strangers is usually very cordial: Indigenous peoples consider meeting new people an opportunity for discovery and enrichment in terms of ideas and personal growth. Since they don't tend to ascribe bad intentions to others at first glance, they naturally express their warmth in meeting you and making you feel welcome. There is not the fear of "the other" that is so typical in Western cities.

A deep sense of responsibility for future generations: In indigenous cultures, the ancestors are always acknowledged. Along the same lines, they acknowledge the coming generations. In this way, they are careful about how they conduct themselves, aware of the repercussions on future generations. For this reason, they are stunned to see Western industries exploit the resources of the earth with so little consideration for the consequences of these actions.

Teaching the younger generations: They don't teach by explaining, but by guiding toward direct experience, bringing individuals into an intimate relationship with life in all things. That's why they do not only acknowledge life in human beings, but also the consciousness of trees, rivers, and clouds—because they are all connected to the flow of life.

Reality perception: Being in harmony with the natural flow of life is a very important understanding of indigenous people, and rightly so. Why should anyone hope for anything less? When one becomes more attuned to the indigenous way of perceiving reality, one becomes aware of the way in which Western thinking has mentally compartmentalized reality in the aim of better controlling it. By limiting the evidence of how everything is linked, how all is fundamentally One, Western thinking has created much pain for all life on this planet.

There are purposes and lessons to be gained here, as in all things, and no accusations are being made. But more and more, the Western world must attune to the ways in which indigenous people perceive the natural flow of life, which is the flow of the Divine. As part of this world, we must feel that we cannot control reality to fit a personal agenda, but simply learn to attune to the holistic energies of the present moment.

Studying these issues and how they can be applied in the modern choices of our society is the goal of Convergence Foundation. We would like to participate in being one of the many "bridges" now being built between indigenous wisdom and modern society.

That is why the Council of Elders [indicated by Kryon] has interested us so much. Recently, we have learned that the Commission on Human Rights of the United Nations has approved the formation of the "Permanent Forum for Indigenous People" with a high-level status. In February 2000, 315 delegates of 47 governments, 3 specialized agencies, and 59 indigenous and nongovernmental organizations established the basis for this forum.

Although the U.N. has been criticized in the past, and still has problems to overcome, we recognize that they continue to do much good work. Until it becomes evident that this is not the right path for us, our foundation chooses to work alongside this international body, closely studying what is being done at this forum. We are also currently involved with the *Earth Charter Project* (for information, please see [www.earthcharter.org] on the Internet).

Since informing the public and the media is an important aspect of this work, we plan to be quite active on this level. Furthermore, we have been linking with associations in Canada, the United States, and Europe involved with indigenous groups for several years now so that we may all provide support for one another.

For more information, please contact us at:

> *Convergence Foundation*
> 1209 Bernard Ave., Suite 110
> Outremont, Quebec, Canada, H2V 1V7
> Phone in Canada: (514) 276-3546
> E-mail: ariane@mlink.net

Donations should be made out to:
Convergence Foundation

— Mark Vallée

"A Sacred Journey"
The World Council of Elders
by
Woody Vaspra

A Prologue—Meeting the First Elder

On August 21, 1999, my wife, Catie, and I were at a gathering of friends in the Rocky Mountains just north of Woodland Park, Colorado. We were emerging from a tepee where we had participated in a drumming ceremony and meditation session earlier that afternoon. Suddenly I was summoned to the main house to respond to a phone call. The caller was a new friend who is part Hopi, part Shoshone, and part Choctaw. He said that he had just had a conversation with a traditional Hopi Elder (*Grandfather*), and that a meeting had been arranged for Wednesday—four days away. I immediately responded that we would be there on Tuesday. At the end of this conversation, Catie and I packed up and headed back to Boulder, Colorado, to repack and prepare for the trip.

Catie and I had met our new Hopi acquaintance in May 1999 through a female friend whom we had met a year earlier at a Kryon "Journey Home" retreat in Breckenridge, Colorado. It was through this female friend that I found out I had a Hopi spiritual brother and realized we had grown up together in an earlier incarnation. There was a very special energy between us, and we knew that something special was to be played out in the near future.

On Monday, we headed west through Grand Junction, Colorado, and into eastern Utah. Then we traveled south toward the northeastern corner of Arizona. The day was long and hot, and we decided to camp for the night at the Devil's Canyon campground in Blanding, Utah. This overnight stop was very good for us, as it gave us the opportunity to relax, get grounded, and connect with Mother Earth. The last couple of days preparing for our trip had been hectic.

The next day, we continued the drive south to Arizona, then on to Hopiland and Hotevilla. Upon entering Hopiland, we carefully followed the directions given by our friends. After missing a road entrance and doubling back, we finally recognized their van by their license plates. Our accommodations were at a modest house owned by a woman friend. It was a typical house on a part of Hopiland that had no plumbing or electricity. Water was collected in barrels from the previous rainfall, and electricity was derived from solar panels on the roof. The toilet was located in an outhouse about 100 yards away from the house. Nevertheless, there was a very special feeling about the area. You could sense the connection between Mother Earth and all of the people in the group. We felt honored to be at Hopiland with our special friends.

Once we got settled, we started talking about our recent trip to Hawaii. Catie and I had attended the World Indigenous Peoples Conference on Education in Hilo, Hawaii; visited my Mom and family on Oahu; and attended very special Hawaiian ceremonies at the Pu'u Ko'hola Heiau on the Big Island. Our discussions went late into the night. We were filled with heightened anticipation and excitement regarding our visit the next day with *Grandfather*, the Hopi elder.

The next morning, we drove to Hotevilla and made the necessary arrangements to meet at two o'clock that afternoon. This gave us the opportunity to visit Prophecy Rock and prepare for the meeting. The visit to Prophecy Rock was very special, and the message on the rock is very clear. It says that mankind can decide to go in two directions: One direction is to destroy itself; and the other direction is live in peace, harmony, and love.

This is a very sacred site, with a spiritual energy that is beyond human description.

About two o'clock in the afternoon, *Grandfather* came over to the house as scheduled. We did the customary ceremonies that had been taught to me a month ago by a friend from Hawaii, and we presented gifts to pay our respects to *Grandfather*. Then we sat down to begin our discussion about a sacred journey that was to involve Elders from indigenous peoples from around the planet. A very brief introductory description of the journey was presented to *Grandfather* to explain why we were having this meeting. After my message was translated in Hopi back to *Grandfather*, and his response was translated back to me in English, the message was that this work I was presenting was in the prophecies! Upon hearing this response, I felt a fantastic sensation of confirmation that this sacred journey to develop a World Council of Elders of indigenous peoples was authentic. Catie and I looked at each other, and we both knew that we were heading in the right direction.

For the next two hours, we discussed the basic concepts for a World Council of Elders (WCOE). At one point, we asked *Grandfather* if he would be interested in participating in the Council. He enthusiastically responded that he wanted to be a part of it, but needed to stay close to his land. He was concerned about traveling to far distances that would keep him away too long. Throughout the afternoon, the entire meeting was spoken in Hopi and translated into English. It was finally pointed out by his son-in-law that *Grandfather* considered this meeting very sacred, so it had to be spoken in the Hopi language. When we heard this, we felt honored by this spiritual act. After having a wonderful discussion, we exchanged pleasantries and ended our meeting. We all said our farewells, and *Grandfather* and his translator left.

The feelings that overcame us were beyond what any of us had ever experienced. We all felt euphoric, but most important, the meeting produced a very strong verification of the work that was about to begin. We all felt the Great Spirit during the meeting and that confirmation would be sent in some way or another.

My Hopi brother went out to the front porch to get some fresh air, but then came flying back in excitedly, motioning for us to come and see what was going on. When we stepped outside, we experienced a sight that none of us had ever seen before: There were two fully developed rainbows that were displaying very bright colors, extending from one horizon to the other. They remained like this for a full 30 minutes. We knew that the Great Spirit was sending a confirming message for his very sacred journey.

The next morning, Catie and I packed our stuff, loaded our vehicle, and said good-bye to our friends, thanking them for this most wonderful experience. As we left Hopiland, the Navajo Reservation police had a roadblock in progress, reminding us that there is still strife going on in this country among the indigenous peoples and our government.

What Is Happening, and Why Now?

What was the impetus for having such a meeting with a Hopi Elder? What was the inspiration to start such a sacred journey?

There is an awakening taking place all around this planet, both within the modern society and among indigenous peoples. They are sensing the major changes in energy shifts going on—not only on this planet, but also throughout the universe. The Spiritual Elders of indigenous peoples are feeling this transformation intensely, and they're ready to take action. As we visit the Elders themselves, many emphatically say, "It is now the time for the gathering of the Elders, for all peoples to unite and to heal Mother Earth." Every time we hear these words, it gives us chills up and down our spines, but it also gives us verification that the prophecies and channels are right on target.

There are already many simultaneous activities happening between indigenous Spiritual Elders throughout many continents. Many religions are starting to gather together to resolve their differences and begin working together for the good of humankind. If one were to look at the big picture of the planet, Jesus and the other great masters were doing just this type of work to convince humans that love is the most powerful tool in the universe.

We all know intuitively that this is a special time—an amazing opportunity for great personal and universal growth. We are experiencing the changes in our world and the accelerated frequency of synchronous events in our lives. When we listen with our hearts, we are aware of our connectedness with all entities in the universe. The veil is lifting. There is a reawakening of the wisdom that each of us holds inside. All that is inconsistent with what we know to be true is revealing itself and falling away. The long-anticipated time of transformation is upon us. Indigenous peoples know that we are all one with the Creator, and we are powerful creators ourselves. The Elders can teach us to remember who we really are and what humanity's role is here on Earth. This is the time and energy we gave intent to be a part of. This is the time to rejoin with family. *"Mitakuye Oyasin"*—we are all related.

Bringing forth universal peace through our own inner wisdom and that of the Elders in conjunction with the power of co-creation is a momentous challenge requiring the pure intent of each member of the human family. Each of us must realize and exercise our gift of free choice. It is also the time for each human to reclaim their individual potentials and to apply these capabilities. The action taken must be from the heart of each human being. It is a spiritual undertaking, and we all have the ability to create a spiritual consciousness that can affect the planet. There has never been a more appropriate time for all peoples to unite in love, peace, and harmony.

Spiritual Communication Through Prophecies and Channelling

There were many events throughout the history of humankind that planted the seeds for the gathering of indigenous Elders and the unification of all peoples. There have been recent channellings and prophecies, as well as those that have been around for more than a thousand-plus years, which confirm that this is the time for this gathering of Elders to occur. This is the time to form councils to help bring love, harmony, and peace to this world. There is a subtle cry for help around this planet to bring out the truths that have been hidden throughout the ages. The indigenous peoples have been on this planet for many thousands of years and know how to connect and live in harmony with Mother Earth and keep open the conduit to Spirit. The Western world has lost this connection, but many people are coming to an awareness that this cannot go on much longer. We must take action—for the answer is on this planet.

Many indigenous peoples have carried prophecies and visions down through the ages that tell us that this is the time for a reunification of all peoples in wisdom and harmony with Mother Earth and among themselves. This wisdom went underground when the white man arrived on the shores of many lands. It is the time now for this wisdom to emerge and be shared among the peoples of the planet. A Lakota (Sioux) holy man, Black Elk, had an epic vision at age nine, which included the unification of all peoples on this planet. Here is a brief excerpt:

The sacred hoop of my people was one of many hoops that made one circle, wide as daylight and as starlight, and in the center grew one mighty flowering tree to shelter all the children of one mother and one father.

Behold the circle of the sacred hoop, for the people shall be like unto it; and if they are like unto this, they shall have power, because there is no end to this hoop and in the center of the hoop these raise their children.

(The sacred hoop means that the continents of the world and peoples of all colors shall stand as one.)

The Spiritual Elder's message is all about love and about living from the heart, in peace and balance with each other and Mother Earth. It's about forgiveness and nonjudgment. Now is the time for merging ancient wisdom and technology in a harmonious balance. Specifically, we understand that the Algonquin peoples in Canada have held such a prophecy of this special time of choice for humanity and for the planet herself. The Aboriginal peoples of Australia, the Mayans, the Celtics, the African peoples, the Tibetans, the Alaskan peoples, the Hawaiians, and the Hebrews, as well as many other indigenous groups, also hold keys for unlocking the ancient wisdom and bringing forth the truth into the light for all to share.

They have been the faithful wisdom-keepers. Now is the time for them to come together and meet in a traditional council to share their wisdom. As a matter of fact, we've learned that Elders of indigenous peoples have been meeting in small groups from time to time and creating networks for this very purpose. In addition, the Hopi, who are considered by many indigenous groups to be the keepers of the truth in this special time in our earth's history, have also long carried prophecies of the challenges in this special time. They have gone four times to specifically address the "House of Mica," normally known as the United Nations.

In more recent events, Lee Carroll, the channel for Kryon, was invited to the United Nations (U.N.) in New York City on three occasions to channel Kryon. At two of the three U.N. channellings, Kryon mentioned the need to consider forming an advisory council of indigenous peoples so their wisdom can be made available for the good of all humanity. Below is a brief excerpt from the November 1996 Kryon channelling at the U.N.:

Now we have a question for you: If you were to build an organization of nations such as this from the beginning again, would it make sense to you in these times, with the millennium approaching, to have the wisdom of the planet's ancients present in your planning? Could you use their collective ideas, or perhaps their secrets, previously hidden? I think you would say, "Yes! That is an excellent idea."

Why is it, then, that there is no place in this vast organization for that very wisdom? Did you forget that it is available? Do you discount that it would be valuable? Even on this continent, there are the native ancestors of the ancients that still carry the understanding of the old Spiritual Earth ways. They understand the spiritual nature of the land, and of peace. They understand coexistence with the elements; and the energy of the west, east, north, and south.

Those ancients who founded the tropical islands of the entire Earth fully understood their own star ancestry! And their human ancestors still teach it to this day in an unwritten language, and know how it all fits together with the energy of Earth.

Those on the other side of the planet from you right now who are today building fires with sticks for warmth and gathering around in a primitive fashion may understand better than any wise person in this building how things actually work! There are ancestors of ancients on every continent, and their knowledge fits together—did you know that? For the truth of the planet never changes, but the basics are often lost to the modern ones.

Yet none of these wise ones are represented in this building, since they do not own the land they are on. They carry the greatest wisdom that this planet has to offer to humanity today—but because they are not politically powerful, they are ignored.

And so we say that it is time to consider a Council of Elders, of the spiritually wise, to advise the rest of you— validated by their planetary lineage and not their governmental credentials. If you do this, it will indeed bring results for you—all of you! There is no greater time than this for such an idea. Perhaps it will now occur—in the big room down the hall.

Lee was again invited to speak at the U.N. in November 1998; Kryon again restated the need for the wisdom of the indigenous elders (page 315).

Why a World Council of Elders?

The World Council of Elders (WCOE) is a developing group of indigenous or native Elders from all across the globe— coming together to counsel and educate humanity about world peace. The mission of the WCOE is to rejuvenate ancient wisdom and sacred knowledge, and to integrate it with modern cultures and technologies to assist humanity and Mother Earth in realizing unification, harmony, and full spiritual awareness.

The indigenous peoples who have remained connected with Mother Earth understand that we each have a role to play in this reunification. Consequently, they can offer much spiritual insight and practical solutions to correct the global problems currently confronting humankind.

The Elders typically share a deep spiritual awareness and power, connectedness with Mother Earth, simplicity, humility, dignity, and, of course, a sense of humor. The Elders also share an astonishingly common knowledge of who we are, where we come from, and where we have the potential to go when we listen to our hearts and follow our own "inner knowing." This wisdom has been kept safe, often hidden away, and passed down for many generations of indigenous peoples until it could be shared in the energy of this special time.

On a daily basis, they sought the counsel of the Great Spirit and Mother Earth to help them understand the principles of life on this planet. From these teachings, these Spiritual Elders understood the energies and vibrations of the planet and its connection to the universe. This knowledge helped the indigenous peoples to live in close partnership with the elements of Earth. They kept life simple and basic. Historically, whenever a society became too complex and lost its connection to the Great Spirit and Mother Earth, it self-destructed or eventually disappeared.

Many indigenous peoples still govern themselves by councils of Elders and have done so for thousands of years. Indigenous peoples respect the wisdom of their Elders, who have life experiences and inner knowledge beyond anyone younger. They have faced the hardships and lessons of life as presented on this planet. Elders possess the inner knowing, which takes time to obtain and pass on to the younger generations. History confirms that councils were comprised of Elders who governed their people wisely. These councils were formed to ensure harmony and peace among themselves and other peoples. It is the oldest form of leadership on this planet.

How It All Got Started

With the ancient prophecies of the indigenous peoples and the recent channellings by Kryon being made public, the necessity and validity for a World Council of Elders has been recognized. The present, ongoing devastation of Mother Earth, and the atrocious behavior of humans against each other is making it very clear that life as it exists on this planet is in a precarious balance. The indigenous peoples of this planet have experienced these painful changes and now know that action has to be taken. One way to mitigate all that has taken place is to develop this World Council of Elders of indigenous peoples.

In my case, some very strong inner voices began to cause a stirring within me, telling me that "something needs to be done." My life on this planet was intended to accomplish a certain mission. How this task was to be realized involved many individuals whom I have contacted at particular times through-out my life, who would be teachers and mentors. Their patience and understanding helped develop the impetus for this work. I would like to thank them for all the assistance they have contributed to this journey.

A recent insight for starting this work was initiated in August 1998 when I talked with Lee Carroll at the second "Journey Home" retreat in Breckenridge, Colorado. Our discussion en-compassed the fact that I strongly felt that I had a mission, but did not know what it would entail or even how it would start. I mentioned that in November 1997, I went back home to Hawaii to be with my family. While there, I had several personal spiritual experiences, which guided me to seek answers. From those experiences, I knew that I was to work as a liaison with indigenous tribes, but I did not know any of the details. I had a feeling that Kryon and Lee knew but could not tell me until I figured it out myself. After my talk with Lee, I left the retreat with a more positive attitude that something was in the making, and it was up to me to figure it out.

I also met Catie at the "Journey Home" retreat! We immediately became friends without realizing that our paths would cross again in the near future (to eventually include marriage). I labored over the discussion I had with Lee for the next two months. Then the journey became more evident in October 1998 at a Kryon "at home" meeting in Lakewood, Colorado. Lee specifically talked about the Kryon channelling at the United Nations and discussed the necessity to organize a Council of Elders. It was at this moment that it really became clear that I had to do something related to what was being said. For the next three months, I read and reread the Kryon United Nations channellings and discussed with Catie the possibility of this mission. In January 1999, I wrote Lee a note and told him that I finally needed to do something about organizing a Council of Elders of indigenous peoples around the world.

Lee responded quickly that I should contact a gentleman in Montréal who had a similar vision. This person was forming a foundation dedicated to the goal of realizing world peace. This is how Marc Vallée and I met. Marc, with his sister, Martine, are cofounders and owners of Ariane Editions, publishers of all the Kryon books, as well as many other metaphysical works in the French language worldwide.

Marc and I communicated via e-mail and on the phone to see if we were on similar paths. We decided that we were close, because one of the final outcomes was to achieve world peace. Thus, we needed to have a face-to-face discussion. On May 1, 1999, Marc and I had a meeting in Montréal at a Kryon Conference hosted by Ariane Editions. During our meeting, we found out that we both knew in which direction to head. However, it was all very new to both of us. We both agreed to officially start our two journeys. Marc was to continue with his passionate desire to find a way to achieve world peace, and I would continue with my aspirations to organize a Council of Elders. With this agreement in place, we feel that we gave each other permission to fulfill our contracts—that of having a positive effect on this planet.

Prior to the Montréal meeting at the end of March 1999, I met with Jennifer Borchers, who was at that time president of the SEAT (Society for Enlightenment and Transformation) at the United Nations. I went to see if Jennifer had any information that could help me in gaining a more understandable picture regarding how a Council of Elders could assist the United Nations. As recently as November 1998, during Jennifer's tenure as president, Kryon again channelled at the United Nations the need for a Council of Elders. I wanted to meet with Jennifer to see if she had any insight on what challenges I was about to undertake. After explaining what my intentions were regarding the Council, her response was one of wonder. She said that it was a considerable task, and massive hurdles would have to be overcome. The U.N. would be one of those hurdles. Jennifer could not speak for the U.N. as a whole, but from her position, the task would have support from the Enlightenment Society (SEAT). We both agreed to support each other as much as we could. There is still much more to be done at the U.N., and a Council of Elders can make an enormous contribution to their uphill struggle for peace, harmony, and unity throughout the planet.

Who Are the Elders?

During the course of our work, we are finding that we are meeting two types of Elders. The first kind is the older Elder, usually aged 70 to 120 years old. They have learned the wisdom of their ancestors through lessons and experiences. Most of them were chosen from an early age to be who they are. They feel the strong connection to Mother Earth through the land, water, sky, and fire, and live their spirituality every minute of every day. They relate to the energies that emanate from their local environment. That is why these Elders feel strongly about preserving their sacred lands. Knowing these energies and how to relate to them is very important in keeping the balance with Mother Earth. It is a strong attachment that they find difficult to break, even when it comes to temporarily leaving their homeland.

Many of these Elders carry the ancient prophecies of their ancestors within them. They know that it is time for these prophecies to be made known to the peoples of this planet, and many of the prophecies relate to this specific time. Some of these prophecies convey doom-and-gloom for the planet, and some of them seem appropriate as we watch the planet being desecrated to the extreme. Much of Mother Earth's resources are being extracted with no reparation to create balance. The Elders call the reparation, *payment*. The current Western world is not making enough *payment* to compensate for what is being used to fuel this modern society. In fact, most Westerners are seemingly disconnected from who they are and how things work, and they are unaware of the imbalances being created.

Payments also relate to each human on this planet. The Elders strongly believe that we are privileged to live on Earth. For every lifetime we experience on this planet, we assume a responsibility for its well-being. We honor this responsibility by paying respect to Mother Earth for what is being provided to us as we live here. We do this by making *payment*—ensuring that we put back what we consume as we live on this planet. We also must spend appropriate time thanking Mother Earth for this privilege. The importance of heartfelt gratitude is another lesson the Elders hold for us.

Many of these Elders have lived long enough to have experienced the many extreme hardships endured by their peoples. The loss of their sacred lands and the hatred of those who took it still dwells deeply in their hearts. However, many of them are leading the way to forgive what has been done around the planet. They feel that there is more important work to be done—and that is to create balance and harmony with Mother Earth, and unity and peace among all peoples. Most important is a close connection to the Great Creator. Many Elders speak of the freedom in forgiveness. This "letting go" of old energy and opening the heart allows the free flow of the love and guidance from Spirit that unites us all.

The other type of Elder is younger, ranging from 40 to 70 years of age. Many of them are still in the learning and experiencing process. They are the ones who were sent to schools to be educated in Western ways. Many of these modern Elders tried living in modern society with success, but soon felt an emptiness and separation from Spirit and Mother Earth. They eventually returned home to go back to their roots, because it is on the land that they felt whole and alive. As these modern Elders returned to their lands, they started the process of learning ancient wisdom and spirituality from the older Elders. Some of them became the carriers of the ancient prophecies. They can speak several languages, and they know how to operate in the modern world.

However, as their learning progressed, the younger elders soon discovered that the ancient methods and knowledge had as much validity as the modern technologies. Some modern scientists are finally realizing this fact, as the ancient knowledge is slowly resurfacing. In fact, much of the technology of the Western world owes its existence to the indigenous peoples, who discovered and diligently used the natural assets provided by Mother Earth. Modern scientists used this indigenous knowledge as the building blocks for many of the functions of our present society.

A number of these modern Elders have also taken on the responsibility of sharing their spiritual wisdom with the world. They are sharing their ceremonies with each other to create a strong energy bond to heal the planet and humanity, and they also feel that it's time for all peoples to share knowledge around the planet and help others to retrieve individual powers that were taken from them, or given up at some time. All humans can regain their inner wisdom and spirituality. Some of these Elders we have visited call themselves "Bridges." They can relate to the two worlds and have accepted the responsibility to help the new world to return to peace, harmony, and love. These Elders, like so many of those individuals now awakening, find themselves to be bridges between the ancient wisdom and the "now" time of integration.

How Is an Individual Recognized As an Elder?

There are many different ways in which an individual is recognized as an Elder. The most customary practice is recognition by his or her people. There are other legitimate methods such as appointment by other Elders, growing into the position, and birthright. It is an earned status, not an elected position. One has to be careful about the self-chosen Elder who is allowing the ego to get in the way. Most Elders feel that the acknowledgment by their people is very important. The people feel that the selected Elder must be properly equipped for the job, well respected, and will follow the right path. Not all Elders have to follow the spiritual path to become an Elder. The work they do encompasses many areas. There are those who heal, pray, arbitrate, govern, trade, farm, teach, and so on. However, the individuals that are necessary for the work of the WCOE are the Spiritual Elders.

An Elder does not *demand* respect; he quietly receives it. You can *feel* an Elder. Children are always around them, because they instinctively know that there is wisdom emanating from that person. The Elder knows the importance of children, for these young ones will carry on the teachings, traditions, culture, language, history, and timeless wisdom of our people.

Encounters with Elders

As soon as the intent was made to coordinate a World Council of Elders, synchronicity occurred in every possible way and is still occurring. In July 1999, a formal presentation was made at the Kryon midsummer conference in Santa Fe, New Mexico. The response was very emotional, much to our surprise. Many of the indigenous peoples at the conference resonated to what was presented. There were many tears shed because this work is from the heart, and everyone felt it that day.

Soon after the conference, Catie and I went to Hawaii to attend the World Indigenous Peoples Conference on Education in Hilo. We met Elders from various locations of the Pacific Rim. Again, they all acknowledged that it is time for this work to commence. On several occasions when I approached Elders, they already knew what was to be discussed. We were talking heart to heart even before I encountered them. When I finally opened my mouth to speak, they would stop me and say, "We already know that it is now the time for a Planetary Council of Elders." The trip to Hawaii verified that we were on the right path. After Hawaii, we visited the Hopi, as described at the beginning of the chapter.

In mid-September 1999, our next meeting occurred right in Boulder, Colorado, where Catie and I were living at the time. Again through synchronicity, we learned that a shaman from the Andes of Ecuador was coming to a local university to share a prophecy that his people have had for thousands of years. Catie and I learned that the prophecy the shaman was disclosing was very similar to a Hopi prophecy: "Those from the Center make us unite the Eagle from the North and the Condor of the South. We will meet with our relatives because we are One."

We established a connection with this Andean shaman and explained the work of the WCOE to him. He understood immediately what was going on and invited us to visit with him and the other Elders of his area. However, much to our amazement, the realization of the prophecy was to occur within a matter of months. This would prove to be another prime example of synchronicity and the ripeness and acceleration of current time.

A few weeks later, Catie and I flew to Washington, D.C., to attend the Prayer Vigil for the Earth on the mall next to the Washington Monument. Here again we met Elders from the United States and Canada. They represented the Algonquin, Choctaw, Cherokee, Delaware, Lakota, Mohawk, Ojibwe, Oneida, and Shawnee tribes, and many others from around the world. Again, we received the same quiet response of knowing that the time is now. From these introductions and discussions, we all knew that it was just the beginning and that we would meet again many times.

A few weeks after this meeting, I headed to Massachusetts to meet Mayan Elders from Guatemala. Two people from different backgrounds contacted Catie and me to say that we should make a strong attempt to see these people. It was a meeting that was to have a large impact and bolster the work on the WCOE.

In the morning, I attended a fire ceremony for the first time. The energy that was being emitted from the flames was beyond my previous experience. I could feel the spiritual uplifting that was occurring.. It was during this very special ceremony that I felt a close connection to the Mayan Elders. After the fire ceremony, I visited with them and explained why I was there. During these special moments, I knew that I had met a sister and brother. After the afternoon session, I again met with the Mayans to discuss the work. They both knew the significance of what was occurring and suggested that Catie and I attend a special gathering in Guatemala in February 2000. That gathering would change the lives of all who attended.

In November 1999, Catie and I went on a five-week tour of the northern tier of the United States to visit Elders from a variety of Native American nations. Most of these Elders were of the younger age, and each one of them also referred to themselves as "bridges." A couple of these Elders were authors of books that introduced their native spirituality. They were mentored by well-known Spiritual Elders and had taken on the responsibility of writing these works. Some of these Elders are working with us to promote the WCOE throughout the United States. They were from the Hunkpapa, Oglala, Teton, MicMac, Abenaki, Cherokee, and Objibwe nations.

A couple of weeks later just before Christmas, Catie and I headed to Quebec City in Canada. It was here that we met a Huron Spiritual Elder who was working in a council with his people to develop the means (with supporting documents) for his people to govern themselves in their traditional ways. The Canadian government was working with them so they could become autonomous. It was a good opportunity to reconsider going back to the time-honored ways of self-government. They were creating councils from the grass-roots levels within the village.

These councils would consist of Spiritual Elders, who would oversee another Elder acting as a political liaison with the Canadian government. This was a way to keep politics as much out of the picture as possible. The purpose of these councils is to preserve the culture, heritage, history, and language. The main objective was to pass this knowledge to the children. This was a significant move in Canada and particularly for the Huron. This was their last village in existence and their last chance to save their identity as a First Nation. A long-lasting relationship developed from this first meeting.

In February 2000, a momentous gathering of Elders from North, Central, and South America took place at several Mayan sacred sites hosted by Gerardo Barrios, Carlos Barrios, Mercedes Barrios, and Mariano. They originate from the Mam Tribe, who are the Keepers of the Knowledge. The Elders gathered to observe the Mayan New Year, celebrate the last phase of the Mayan sacred calendar, which concludes in 2012, and conduct ceremonies to have the Condor fly with the Eagle. The Mayan New Year was the first of two New Years celebrations that will take place this year. This happens because the sacred Mayan calendar year is 260 days long and provides the possibility of two Mayan New Year celebrations in one Gregorian calendar year.

We learned that according to the sacred Mayan calendar, December 21, 2012, marks the turning point of three of the Mayan calendars: one a 3,600 -year cycle, one a 5,200-year cycle, and one a 67,600-year cycle. With the ending of the sacred Mayan calendar in 2012, the Mayans do not necessarily envision a doom-and-gloom scenario. They consider the end of these cycles to be the start of a new beginning, thus giving the human race more opportunities to do things right on this planet.

In addition to the celebrations, ceremonies were conducted between the Elders of the Americas to facilitate the North and South American prophecy of having the Condor unite with the Eagle. According to Mayan prophecy, they are to be the facili-tators for the South Americans to meet the North Americans. The two birds mentioned in the prophecies have diverse traits. The Eagle is aggressive and goes for its prey. It also represents the energy of the North, which tends to have more of a mental nature, whereas the Condor is patient and waits to complete the cycle of life. The Condor also represents the energy of the South, which tends to be more heart-oriented. When both these birds meet and fly together in harmony, they will create a balance. This unification of energies is needed to create balance on Mother Earth and within her people. Other groups of Elders are also meeting to assist in fulfilling this prophecy as well. There is a subtle urgency to complete this work.

Elder meetings were held along with ceremonies. These meetings resulted in a short list of priorities:

(1) The Elders felt that the healing of Mother Earth was an immediate priority. She is in pain and reflecting it in many parts of the world. This is observed through the climatic changes that are affecting the surface of the planet, causing fertile areas to dry up and temperatures to rise above normal in many areas. To the Western world this is known as global warming, which is being caused both by human intervention and natural Earth cycles. The human intervention may be accelerating these changes. This is why the Elders feel that healing Mother Earth is most important.

(2) Another priority voiced by the Elders is the preservation of sacred lands. Many of these lands are sacred, for they hold the energies of Mother Earth. If these lands are not properly cared for and stripped of their natural resources, the changes that occur in the energies of that area create an imbalance, which eventually affects the whole planet. These areas must be cared for and respected. The Elders who are connected with these lands know how to heal them, and they can teach us how to live in harmony with our Mother Earth when we are ready to listen.

(3) A third major priority is the healing of the entry points where the dominating societies came into the continents of the Western Hemisphere. The Elders feel that we all must heal and forgive. It is time for all peoples to come together and reconcile

their differences. We must stop wars and exploitation. The genocide of races must end now. This is a time of unification and peace. We all must work together to heal Mother Earth and prepare for the spiritual period that has been predicted by many persons around the planet. The Elders feel very strongly about these priorities. More unification work is in the making, but these three priorities are most important for the survival of the planet and its inhabitants at this time.

The Spiritual Elders believe that it is essential to heal the wounds of Mother Earth and balance the energies first, in preparation for the new time that is fast approaching. The Elders know that once this healing work is sufficiently in progress, the energies will be in place and the synchronicities can come together to support the work that will come forward as a natural result. The WCOE may become an advisory body to the U.N. or other world governments. However, this can only occur after a period of shift in the mind-set of those operating in these institutions of modern culture. Resulting work will also involve teaching and experiential programs led by the Elders. The Elders are particularly interested in the education of the children, especially those special kids coming in at this time with increased creativity, receptivity, and other abilities to integrate the ancient wisdom with the modern technology. With the wisdom of the Elders, these children will be equipped to manifest the true potential of humanity in the "now age."

The Journey of the Feathered Serpent

Over 20 years ago, Gerardo Barrios, Mayan Elder, began a quest to validate and understand the sacred Mayan calendars. He traveled to different villages in Central America searching for the most traditional Mayan Elders in very remote areas. He wanted to know if they were all using the same calendars. Except for some variation in names and small language differences, most of them matched. As part of this research, in 1988, he and nine other Mayans traveled to a very remote village where the traditional Mayans have dedicated their lives to keeping the temple fire for over a thousand years. The Mayans maintain this fire 24 hours a day as a prayer for peace on Earth. After a five-day walk through the deep forest, Gerardo and his team finally reached this village. The Elders had known through their own visions that this group was coming. The ten Mayans were given divinations, and only five were welcomed into the village's sacred temple. Gerardo was one of them.

Once inside the temple, one of the Elders took Gerardo aside to talk to him privately. The Elder began to introduce him to the story of the *feathered serpent* Kulkulkan, a snakelike sacred Earth energy that moves throughout the land. It took two more visits to this village to complete the story. The Mayan Elders of the village explained how this energy rises periodically and showed him on the map he had brought with him, where and when it had appeared. Later, when Gerardo tracked through history, he found along its path events such as the great spiritual awakening of Tibet in the 1950s, the anti-Vietnam War movement of the '60s, and leaders such as Martin Luther King.

These Elders said this that this *feathered serpent* has the intention to move down the Americas via the spine of Mother Earth to Lake Titicaca in the Andes, to be there in 2012. If one were to open a map of the Western Hemisphere and track the mountain ranges from Alaska in North America to Chile in South America, you would see them extend in a continuous line from North to South. This was described as the spine of Mother Earth.

This movement of energies must be completed to keep Mother Earth in balance. The energy also has a cycle that it must follow and fulfill in order to create the balance needed to keep things harmonious on this planet. However, this movement has encountered a barrier stopping its movement. It is backing up at the Panama Canal, where the ground was excavated and a water current was forced across the spine of the continents. When this energy is blocked, it can have disastrous results in the same way a spinal fracture can affect the function of the entire human body. Gerardo learned that spiritual ceremonies must be conducted to help the harmonious and natural flow of this energy of the *feathered serpent*. When Gerardo expressed concern about the magnitude of the task, the Elders told him not to worry about how it was to be done, for helpers would appear. These helpers began to appear in Guatemala in November 1995.

The Healing of Mother Earth

Other peoples have also expressed their concerns for the healing of Mother Earth. The Witoto tribe in South America has been in tune with the energy of the *feathered serpent*, and they have been conducting ceremonies to honor it. They feel strongly that it must complete its movement in order to balance out the whole planet.

The Tairona peoples, who inhabit the Sierra Nevada de Santa Marta in Columbia, South America, consist of the Kogi, Arahuaco, Arsarios, and Cancuamos. These peoples have only recently revealed themselves and have stepped down from the mountains of the Sierra Nevada de Santa Marta to convey strong messages about the devastation of Mother Earth's environment. This was presented in a BBC documentary made by Alan Ereira in 1993 titled *From the Heart of the World—the Elder Brothers' Warning*. The peoples of Tairona refer to themselves as "the Elder Brothers," and the Westerners as "the Younger Brother." They believe that it is their duty to look after the mountain, which they call "the Heart of the World." They are very concerned because they feel that the Younger Brother is destroying the balance of the planet. Their work to keep the planet in balance is being made increasingly more difficult by all the destruction. They can see that something is wrong with their mountain, the heart of the world. The mountain rivers have stopped flowing, and vegetation areas are drying up where before it was very green and fertile. When the mountain is sick, then the whole world is in trouble.

Even when the Younger Brother is hit between the eyes with truth, he often still does not understand what he's doing. In many ways, the current societies are not progressing, but regressing. One just needs to look at the big picture. Just look at the wars, atrocities, greed, oppression, domination, hatred, racial discrimination, abuses to Mother Earth, and so on. This presents a very bleak picture.

However, there is an underlying current weaving its way among many individuals in both the modern and indigenous worlds. Many now believe that it is their duty to look after the mountain that they call "the Heart of World." They are beginning to realize what is happening and want to make a positive contribution. There is still much good being done on this planet. It is time to take action.

The Collective Journey Continues

The journey to establish the WCOE is a very sacred one. It is a spiritual journey that has been in the making for thousands of years, and one that each of us is responsible for bringing into manifestation. It is time to gather the spiritual indigenous Elders from all the continents of this planet to bring forth the universal truths that they hold. It is time to find that place of quiet within ourselves in order to simply listen to what we know to be true within our hearts. It is time to remember who we are, why we're here, and to put the teachings of the ages into practice to restore balance, harmony, and peace to humanity and our precious Mother Earth.

Many individuals from around the world are awakening and beginning to resonate with the shift occurring at this extraordinary time. Humanity has "passed the marker," and the groundswell of hope and positive, loving energy is growing exponentially. Like no other time before, now is the time for each one of us to reclaim his/her power and exercise free choice to support the loving, healing work of the Elders. Now is the time for humanity and Mother Earth to step into their rightful place as conscious spiritual partners with the universe of all creation.

What You Can Do

We are so grateful for the generous contributions of time, energy, and funding from those beautiful and courageous humans with the vision to step forward in support of the WCOE. Of course, the monumental task at hand requires the love, prayers, pure intent, heart-centered commitment, and financial support of many enlightened people. A nonprofit organization has been developed to coordinate funding, as well as the logistics of bringing the Elders together and facilitating communication of their wisdom.

Please feel free to contact Catie and me for more information regarding the work of the WCOE. This is a journey from the heart, and is driven by the energy of synchronous events and contacts with people like you. We'd love to hear from you, and of course, your financial contributions are welcome and greatly appreciated.

For more information, please contact us at:

> *World Council of Elders*
> P.O. Box 5640
> Woodland Park, CO 80866
> Toll-free voicemail/fax: (877) 750-4162
> E-mail: wcoe4peace@earthlink.net

Donations are tax deductible and should be made out to: *World Council of Elders Fund*. Also, be on the lookout for our upcoming Website: [www.worldcouncilofelders.org].

— Woody Vaspra

P.S.: From Lee—

At noon on July 16th, 2000, in Santa Fe, New Mexico, Jan and I were honored to help unite Catie Johnson and Woody Vaspra in marriage. The ceremony was held before the attendees of the Kryon annual midsummer light conference.

"Science"

Lee Carroll

Chapter Fifteen

"Science"
by Lee Carroll

As you can see, this is the science section for this Kryon book. Much like other topics, it is a brief discussion of what has taken place since the last book in the area of science, which validates the potentials that Kryon has given us. As I have said before, I am not a scientist, so the discussions that follow are not filled with science-speak (the language most comfortable to the science-minded). Instead, it is an attempt to show relationships between what Kryon has given in channellings, to what is happening in the real world around us. I have always enjoyed the synchronicity in this, and in the last year, the distance between Kryon's words and the science validations has dramatically shortened, often coming in months instead of years.

If you have followed previous Kryon books, you know that some very profound channellings regarding specific scientific potentials given in the early 1990s have been validated within these pages. Some of them include: the faster-than-light *twins* (Kryon Book Six, page 370); the discovery of Deinococcus Radiodurans, the bacteria that eats nuclear waste (Kryon Book Seven, page 334); Kryon's comments regarding the Big Bang [that wasn't] (Kryon Book Six, page 374); the continuing hints regarding gamma ray activity and what it means (Kryon Books Six, page 367, and Kryon Book Seven, page 132); the way disease works (Kryon Book Six, page 376); and crop circle math (Kryon Book Six, page 365). For 11 years now, Kryon has been actively telling us the "way things work," and has invited us to discover it.

Here is some of the latest information since the last Kryon publication. I think that readers will be particularly interested in three areas of discussion: (1) DNA, (2) physics and the Cosmic lattice, (3) anthropology, and (4) totally weird stuff turned scientific (my favorite). There are more quotations in this Kryon book from valid science sources than in any other, showing more and more that, indeed, the weird is becoming more scientific every day!

The Search for Magnetic DNA

DNA (deoxyribonucleic acid) is a molecule of two chains— strands of chemical compounds called nucleotides. These chains are arranged like a twisted ladder, in a double helix (spiral).

Chromosomes are almost entirely composed of protein and nucleic acids, and in 1944, Canadian bacteriologist Oswald Theodore Avery proved that DNA is the substance that determines heredity. In 1953, American geneticist James Watson and British geneticist Francis Crick worked out the structure of DNA. They found that the DNA molecule is formed of two long strands in a double helix, somewhat resembling a long, spiral ladder. To make an identical copy of the DNA molecule, the two strands unwind and separate. New matching strands then form with each separated strand. DNA was actually discovered by Rosalind Elsie Franklin, who photographed it in the early 1950s.[*]

This paradigm of DNA has remained since its initial discovery, and has been well received and accepted by biologists and biochemists for almost 50 years. Now we know that within the chemical DNA there are "instructions for life," and in the year 2000, we have finally mapped the Human genome, and we are discovering the inner workings and codings of this marvelous puzzle. But Kryon says that there are far more than chromosomes and genetic life codes within this structure.

---

[*]*Encarta* ® *98 Desk Encyclopedia* © & 1996-97 Microsoft Corporation.

Eleven years ago, Kryon told us that Earth's magnetic field somehow "talked" to DNA! In subsequent books, he has given us some of the mechanics of this transfer, and has indicated that DNA is a magnetic engine of sorts and is very susceptible to outside magnetic influences. He has gone on to indicate that profound magnetic instructions are possible to be given to DNA, literally awakening hidden potentials that "rest" there, ready to be activated. In 1994, he even informed us how we did some ancient magnetic tinkering, using the Temple of Rejuvenation in Atlantis, which extended our lives—all using magnetics and DNA (Kryon Book Two—*Partnering with God*).

Back then, this information was greeted with howls of laughter from scientists, and provided fodder for attacks and fear-based messages from old-energy metaphysicians. When Kryon Book One entered the market in 1993, it seemed that Kryon and I instantly had enemies from both sides of the fence—established science and established metaphysics. As I have previously written, I expected ridicule from the scientists, but I didn't expect to be attacked by other lightworkers simply because Kryon spoke of magnetics and DNA.

To this day, there are still old-style, fear-based teachings that say that the magnetic grid of the earth is somehow evil in nature, a result of some battle between good and evil in the past. Each time I am confronted with this information, I wonder if they also feel that air is devil's food, dirt is satanic, or that the ionosphere of the planet is an evil plot against humanity. In other words, to me these things are basic elements of the planet, given to us in natural ways for our ongoing, balanced existence. I don't consider them to be a result of some mystic battle or fable that created the planet.

To me, developing fear-based scenarios around basic Earth elements is a disservice to Gaia itself, and also an insult to the indigenous peoples of the planet who regularly honored and celebrated the magnetics of Earth—the east, west, north, and south. Kryon tells us that the magnetic grid was created for us, and helps to posture both the duality, our enlightenment, and even carries the engine for astrological attributes. I look at all nature as something given to us carefully, with the greatest love. But for some, since Kryon deals with the magnetic grid, he must be the cosmic evil [sigh].

Science was far gentler on Kryon—simply ignoring everything that was said. This is still the case today, and is the expected reaction from credible scientific sources. After all, channelling is weird, spooky stuff, right? No basis in fact. Not science. Even as some of the information brought to us back then is starting to become reality, it still isn't prudent for biologists, physicists, or M.D.'s to publish anything that might have Kryon's name associated with it. I truly understand this, and it is acceptable to me.

The interesting part of our work at the moment is that we now attract many M.D.'s and scientists to Kryon seminars all over the world! They are lightworkers, too, you know—they just can't tell many of their peers about it. Many of these professionals enjoy the Kryon books just as you do. I happen to know that there are Kryon books hidden in drawers of the United States Missile Command in Huntsville, Alabama; the Livermore Laboratory in California; and in countless hospitals and research laboratories throughout the nation. The reason? Many of the owners of those books have attended the Kryon seminars and have told me so—and most of them had impressive initials after their names.

Before I let you in on some of the recent discoveries about DNA, I want to bring you up-to-date on some very basic Kryon admonitions: (1) Stay away from stray magnetic fields that you might live or work in, and (2) be careful about electric blankets (Kryon Book One—*The End Times,* page 20).

When these two admonitions were given back in 1989, the scientific community was not convinced that either was a problem. As I have previously written, both of these admonitions are oversimplifications of what Kryon has spoken about regarding magnetics. Not all fields are bad for you, but you should at least be aware of what you decide to sleep around, or live within. There are many kinds of magnetic fields, and lots of attributes to consider.

Saying that magnetic fields are bad for you is like saying that water is bad for you. It is, if you're drowning in it, or drinking it loaded with bacteria. Otherwise, it might also heal you, or at the least, hydrate your body and quench your thirst. Magnetic fields are in the same category. You can't just take a generality that says that "magnetic fields are bad." Are they active or passive fields? Strong or weak? Random or designed?

Power lines can be horrible for you—or not affect you at all, depending on the current they carry, and the patterns—how their fields combine at the point where you live or work. Each case is different, but in general, we are warned about a condition of active fields that generate fields around the Human Being strong enough to move a compass.

Back in 1989, this Kryon information was also suspect by science, and many of you had a difficult time finding anything to validate it. There was no scientific experimentation regarding Kryon's words of wisdom. This has now changed. I present for you evidence of what science is now looking into. David A. Savitz, an epidemiologist at the University of North Carolina; and Antonio Sastre at the Midwest Research Institute in Kansas City, have both published works on a very interesting study:

The two researchers and their team now report that compared with men who worked in low-EMF jobs, men in trades exposed to high EMFs—such as linemen and power-

plant operators—were far more likely to have died from heart attacks and heart conditions related to abnormal rhythms, or arrhythmias.

Moreover, risk of death from these conditions climbed as average EMF exposure increased. Savitz notes that men in the highest risk group tended to have worked in EMFs at least twice as high as those that people typically encounter in their homes.

Taken together, these "suggest a possible association between occupational magnetic fields and arrhythmia related heart disease," the researchers conclude in the January 15th American Journal of Epidemiology. [1]

Remember Kryon's electric blanket advice? Although there is still no solid science supporting that they might be bad for you, the manufacturers are taking no chances. This, from *Science News*. In answer to the question, *"The biological effects of electric and magnetic fields remain questionable. Has anyone specifically checked the electric bed-blanket?"* [2]

Several research teams have investigated risks that might stem from spending long periods under electric blankets. We reported that manufacturers were re-engineering blanket wiring to reduce a sleeper's exposures to electric and magnetic fields.[2]

So, magnetics may affect cellular structure? It seems that way with some of the science articles that are being seen now. I have ignored this big DNA question now for ten years. There simply was no evidence at the molecular level that magnetics

---

[1] *Science News*; Janet Raloff; Volume 155; January 30, 1999; "Electromagnetic fields may damage hearts"; page 70.

[2] *Science News*: Janet Raloff; Volume 156; August 28, 1999; "No blanket answer on EMFs"; page 131.

might be a part of DNA. But last year my heart skipped a beat with two distinct discoveries that landed in the news. These discoveries finally opened the door for known scientific principles to explain how DNA might possibly have a magnetic component, or at least it could have the attributes of a magnetic reception device. (Kryon said it did, even in this book.)

I find that I'm not alone in my quest. Science is also looking for a biological mechanism that might help explain how magnetics affects cells:

> *Although the data linking electric and magnetic fields to cancers or other diseases is weak, a new federal review concludes that exposures to these fields "cannot be recognized as entirely safe."*
>
> *Seven years ago, Congress established a federal EMF Research and Public Information Dissemination Program to try to find biological mechanisms that might explain the epidemiology linking EMFs to cancer.*
>
> *Overall, the report finds, epidemiological studies of Human populations exposed to high EMFs have shown a "fairly consistent pattern of a small, increased risk with increasing exposure" for both childhood leukemia and chronic lymphocytic leukemia in adults.* [3]

What I found next was hiding since 1998! Scientists have been very skeptical about EMFs damaging DNA. Getting cancer from EMF exposure was something that was simply not accepted. This was because scientists could not believe that the fields could *damage cells* from a distance, and with that low of an energy (gauss). Now what is finally being realized is what Kryon

---

[3] *Science News*: Janet Raloff: Volume 156; July 3, 1999; "EMFs—doubts linger over possible risks"; page 12.

has said all along. Magnetics (EMFs) are not *damaging cells!* EMFs are giving instructions to cells at a low level, through the DNA, and the instructions could be harmful. This is old news to readers of Kryon, but suddenly science is agreeing.

> *For about 6 years, pediatric oncologist Faith M. Uckun of the Wayne Hughes Institute in St. Paul, Minn., reviewed research proposals on EMFs from people seeking grant money from the National Institutes of Health. Without a mechanism for suspected EMF risks, he says, "I thought it was voodoo."*
>
> *That assessment is now coming back to haunt him, he says. His latest test tube studies show that magnetic fields with a frequency of 60 hertz and a strength of 1 gauss—trigger a cascade of enzyme-driven cell-signaling events. These short-distance communications serve as a means by which cells can relay operational directions to their DNA.* [4]

Can it be any clearer? This article is indicating exactly what Kryon has been saying all along. Cell-signaling events? Operational directions to DNA? This is not EMF *damage.* It's *communication!*

Let me briefly explain exactly what I have been looking for, and to some degree what the quotes I have shown says that research is looking for, also. Within DNA, I have always wanted to find the magnetic "engine." I need to show the possibility of "inductance" (as Kryon mentioned). As an audio engineer, I understand inductance within electrical circuits.

Let me explain and make it simple. When you have two magnetic fields that intersect each other, you have a unique situation where electrical attributes may be transferred though

---

[4] *Science News*; J. Raloff; Volume 153, February 21, 1998; "Electromagnetic fields may trigger enzymes"; page 119.

the magnetic field without any wires touching. Two coils of wire located next to each other can pass current between them without any physical contact. The process is called inductance. It's not very esoteric, either, for transformers of every kind and size do it daily in millions of devices all over the world. It's very well known, and is probably in everything you own, from your toaster to your computer.

Lately, science has been given more and more credit to magnetics, and also to electric attributes within the body. Suddenly science is also climbing on the magnetic healing bandwagon (even though for some reason they won't admit that stray magnetics is bad for you!). I'm looking carefully for scientific evidence of inductance, and I found it in several places already!

Most news reports about EMFs have focused on emanations from power lines, building wiring, and appliances. They have chronicled the continuing controversy over whether these fields have unhealthy effects, such as perturbed sleep patterns, altered heart rhythms, and cancer. Yet while these risks have grabbed headlines, EMFs have been quietly edging into medicine.

Over the past 20 years, FDA has approved EMF generators for two medical uses. The devices are used frequently to treat bone fractures that have stopped healing, and EMF treatment is also increasingly being applied to fuse spinal vertebrae in people with intractable back pain.

More recent techniques enable fields to be delivered without electrodes touching the body. "This is the most important therapeutic advance in recent years," suggests Arthur A. Pilla, a biophysicist at the Mount Sinai School of Medicine in New York City. He explains that the newer devices transfer a field's energy into the body from wire coiled around, but not touching, the injured area. [5] *(bottom of next page)*

What? Not touching the body? How weird!... call the priest and get the exorcist! Oops, never mind, it's science now. (I'm having fun ... don't send me letters.) That's exactly what I'm looking for—a coiled wire around the injured area? That's inductance! I have to ask, "How then does the body receive this healing?" There absolutely has to be something molecular receiving the information from the coiled wire being used on the outside of the body. Are any of you projecting this potential of inductance (just validated in the article on the previous page) with the very spooky (science talk) action of metaphysical energy work? The next time you see it, do it, or have it done on you, remember the scientific healing technique above, where EMF work is being done in a laboratory *without touching* the Human! And they said *we* were weird?

While searching for inductance in the Human body's cellular structure, I also stumbled onto a known biological phenomenon that blew me away! I had never realized that the basis of synapse within the brain depends on inductance! We have the world's most powerful computer in our heads, and we now understand that none of the "wires" (nerves in our brains) in that big computer connect to each other! The nerve endings that carry our thoughts and memories—called synapses—surge with tens of millions of instruction sets per day through our brains and never touch each other. They only come close to each other!

We already know about the electrical characteristics of the brain. This is very well acknowledged, and even measurable using an EKG machine. So (follow me here), here is the Human brain, a computer using electrical current, where the "wires" don't touch. This is a wonderful example of inductance within the Human biological system. It's obvious that synapse is a type of "information" transferred between nerves using inductance.

[5] Science News: Janet Raloff: Volume 156; November 13, 1999; "Medicinal EMFs"; Page 316.

This also indicates that a magnetic field must surround each nerve ending. This follows basic electricity rules, and makes sense. In addition, it also helps us understand how our brains can often "rewire" themselves in case of injury or trauma. Many times the brain retrains itself to use other parts when one is damaged. Since it isn't "hard wired" (with nerves connected), it can then reroute the electrical paths—and it does!

I bring this up so that you might understand that there is now a protocol of the very thing I'm looking for within DNA, as a known part of the way our bodies work. Therefore, it's not so strange, after all, to be looking for this process in other areas of our chemical makeup. Nerves carry electrical energy, however. It's understandable how they might have a magnetic field. DNA isn't known for its electrical attributes, so I still have a way to go to find my DNA magnetic engine.

I found, however, an overall statement that I have been hoping to see for years: an acknowledgment of the importance of electrical characteristics within ALL biology (that's DNA, too):

> *THE GLUE OF MOLECULAR EXISTENCE IS FINALLY UNVEILED: Of the roughly 20 million chemical substances scientists have catalogued, ranging from simple ones like water to gigantic compounds like DNA, nearly all are assemblages of atoms linked together by electronic bonds. The quest to understand these tiny bonds—the very glue of material existence—is the heart of chemical science.* [6]

My quest as a nonscientist to find a magnetic property of DNA was lifted a few notches as I read this conclusion. Scientists

---

[6] *The New York Times*; Malcolm W. Browne; September 7 1999; "The Glue of Molecular Existence is Finally Unveiled"; Science Desk.

are starting to talk like Kryon! But I'm still missing some profoundly needed things to even begin to postulate something as odd as magnetic DNA. I need to show the possibility of natural electrical current within DNA. This is tough! First, for current, you need a loop. Second, it is a known fact that chromosomes conduct electricity very poorly—if at all! For ten years it looked like I would never find the potential information I was looking for—until now. Last April (1999), someone E-mailed me the first line of a tantalizing science article that shocked me:

> *DNA is a building block of life, but it might also some day be a building block of minuscule electronic devices. That is the tantalizing possibility raised by new research that shows that DNA conducts electricity.* [7]

I couldn't believe I was reading this! I located the full article on-line, and printed it out. Here is more:

> *The study found that while DNA will never be a substitute for copper wire, it does conduct electricity about as efficiently as a good semiconductor.*

A semiconductor? That device is the heart of almost everything electronic you and I own (okay, maybe not your toaster). I searched and found more on this subject:

> *"DNA transports electric current in much the same way as semi-conductive material," says physicist Hans-Werner Fink and Christian Schoenberger of the University of Basel's Institute of Physics in Switzerland. "You get not just a scaled-down*

---

[7] *The New York Times*; Henry Fountain; April 13, 1999; "Observatory"; Science Desk.

*version of a wire, but very different properties," says Fink.
"With DNA, the width of the conductor is comparable with the
wavelength of the electron. We might be dealing with ballistic
electron transport. Ballistic means that no scattering of slowing
of the electrons takes place." This could mean faster connections
that are free of the impurities found in even the best semicon-
ductors. [8]*

Ballistic electron transport? Suddenly, after all this time,
DNA conducts electricity... and in a way not seen before! What
is odd is that chromosomes don't! Therefore, the parts don't, yet
the whole does! Go figure. Still missing, however, is the circle.
You need a circular path to get electrons going in a continuous
route to create current. But alas, chromosomes and DNA are
built as a strand, not a loop—or are they? After 50 years, could
there indeed be something dramatic about the shape of something as well documented as DNA? Yes! I found it only one
month later than the article regarding the conductivity of DNA.

> *It is almost as surprising as discovering a new bone in the
> human body. Biologists reported that chromosomes—the lengthy
> DNA molecules that carry our genetic instructions—end in
> neatly tied loops. Biologists must have gazed thousands of times
> through microscopes at the 46 chromosomes in the nucleus of
> every normal human cell without perceiving what has now been
> discovered: the ends of the chromosomes—the immensely long
> molecules of DNA that carry the genetic information—are
> neatly tied in large, firmly knotted loops.*
>
> *The loops provide the answer no one had divined: Normal
> chromosomes have no ends, only the perfect topological con-
> tinuum of a circle. [9]*

---

[8] *Popular Science*; Hank Schlesinger; August, 1999; "DNA Conduc-
tors"; electronics section.
[9] *The New York Times*; Nicholas Wade; May 14, 1999; "Chromosomes
End in Tied Loops, Study Finds"; National Desk.

Science News also reported this, and brought in more detail regarding telomeres.

> *Scientists had thought that telomeres consist of a linear DNA molecule, with one of the DNA's usually paired strands slightly longer than the other. This telomeric overhang posed a dilemma: Cells don't tolerate single-stranded DNA. Why haven't biologists observed "t-loops" before? Telomeres are only a small portion of a chromosome's DNA. "Unless someone had been looking for a loop, it would be easy to miss," says (Jack D.) Griffith.* [10]

I now have my electric DNA engine! Within a few months of each other, unrelated research shows that DNA conducts electricity, and loops in a circle. Okay, okay—nobody said that DNA was magnetic, and nobody has yet to discover any kind of current lurking in a DNA loop.

But let me paraphrase the above science into my own future quote: "Why haven't biologists observed *the magnetic field* before? Unless someone had been looking for a *magnetic field*, it would be easy to miss." If science could have missed the obvious loop for 40 years, who knows what else they missed? At the rate this is going, we might even get this statement this year . . . or by the time this book is printed.

My contention is that DNA is now being shown to have the potential to carry electrical current much like the brain does. Perhaps there is a very tiny magnetic field around each chromosome? Who knows—but I firmly believe that our own science will shortly give Kryon full validation that the heretofore eye-rolling postulate that DNA is magnetic—will become science.

---

[10] *Science News*; J. Travis; Volume 155, May 22, 1999; "Closing the loop on the end of a chromosome"; page 326.

When it does, it will explain how power lines and electric sleeping blankets might affect us, as well as magnetic mattresses and chairs . . . and, oh yes, how something called the magnetic field of Earth might "talk" to the cellular structure of the Human DNA. Yesterday's weirdness is starting to become today's fact.

Physics and the Cosmic Lattice

I don't ever expect that physicists or astronomers will someday discover hidden energy in the darkness of space and call it the "Cosmic Lattice." That is the name given by Kryon to a carefully balanced energy that pervades space, and was explained and published in Kryon Book Seven—*Letters from Home.*

I am, however, looking for scientific discoveries that would work hand-in-hand with what Kryon has described. Without going into an extensive Cosmic Lattice review, suffice it to say that I am looking for science to find Kryon's description of the unique and elusive "cosmological constant" that the Cosmic Lattice represents. In addition, anything about hidden energy or magnetic fields in free space would be a wonderful hint, too.

Again, I report to you that I found both concepts in science articles written in 1999 and 2000! You would have to understand the overview of my search. I have been waiting for anything of this sort for a very long time, and suddenly it appears all over the place within months of each other in 1999 and 2000. Coincidence? Or are we being given some wonderful new energy of discovery at a time when we are also being released from "the end of days"?

There was a wonderfully extensive article by James Glanz in the October 1999 issue of *Astronomy* regarding the cosmological constant and a new discovery about missing energy. It is well written and worth finding if you want a complete story.

Remember the original cosmological constant? Albert Einstein postulated it in 1917 as his "fudge factor"—an *add-on* to his Theory of Relativity. Evidently this theory didn't quite work for things as large as the entire universe, and by applying his cosmological constant, he got it all to balance. Later he called this idea his "biggest blunder," and apologized.

What Mr. Glanz reports is that Einstein was right, and the cosmological constant is now being rediscovered. What has been found is shocking astronomers and physicists alike. And, according to Glanz's article, it hasn't been an easy sell. The discovery is simple: The expanding universe is expanding past the potential of the energy that created it! In other words, gravity should be acting like a brake over time, slowly making the acceleration and expansion decrease, and eventually bringing it to a halt altogether (gravity does that, you know). The discovery is that, instead, it's speeding up! In order to have an accelerating cosmos, there has to be hidden energy working against gravity— and that's the subject of *"one of the more important developments in any field of science in the 203th century,"* [11] says Glanz.

> *"It would be a magical discovery," said (Michael) Turner [who predicted that the cosmological constant would be found]. "What it means is that there is some form of energy we don't understand."* [11]

The famous scientist Stephen Hawking, the University of Cambridge cosmologist, initially said that the ongoing cosmological constant discoveries were *"too preliminary to be taken seriously."* [11]

---

[11] *Astronomy*; James Glanz; October 1999; "Accelerating the Cosmos—Cosmologists have discovered a new kind of energy that is speeding up the universe's expansion"; page 44.

Now, Glanz reports that Hawking says, *"I have now had more time to consider the observations—I now think it is very reasonable that there should be a cosmological constant."* [11]

Glanz sums up his article with this statement:

> *What physical energy is responsible for the constant? Nobody knows. The so-called "funny energy" could be anything from the evanescent particles that quantum mechanics says should pop in and out of existence, to a weird, fluid-like substance called quintessence. Oddly enough, now that particle theorists have started thinking about this new funny stuff, their calculations are producing too much of it rather than too little.* [11]

I love the term "funny energy." It's much better than the Kryon name, the Cosmic Lattice! Hey, Kryon, why didn't you call it "funny energy"? Another interesting discovery regarding what is now being found in space with our ever-better instrumentation also goes right along with Kryon's Cosmic Lattice. Kryon spoke of electromagnetic forces that keep energy balanced at zero—or what he called a "null" state. He also spoke of some regular unbalancing of the Lattice that we could see, including how black holes were a part of it all. If this is the case, then we should expect to see magnetic energy outside of the influence of galaxies or other physical "seen" matter. This would help show the workings of some kind of electromagnetic force unrelated to gravity. In May 2000, this was reported:

> *Hunting for magnetic energy in intergalactic space, researchers have found an unexpected motherlode of it. Both in the gaps between galaxies that are clustered and in the lonelier neighborhoods outside those clusters, magnetic fields are remarkably strong, a scientific team reports.*

"This is evidence of a tremendous energy source that astronomers have overlooked," comments theorist Stirling A. Colgate of Los Alamos (N.M.) National Laboratory.

"That tells us there's significant energy in space contained in the [intergalactic] magnetic fields," says Philipp P. Kronberg of the University of Toronto, responsible for the decade-long search.

"I'm surprised, very surprised," says Russel M. Kulsrud of Princeton University, adding that he harbors some doubts that the strengths are quite as high as Kronberg says they are, "but even if the field strengths are a bit smaller," he adds, "they are still very difficult to explain." [12]

So, it seems that science is finding some of the formerly weird and eye-rolling attributes of the Cosmic Lattice. Almost all of these reports are filled with the words *unexpected* or *surprising*. (I still like "funny energy.")

Another very surprising revelation from physics is also in the news, and it, too, is reinforcing information we have learned from Kryon almost since the beginning regarding discussions about the essence of the atom. Kryon has taught many times (in channellings) about the interdimensionality of matter. He told us that much is hidden, and that, like DNA, there are simply things that are working, but unseen.

The whole idea of anything being interdimensional has always been something relegated to the woo-woo or science fiction crowd. To consider regular matter or biology as multi-dimensional stuff is really getting "out there" (kind of like "funny energy" . . . ha, ha). Therefore, when I read the concept within a science journal in February 2000, I was astonished!

[12] *Science News*; Peter Weiss; Volume 157, May 6, 2000; "Intergalactic Magnetism Runs Deep and Wide"; page 294.

Only two years ago, the idea of extra dimensions inhabited a nebulous region somewhere between physics and science fiction. Many physicists had already begun to see the up-and-coming string theory as the next major step for theoretical physicists. In that theory, everything in the universe is composed of tiny loops, or strings, of energy vibrating in a space-time that has six or seven extra dimensions of space and one of time. Those extra dimensions are compacted, as physicists say, crumpled up in a space so small as to be unobservable.

The idea that extra dimensions might be larger—perhaps detectable—was something that scientists mostly talked about "late at night, after a lot of wine," says Gordon L. Kane, a theorist from the University of Michigan in Ann Arbor. Kane therefore felt he was walking on the wild side when he penned a fictional news story about experimenters discovering extra dimensions.

Even by the time his article came out, however, the possibility no longer seemed quite as surprising as it had when he wrote it a few months earlier. Between the submission of Kane's [fictional] story and its publication, two theoretical studies had come out that suddenly pushed the whole idea of relatively large extra dimensions into the spotlight. [13]

The article goes on to say that two studies have shown this unexpected discovery. One study was conducted at CERN, the European Laboratory for Particle Physics in Geneva, and the other one—a combination of Stanford University and the Abdus Salam International Center for Theoretical Physics (ICTP) in Trieste, Italy.

[13] *Science News*; Peter Weiss; Volume 157, February 19, 2000; "Hunting for Higher Dimensions"; page 122.

> *Today, teams of experimentalists in both the United States and Europe are searching for the signatures of extra dimensions. The hunt for such indicates "certainly one of the best chances of making a very spectacular discovery in the next couple of years," says Joseph Lykken of the Fermi National Accelerator Laboratory in Batavia, Ill.* [13]

So now we return full circle to the beginning of this book, where I try to explain the interdimensionality of life in Chapter 1, called "Hard Concepts." Then, of course, Kryon channels about it in Chapters 2 and 3, called "Time and Reality." Now, here we are at the end of this book, and I get to present the fact that science is beginning to do the same thing! I also like to point to page 110 in this book, where Pope John Paul spoke of the "ultimate realities of Heaven and Hell," and how they were not as we were originally told. All this points out that we are beginning to understand that *we* are interdimensional creatures in an interdimensional world. I just didn't expect mainstream religion and physics to say it at the same time! (See page 379)

It's been a banner two years for discoveries in DNA and physics in relation to the validation of Kryon's teachings, but I really didn't expect what follows. Now I get to speak to you about anthropology—the study of the origin of the Human species.

The Humans of Today Are Not a Product of Normal Evolution!

Take a look at the channelling in this book in Chapter 7, starting on page 162. Channelled in California in December 1999, Kryon is speaking about a setup of Humanity. The subject is "Past Intervention of Human Biology." In review, Kryon told us that we, as Humans, represented only one "kind" of Human, and that this really was against everything we understood about natural selection, and the accepted process of evolution on Earth.

Here is what Kryon said:

Dear Human Beings at the top of the evolutionary chain, why is it that there is only one kind of Human? You may ask, "Kryon, what do you mean? There are many differences in Humans." Listen: We wish you to look at ALL other biology on your planet. Look at all the orders, species, and types. You are the top of the chain, yet there are many kinds of mammals, many kinds of whales, many kinds of primates. Every single type has many kinds, until it gets to the Human. Then, an anthropological anomaly happened: Only one kind of Human got placed at the top! [14]

Somewhere, there should be some evidence of this evolutionary anomaly, and I wondered if anyone would ever really notice it, or truly understand what Kryon was speaking about. After all, this is a very strange thing to speak of. We are very used to there only being one kind of Human . . . and most of us don't even think twice about it.

Never have I had such a quick validation of what Kryon channelled—and on a subject that he has never broached before. At the beginning of the year, I spotted the cover of the January 2000 issue of *Scientific American* [15] in an airport (where else?), and I was stunned at the cover story. I present the cover here on the next facing page. Take a look at what this scientific magazine is saying!

---

[14] Kryon speaking about the Human setup; Chapter 7 in this book, page 162.
[15] *Scientific American*; Ian Tattersall; Volume 282, Number 1; January 2000; "Once We Were Not Alone"; page 56.

We were not alone. Our species had at least 15 cousins. Only we remain. Why?

Today we take for granted that Homo sapiens is the only hominid on Earth. Yet for at least four million years many hominid species all shared the planet. What makes us different?

Homo sapiens has had the earth to itself for the past 25,000 years or so, free and clear of competition from other members of the hominid family. This period has evidently been long enough for us to have developed a profound feeling that being alone in the world is an entirely natural and appropriate state of affairs.

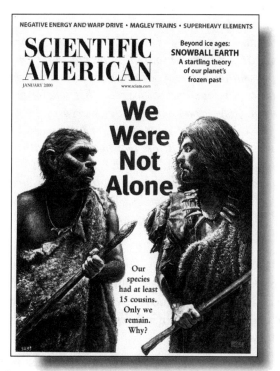

Scientific American; Volume 282, Number 1; January 2000.

Despite our rich history—during which hominid species developed and lived together and competed and rose and fell— H.sapiens ultimately emerged as the sole hominid. The reasons for this are generally unknowable . . . [15]

Now I also realize (and this is for those of you Kryon fans who have all the books), that Kryon gave us a "heads up" on this very fact in Kryon Book Two—*Don't Think Like a Human*. Here is Kryon speaking in 1994 of exactly what we just found . . .

Human History Limits on Earth: *You have a splendid lineage on the planet! Your lineage goes back as much as 300,000 years. You would be well admonished, however (if you must study the history to know who you were), to look at the information that is only as old as 100,000 years. The reason for this? If you consume yourself in the search for knowledge and information that represents a period longer than that, you will be studying humans which are not like you, for there was a marked change at that time (100,000 years ago). The humans that you know around you now conform to the ones of only 100,000 years in age. Before that there was a different scenario, one that might be of interest, but which will not be discussed tonight. We have spoken in the past of your history before the ice (in past channellings), and of the seed biology of your species. The difference is in the DNA. That is how you know of your specific human type.* [16]

It appears that Kryon was telling us all about this whole thing even in 1994. How does the time frame that Kryon gave, stack up to the recent article in *Scientific American?* I again quote Mr. Tattersall:

[16] Kryon Book Two—*Don't Think Like a Human*; 1994; Lee Carroll; "Human History Limits on Earth; Chapter 11; page 164.

> *Although the source of H. sapiens as a physical entity is obscure, most evidence points to an African origin perhaps between 150,000 and 200,000 years ago. Modern behavior patterns did not emerge until much later. The best evidence comes from Israel and environs, where Neanderthals lived about 200,000 years ago or perhaps even earlier. By about 100,000 years ago, they had been joined by anatomically modern H. sapiens . . .* [15]

The time frame is much the same, according to the article, and it all starts to fit together . . . again to what we were given in channelling so many years ago.

So here we are in the new millennium, beginning to learn more about our history from scientific sources that are now beginning to align with the Kryon writings. You think this is something? Wait until we find what Kryon gave us in this book regarding the Human map. Remember Kryon's channelling in Chapter 6 of this book (page 146)? He speaks of revelations regarding the Human genome. It's true that we finished the map this year (2000), but that's not a decoded map. We still have to decode the information. It's like finally finding the entire script of a play that's in a strange language. Now we have to understand what the words mean. Kryon tells us there will be some surprises—ones that might point to intervention, or at least a curiosity of logic and evolution. Perhaps by the next book I will be able to quote from science on that, too?

The Weird and Amazing—Turned Scientific

This will be short . . . since this section is a new one, but I fully expect it to grow with time. I think I will name it "*The Eye-Rolling* Stops Here*" department of the Kryon books. Below are

---

* *"Eye-rolling"*—Defined as unbelieved, inconceivable, unthinkable, unimaginable, staggering, and associated with channelling and other weird stuff.

items I found in mainstream magazines, both scientific and general, regarding issues that have formerly been eye-rolling to most.

How long has it been that Kryon (and most other metaphysical types) have been telling humanity that a focus on the inner self will create long lives and healing? In fact, Kryon has been telling this to us from the very beginning. One of the anchors of Kryon's message is that we can have much longer lives when we find the peace of who we really are. The end of worry, the reduction of stress, and the balance of being will be the result, along with direct biological intervention and change. Take a look at what is now being "discovered" by science . . . all in the year 2000.

Medical Mantra

While it's no surprise that transcendental meditation reduces stress, researchers now show that using TM to reach a higher state of consciousness may help unclog arteries. African Americans with high blood pressure who practiced meditation for six months saw a .098-mm decrease in the fatty buildup in arterial walls, compared with an increase of .054-mm among folks who simply tried to change their diet and life-style. Getting results takes some effort. First you need to learn how to meditate, which can take hours, and then you should do it for 20 minutes each morning and evening. [17]

Say what? The health page of *Time* magazine is advocating doing meditation to unclog arteries (eye-roll, eye-roll)? It's true! What about living longer using spirituality as your guide? You think that's ever going to be a scientific issue? Think again . . .

---

[17] *Time* magazine; Your Health—"Good News—Medical Mantra"; March 13, 2000; page 98.

Religious Commitment Linked
to Longer Life

Regular involvement in religious activities goes hand in hand with better physical health and a longer life, according to a statistical analysis of 42 independent studies published since 1977 that have addressed this issue.

"Scientists now need to examine the pressing matter of what causes the association between religious activity and mortality," asserts a team led by psychologist Michael E. McCollough of the National Institute for Healthcare Research in Rockville, MD.

"This is a phenomenon that deserves a lot more attention than it has traditionally received," says McCullough. [18]

Can you believe what you are reading here? This came out of a major scientific magazine! An association between spiritual activity and life span? Okay, everyone, I want to be fair. Within the same article, however, even after 42 independent studies over 23 years showed scientific correlation . . . it was just too much of an eye-roller for George Kaplan, a social epidemiologist at the University of Michigan in Ann Arbor. He states: *"There is absolutely no basis for recommending religiosity as a preventive strategy in heath care."* [17]

It's okay, George (eye-roll, eye-roll). Nobody's going to make you get weird or spiritual if you don't want to. However, this scientist, as well as many others, must hate this trend toward the verification of the formerly laughable creeping into their professional lives and periodicals. I can relate to this (oddly enough), and I also feel it's part of the message within the channelling of this book. I remember as an engineer with more than 20 years' experience how I fought the idea that there might be energy within Human consciousness. Now I believe there is, and it has expanded my thinking. I gave away nothing in my transition, and my engineering mind is still with me to this day. It's just a bit larger in the scope of what the Universe might include in the workshop of elements that make up the whole picture.

Regarding those who won't budge: Will these folks deny this evidence to the end, or will they investigate with integrity? Only time will tell, and, according to Kryon, they will have to make a decision to eye-roll or not to eye-roll. It's all part of "No More Fence-Sitting," explained in Chapter 10 in this book.

Are you ready for something you never thought you would see in your lifetime? Remember the *20/20* TV program several years ago where the idea of hands-on healing was "proven" to be bogus? Or how about the science fair project that made the national news, presented by a young person who also "proved" that this "eye-rolling" work wasn't viable?

Both of these examples from the national press, mentioning the ability of a Human to affect another Human with energy work of some kind, were highly suspect. The details and procedures of the "studies" were taken to task by many. But, seemingly, the damage was done, and some of us thought that this mainstream "eye-roller" was doomed to stay that way . . . its reputation continuing to be tarnished and devalued even though "hands-on" is practiced in major religions as well as metaphysical circles worldwide (the indigenous, too). Now comes this:

Going the Distance

It's enough to make a skeptic squirm. After analyzing the results of two dozen trials, researchers say there may be some merit in the alternative art of "distance healing," which includes praying for someone's well-being, and "therapeutic touch," in which healers move their hands over (but not on) a patient's body. In 57% of the studies, these practices appeared to accelerate recovery or reduce pain. As for how distance healing may work, that's for a higher authority to say. [19]

I think I will take a deep breath now . . .

What can I say? Finally someone is not afraid to scientifically test some of the strangest ideas—issues that were formerly relegated to areas of non-science, or at least what many are calling pseudo-science. Indeed! Perhaps there should be a separate area where these things belong, but it needs to be an area that is as respected as any other, and one where those studying it no longer need to hide the books they are reading, or experiments they are doing . . . and it should not be called paranormal. It absolutely *is* normal. That's the issue, isn't it?

Finally, I bring you this: Is it weird? No. Is it amazing? I think so—amazing to me, anyway. For many years we have tried to break through the kind of thinking that was so revered that to even postulate it wasn't so would bring you trouble. Now it's beginning to surface by itself. It's about time, and I honor the courage of those brave enough to step forward and report it. There are many things Kryon has told us about the universe and physics. Some are still eye-rollers, but there is one that is the "Holy Grail" of scientific thought.

[19] *Time* magazine; Your Health—"Good News—Going the Distance"; June 19, 2000; page 145.

The speed of light is so well accepted as the absolute speed of anything in the universe that we measure universal distances using it. It has been plugged into physics formulas, math formulas, and has played the part of "the standard" for so many years that it is in danger of becoming sacred. It has shaped what we think, and has limited us to what is possible.

Kryon told us long ago that the speed of light was not the absolute speed at all. He tells us that the Cosmic Lattice has transmission of vibrations that far exceed anything we can even conceive of (Kryon Book Two, page 220; Kryon Book Six, page 369; and Kryon Book Seven, page 359).

Here is yet another wall of existing belief beginning to crumble as physical possibilities overcome tradition—much like those who tell us that atomic structure is now interdimensional (eye-roll, eye-roll). I honor those who bring us this!

Warp Speed

That Einstein guy—pretty smart, right? Here's a puzzle for him. Last week two independent groups of researchers, one in the U.S. and one in Italy, each claimed to have found a way to make light travel faster than its regular cruising speed of 186,000 miles per second. According to the special theory of relativity, that's verboten; the velocity of light is supposed to be the cosmic speed limit, which nothing can exceed. Nevertheless, a physicist, Lijun Wang of the NEC Research Institute in Princeton, N.J., says he revved up a beam of light as much as 300 times its normal speed, using a special chamber filled with cesium gas. Now let's see him prove it. [20]

[20] *Time* magazine; Your Technology—"Warp Speed"; June 12, 2000; page 94.

Three hundred times the speed of light? With two research-ers claiming the same thing, I think there is something here. It might even be the beginning of a breakthrough. I hope so. I don't want this stuff to just validate Kryon—I want it for science! I'd love us to get to the place where science doesn't have to compete with spirituality for a place in the sun. I firmly believe that they can and should complement each other in a way that may make some old energy folks very uncomfortable. (See page 378)

Interdimensionality? Living longer though spiritual activi-ties? Long-distance, hands-on healing validation? Magnetic DNA? What's next? Beam me up, Scotty? Yep . . . probably that, too, eventually. Responsible science and responsible spiritual-ity are a team that can't be beat. The best of both is the search for the way a universe works that is far grander than we have been led to believe. We can change reality, change our life span, perhaps even change a very old consciousness on Earth into a peaceful state. It's a millennium shift like no other, and person-ally, I'm very glad to have been here to write this book and again present the loving and informative channelling of Kryon.

Thank you, friends, for your continued support and love.

—Lee Carroll

P.S.: This is the first book where my two pets, Mini, my ever-present seven-pound Maltese dog; and Blondie, my shoulder-sitting, ever-present Cockatiel, have participated in their own ways. Between stained proof sheets, absolutely meant for potty-training paper, and the chewed edges of most of the research paper my desk, these two precious beings have had their own part to play in this Kryon book. They wanted you to know that animals count, too!

More Information on Breaking the SPEED OF LIGHT!
(And perhaps even the linear time barrier?)

SCIENCE: Two new experiments seem to suggest speeds up to 300 times faster are possible.

Nothing can travel faster than the speed of light, according to freshman textbooks. If anything could, then Einstein's theory of relativity would crumble, and theoretical physics would fall into disarray.

However, using a combination of atomic and *electromagnetic* effects, researchers have produced light beams in the laboratory that appear to travel much faster than the normal speed of light. Einstein's theory survives, physicists say, but the results of the experiments, they agree, are mind-bending.

In the most striking of the new experiments, a pulse of light that passes through a transparent chamber filled with specially prepared cesium gas appears to be pushed to speeds 300 times the normal speed of light. That is so fast that, under these peculiar circumstances, *the main part of the pulse exits the chamber even before it enters*.

The New York Times
by James Glanz
May 30, 2000

More information on Scientific
DIMENSIONALITY!
(Eleven of them!)

MIND OVER MATTER:

[Something] that's tangling up physicists who work on string theory—the idea that the whole of nature is sung by the harmonics of 11-dimensional vibrating strings. The math works out so well that many physicists consider it close to magic. But they don't know why it works. They don't know why strings, or why 11 dimensions, or just what the strings are.

Ignorance is not a weakness of science, but its major strength. What's more, total ignorance is surprisingly common—especially for scientists working at the forefront of knowledge.

"The truth of the matter is research is almost always without understanding," says University of Arizona physicist Johann Refelski, whose specialty is the physics of the vacuum—or empty space.

"Physics doesn't require someone who's intelligent. It requires not taking for granted things which are happening around you."

Los Angeles Times
by K.C. Cole
July 8, 1999

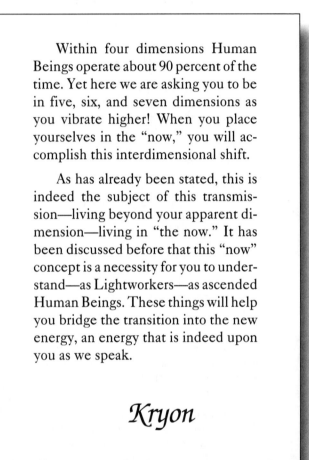

Within four dimensions Human Beings operate about 90 percent of the time. Yet here we are asking you to be in five, six, and seven dimensions as you vibrate higher! When you place yourselves in the "now," you will accomplish this interdimensional shift.

As has already been stated, this is indeed the subject of this transmission—living beyond your apparent dimension—living in "the now." It has been discussed before that this "now" concept is a necessity for you to understand—as Lightworkers—as ascended Human Beings. These things will help you bridge the transition into the new energy, an energy that is indeed upon you as we speak.

Kryon

Kryon News and Products

Chapter Sixteen

Kryon at The United Nations!

In November 1995, November 1996, and again in November 1998, Kryon spoke at the S.E.A.T. (Society for Enlightenment and Transformation) at the United Nations in New York City. By invitation, Jan and Lee brought a time of lecture, toning, meditation, and channelling to an elite group of U.N. delegates and guests.

Kryon Book 6, *Partnering with God,* carried the first two entire transcripts of what Kryon had to say . . . some of which has now been validated by the scientific community. Kryon Book 7, *Letters from Home,* carries the meeting in 1998 (page 289). All three of these transcripts are on the Kryon website [www.kryon.com].

Our sincere thanks to Mohamad Ramadan in 1995, Cristine Arismendy in 1996, and Jennifer Borchers in 1998, who were presidents of that bright spot at the United Nations, for the invitation, and for their work to enlighten our planet.

Kryon

On the Internet
[www.kryon.com]

The Kryon Website features lots of goodies! See the daily updated Kryon seminar schedule, and some of the latest channellings (including all the United Nations transcriptions). See what Kryon products are available, learn about the foreign translations and Kryon Websites in other languages, and read the latest Kryon book reviews.

Receive "marshmallow messages," personally chosen and sent to your e-mail each day. Join in a chat room with others of like mind. Spend time on the message board. Find others in your area of the same consciousness. From the products to the chat rooms, our Website is a "family" area—warm and toasty—filled with love and joy!

*Webmaster—**Gary Liljegren***

The World Finally Notices HAARP!

Playing the Wrong HAARP

"Last January (99), The European Parliament took a stand on electro-magnetic weaponry, nuclear hazards, land mines, and environmental refu-gees. In its decision, the EP considers HAARP (High Frequency Active Au-roral Research Project) by virtue of its far-reaching impact on the envi-ronment to be a global concern.

"It calls for HAARP's legal, eco-logical, and ethical implications to be examined by an international inde-pendent body before any further re-search and testing."

Canadian Journal of Health and Nutrition
As reported by Jean Manning in *Alive magazine*
#203; September 1999; page 42.

The End Times

White · **Kryon Book One**

The First Kryon Book

The first Kryon book, and the one that started it all. This book continues to be one of the best selling of the entire series. Although written in 1989, it sets the stage for all that we are experiencing now.

"The simple manner in which the material is presented makes this a highly accessible work for newcomers to Metaphysics"

■ *Connecting Link* magazine - Michigan

Published by Kryon Writings, Inc • ISBN 0-9636304-2-3 • $12.00

Don't Think Like a Human

Blue   **Kryon Book Two**

Channelled Answers

The second Kryon book, published in 1994. This book was the first one to begin to ask questions about how everything worked . . . mostly asked by the channel—an audio engineer!

"This read is a can't-put-it-down-till-the-last-page experience"

■ *New Age Retailer* - Washington

Published by Kryon Writings, Inc • ISBN 0-9636304-0-7• $12.00

Books and tapes can be purchased in retail stores, or by phone
~ Credit cards welcome ~

1-800-352-6657 - <kryonbooks@aol.com>

Alchemy of The Human Spirit

Fuchsia   **Kryon Book Three**

Human New Age Transition

*Kryon Book Three was published in 1995. It contains much
explanation of formerly difficult Kryon attributes (such as
the implant), and also broaches base-12 math. This is the
book that begins the science sections, common to all the books
that follow it.*

*"The Kryon channelled messages are growing to be as
valuable as the Seth teachings"*

■ *The Book Reader* - San Francisco, California

Published by Kryon Writings, Inc • ISBN 0-9636304-8-2 • $14.00

*Books and tapes can be purchased in retail stores, or by phone
~ Credit cards welcome ~*

1-800-352-6657 - <kryonbooks@aol.com>

The Journey Home

Kryon Book Five
A channelled novel!

This is the book that has created "The Journey Home Retreats," held in Colorado twice a year. These retreats take 50 attendees and walk them through the journey of Michael Thomas, as presented in this channelled novel. Perhaps the most profound of all the Kryon books, sacred messages hide in metaphor after metaphor . . .

■ *Also available unabridged on tape, read by Lee Carroll*

"The Journey Home is the latest work from one of this reviewer's favorite authors. It is also his best. Lee Carroll has given us a well-written book that flows like a mighty river. And that river takes us to places like truth, hope, destiny, awareness, and home!"

■ **Richard Fuller, Senior Editor**
Metaphysical Reviews

Published by Hay House • ISBN 1-56170-552-7 • $11.95

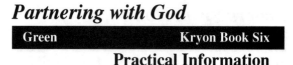

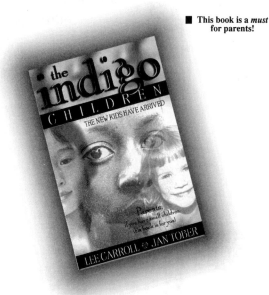

Timely. Informative. Provocative.

M A G A Z I N E

The *Kryon* magazine brings you timely information about our transformation into the New Age with several information-packed issues per year. It's filled with the latest Kryon channellings and parables, science and medical news, reader questions, inner child features, how-to information about working with your New Age tools, upcoming seminar schedules, and much more. Stay tuned to the latest news about these changing times by subscribing to the *Kryon* magazine. Just $24 for four issues; $40 for eight issues. (*Australia and New Zealand - see below**)

TO ORDER THE *KRYON* MAGAZINE:

- PHONE (credit card orders only): Call 1-800-945-1286 or 1-303-642-1678
- FAX (credit card orders only): Complete this order and fax to: (303) 642-1696
- E-MAIL (credit card orders only): E-mail all information contained in form below to: Kryonqtly@aol.com
- MAIL completed coupon below, include check, money order or credit card information to: *Kryon* magazine, PO Box 7392, Golden, CO 80403 - Make checks payable to *Kryon* magazine.

Name _____

Address _____

City _____ State _____ Zip _____

E-mail address (optional): _____

❑ Four issues $24* ❑ Eight issues $40* CO residents add 4.2%

*U.S. dollars. Orders outside U.S., please add $10 *per year* for shipping.

Payment: ❑ Check/M.O.   ❑ MasterCard   ❑ VISA

Credit Card Number: _____

Expiration Date: _____

Signature: _____ Phone: _____

---

* From within Australia and New Zealand, call direct: 800-44-3200 <crystals@senet.com.au>

Get together for a personal afternoon or evening with Kryon and Lee Carroll . . . in the comfort of a cozy living room or community center with a small group of dedicated lightworkers. It's called *At Home with Kryon,* the latest venue for joining in the Kryon energy. The special meeting starts with an introduction and discussion by Lee Carroll regarding timely New Age topics, then it continues with individual questions and answers from the group. Next comes a live Kryon channelling! Group size is typically 50 or 60 people. Often lasting up to five hours, it's an event you won't forget!

To sponsor an *"At Home with Kryon"* event in your home, please contact the Kryon office at 858/792-2990 - fax 858/759-2499, or E-mail <kryonmeet@aol.com>. For a list of upcoming *At Home with Kryon* locations, please see our Website at [http://www.kryon.com].

Kryon Live Channelled Audio Tapes

▶ **Ascension in the New Age** — ISBN 1-888053-01-1 • $10.00
Carlsbad, California—"Kryon describes what ascension really is in the New Age.
It might surprise you!"

▶ **Nine Ways to Raise the Planet's Vibration**—ISBN 1-888053-00-3 • $10.00
Seattle, Washington—"Raising the planet's vibration is the goal of humanity!
Find out what Kryon has to say about it."

▶ **Gifts and Tools of the New Age**—ISBN 1-888053-03-8 • $10.00
Casper, Wyoming—"A very powerful channel. Better put on your sword, shield,
and armor for this one."

▶ **Co-Creation in the New Age**—ISBN 1-888053-04-6 • $10.00
Portland, Oregon—"Tired of being swept around in life? Find out about
co-creating your own reality. It is our right in this New Age!"

▶ **Seven Responsibilities of the New Age**—ISBN 1-888053-02-X • $10.00
Indianapolis, Indiana—"Responsibility? For what? Find out what Spirit tells us
we are now in charge of . . . and what to do with it."

Music and Meditation

▶ **Crystal Singer Music Meditation Tape**—ISBN 0-96363-4-1-5 • $10.00
Enjoy two soaring 17-minute musical meditations featuring the beautiful singing
voice of Jan Tober.

▶ **Guided Meditations Tape**—ISBN 1-888053-05-4 • $10.00
Jan presents two guided meditations similar to those delivered at each Kryon seminar
throughout the United States and Canada, with beautiful Celtic harp accompaniment
by Mark Geisler. **Side One: "Finding Your Sweet Spot" Side Two: "Divine Love"**

▶ **Color & Sound Meditation CD**—ISBN 1-888053-06-2 • $15.00
A complete color/sound workshop — an exercise to balance and harmonize the chakras.
Jan guides us through the seven chakra system using the enhancement of the ancient
Tibetan signing bowls. **Side One: 30-min meditation Side Two: 12-min meditation**
Available in English or French! - please specify

Kryon Audio Books

Published by **AUDIO LITERATURE** *Read by Lee Carroll*

▶ **The End Times**—ISBN 1-57453-168-9
▶ **Don't Think Like A Human**—ISBN 1-57453-169-7
▶ **Alchemy of the Human Spirit**—ISBN 1-57453-170-0
Each audio book contains two cassettes, 3 hours, abridged - $17.95

▶ **"The Parables of Kryon"**—*Read by Lee Carroll*
Published by Hay House and scored with music! ISBN 1-56170-454-7 -$16.95

▶ **"The Journey Home"** *Unabridged!*—*Read by Lee Carroll*
Published by Hay House—a six-tape set! ISBN 1-56170-453-9 -$30.00
(seven-hour listening experience)

Books and tapes can be purchased in retail stores, by phone or E-mail
Credit cards welcome ~ 1-800-352-6657 ~ <kryonbooks@aol.com>

Would you like to be on the Kryon mailing list?

This list is used to inform interested people of Kryon workshops coming to their areas, new Kryon releases, and Kryon news in general. We don't sell or distribute our lists to anyone.

If you would like to be included, please simply drop a postcard to us that says "LIST," and include your clearly printed name and address.

The Kryon Writings, Inc.

422
1155 Camino Del Mar
Del Mar, California 92014

The Kryon Master Index
An index for the eight Kryon channelled books

Kryon Master Book Index

The Kryon Master Book Index

Bk 1 - *The End Times*   Bk 2 - *Don't Think Like a Human*   Bk 3 - *Alchemy of the Human Spirit*
Bk 4 - *The Parables of Kryon*   Bk 5 - *The Journey Home*   Bk 6 - *Partnering with God*
Bk 7 - *Letters from Home*   Bk Ind - *The Indigo Children*   Bk 8 - *Passing the Marker*

The Kryon Master Book Index

The Kryon Master Book Index

The Kryon Master Book Index

The Kryon Master Book Index

The Kryon Master Book Index

The Kryon Master Book Index

The Kryon Master Book Index

The Kryon Master Book Index

The Kryon Master Book Index

The Kryon Master Book Index

The Kryon Master Book Index

The Kryon Master Book Index

The Kryon Master Book Index

The Kryon Master Book Index

The Kryon Master Book Index

The Kryon Master Book Index

Index for this book only
"Passing the Marker"

Book Index

Index for this book

Index for this book

Index for this book

Listen: This is important for you to know. You are empowered!

There is not one of you here who has to come back to this room to experience this. No person ever has to read these words again if they choose not to. No Human has to join anything or profess any system of belief to find the divine inside. The Third Language is your guide! We are all available—all in that closet, if you will. YOU ARE all God!

And so it is that the new energy of the planet fills this space and gives you the wisdom of God. And so it is that you have asked for, and have received, instructions this day about the potentials of the planet and who you really are.

And so it is.

Kryon

And so, dear family, it is with some sorrow that we retreat from this room and from the area where you are reading. Again, we tell you this: You are never alone! The energy you have felt today may visit you anytime you want it to. You can join us in that circular place. Feel stuck on your path? Celebrate it while the synchronicity moves toward you. Feeling stopped with no apparent direction? Celebrate the knowledge that all is relative and that you are stopped so that others may catch up or come from the front or the side or even from behind (the past) in their time. Celebrate the fact that all is in motion, but that your linearity simply looks like a halt. Actually, the family is in motion around you all the time—just like the incredible love that we have for you is never still.

And so it is.

Kryon